The Story of Ourselves

The Story of Ourselves

Teaching History Through Children's Literature

Edited by   Michael O. Tunnell & Richard Ammon

HEINEMANN
Portsmouth, New Hampshire

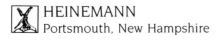

Heinemann
A division of Reed Elsevier Inc.
361 Hanover Street   Portsmouth, NH 03801-3912
Offices and agents throughout the world

We would like to thank the following for permission to reprint material from copyrighted work:

Page 9: From *Prince Henry the Navigator* by Leonard Everett Fisher. Copyright © 1990 by Leonard Everett Fisher. Reproduced with the permission of Macmillan Publishing Company.

Page 21: From *Pyramid of the Sun Pyramid of the Moon* by Leonard Everett Fisher. Copyright © 1988 by Leonard Everett Fisher. Reproduced with the permission of Macmillan Publishing Company.

Page 24: From *Prince Henry the Navigator* by Leonard Everett Fisher. Copyright © 1990 by Leonard Everett Fisher. Reproduced with the permission of Macmillan Publishing Company.

Page 37–38: Excerpt from *Pedro's Journal: A Voyage with Christopher Columbus, April 3, 1492–February 14, 1493* by Pam Conrad, reprinted with permission of Boyds Mills Press, 803 Church Street, Honesdale, PA 19431.

Page 49: From a poster prepared by Leonard Everett Fisher for The Children's Book Council. Copyright © 1985 by The Children's Book Council Inc. Used by permission of The Children's Book Council and Leonard Everett Fisher.

Page 91: Illustration by Leonard Everett Fisher. Reprinted from *The Railroads* by permission of Holiday House.

Every effort has been made to contact the copyright holders for permission to reprint borrowed material. We regret any oversights that may have occurred and would be happy to rectify them in future printings of this work.

Library of Congress Cataloging-in-Publication Data
The Story of ourselves : teaching history through children's
   literature / edited by Michael O. Tunnell & Richard Ammon.
      p.   cm.
   Includes bibliographical references.
   ISBN 0-435-08725-8
   1. History—Study and teaching (Elementary)   2. Children's
literature—Study and teaching (Elementary)   3. Interdisciplinary
approach in education.   I. Tunnell, Michael O.   II. Ammon, Richard.
   LB1581.S76   1993
   372.89'044–dc20   92-30963
                                                                   CIP

Designed by Jenny Jensen Greenleaf.
Printed in the United States of America.
96 97   9 8 7 6 5 4

Contents

Introduction

Critics, such as Nat Hentoff (1984) and Paul Gagnon (1989), have criticized social studies and history textbooks for failing to tell the full story. Textbook publishers, sensitive to special interests, have reduced spirited moments in history filled with human joy and pathos to bland accounts of wars and battles, names and dates, places and populations.

Recently, social studies educators have engaged in lively debates over curriculum. Many have argued for greater historical content. Others have questioned the traditional lecture-discussion methodology and have urged that the study of history be integrated with the study of literature, art, and other subjects.

At the same time, elementary and middle school teachers have embraced whole language. These teachers do not believe in teaching isolated language skills. Instead, whole language advocates teach children to read from real books (trade books or library books) and to write, not by using workbooks but by composing their own stories.

Whole language teachers also encourage reading and writing across the curriculum. They believe that students will learn more about history, for instance, from reading trade books, which offer clearer, more engaging accounts of the people of history, than from texts. Moreover, they believe that by writing in subjects other than English, learners develop a better understanding of concepts and learn to think critically. These interdisciplinary instructional models provide a natural link between history education and the language arts.

Teaching critical thinking has also gained recent attention. Although critical thinking may represent an innovation in some areas of the curriculum, it has been practiced for years in other disciplines. Science has long emphasized the scientific method, and, more recently, teachers of literature have become familiar with Rosenblatt's theory of transactional analysis, which places the reader in control of interpreting the text.

Teaching history with trade books, then, successfully integrates reading, writing, thinking, and subject-related content. We believe that interdisciplinary teaching restores a vibrance to history education in our elementary and secondary schools.

This collection of writings by trade book authors and public school and college-level educators offers support for using children's literature in history education. It begins with a chapter titled "Why Teach History to the Young?" wherein Terrie L. Epstein makes a passionate case for including history in the school curriculum.

In Part I, "The Creative Process," four authors and an illustrator address the process of writing and illustrating historical fiction and nonfiction. Newbery medalist Joan Blos shares her perspectives on writing historical fiction, whereas artist Leonard Everett Fisher explains the role of illustration in interpreting history. Highly acclaimed nonfiction author Milton Meltzer writes of the importance of primary sources in recounting history. Pam Conrad believes we can learn about ourselves from history, and Newbery medalist Russell Freedman talks about making the past real for today's youth.

In Part II, "Research and Other Considerations," Carl Tomlinson, Michael Tunnell, and Donald Richgels compare and contrast history textbooks and trade books by examining content emphasis and coverage, as well as features of writing such as form, text structure, and style. Nationally known social studies researcher Linda Levstik examines how reading historical fiction affects children's grasp of historical content, whereas Michael Tunnell looks at the coming of age of historical trade book literature.

Authors in Part III, "Practical Applications," share teacher-tested strategies for structuring history units around the reading of children's and adolescent literature. Richard Ammon and Diane Weigard talk about reading topics and genres not typically associated with history and social studies. Curriculum specialist Judith Wooster offers several proven classroom approaches for enabling students to think about what they have read. Gail Tunnell, an English teacher, and Jeannie Ammon, a librarian, tell how they developed a trade book unit on the Holocaust. Likewise, Anita Downs describes a framework for creating history/trade book units, using her unit about life in the Middle Ages as an example.

Finally, we have included a selected, annotated bibliography of trade books about American history. The list is designed to suggest not only possible titles but also new directions for approaching traditional topics.

Ultimately, our task in teaching history is not so much to teach facts as to help students grapple with concepts. Part of this process dictates breathing life into the dusty past and presenting history from varying viewpoints. Trade books provide one of the best mechanisms for helping teachers achieve a livelier and more meaningful history curriculum.

> Our job is not shaping students to [a particular] viewpoint, but assisting them to read so they may shape themselves. The task in teaching literature (and history) is to help students think, not to tell them what to think. (Probst, 1984, p. 16)

Michael O. Tunnell and Richard Ammon

REFERENCES

Gagnon, P. (1989). *Democracy's half-told story*. Washington, D.C.: American Federation of Teachers.

Hentoff, N. (1984, February). The dumbing of America. *The Progressive*, pp. 29–31.

Probst, R. (1984). *Adolescent literature: Response and analysis*. Columbus, OH: Merrill.

Terrie L. Epstein teaches courses in curriculum and secondary social studies at the University of Michigan. She founded the *Magazine of History* and served on the editorial review board of *Theory and Research in Social Education, Social Education,* and the *Harvard Educational Review*. In addition, she has written numerous articles in social studies and history journals.

*   *   *

Why teach history to the young? Terrie Epstein answers her own question by making a compelling case for members of the next generation to connect their lives with those who came before them. She also examines the relevance of history education, stressing the advantage young people gain from understanding how the present is affected by the past.

Why Teach History to the Young?

Terrie L. Epstein

In the 1890s, two nationally prominent professional organizations, the National Education Association and the American Historical Association, each established national commissions to examine the state of precollegiate public education. Both commissions made the case for including history, a relative newcomer to the school curriculum, as a subject taught throughout the public schools. According to the commissions, the purposes of introducing history to the young were many. History served to "broaden and cultivate the mind," "kindle the imagination," "counteract a narrow and provincial spirit," and prepare students in later years for "intelligent citizenship" and "intellectual enjoyment" (Hertzberg, 1981). Today, one hundred years later, state and national blue-ribbon commissions continue to promote the place of history in the school curriculum and the reasons they cite for doing so are as vital and varied as those proposed a century ago (Bradley Commission, 1988; History-Social Science Curriculum, 1988; National Commission, 1989; New York State, 1991).

One of the most widely cited reasons for teaching history to the young is tied to the concept of citizenship. Most educators accept the notion that in order to exercise judiciously the rights and responsibilities of citizenship in a democracy, young people need to know how these rights and responsibilities evolved. It took a revolution, for example, to institutionalize a democratic form of government and to create a constitutional foundation for individual rights. It has taken another two centuries, however, to extend the protections of government and the rights of individuals to greater numbers of Americans. As future citizens, young people need to learn that freedom and equality, although part of their historical legacy, must be guarded and fostered in order to be maintained (Gagnon, 1988).

History also provides a nation and its young with a sense of shared heritage based on common traditions, beliefs, and values. This common heritage is most evident in the political and legal principles set forth in the Constitution and Bill of Rights. The study of history sets the historical context for comprehending the evolution of political and legal rights and institutions. It also provides a platform for comparing democratic government with other forms of rule. Even young children, for example, can grasp in simplified form the development of contending political parties and the differences and resulting consequences between rule by the dictates of one and rule by the consent of the governed.

Americans also share a heritage based on the intermingling of many peoples and cultures. American music, for example, in all its forms and variations, is an amalgam of sounds and structures borrowed from cultural heritages originating in Africa and Ireland, Mexico and France (Lomax, 1975). American literature, art, customs, food, and clothing—not to mention the English language itself—have been enriched by the commingling of cultures (Ravitch, 1990). By being introduced to the cultural history of their country, young people learn something about the legacies of other lands.

History and culture not only provide the basis for a sense of common identity, but they also illuminate the role diversity has played in forging a nation. Just as people from all parts of the globe and under a variety of circumstances have come to the United States, people of all ancestries have contributed to the building and shaping of the country. A multicultural approach to the study of history takes pride in our country's diversity by integrating into the main historical narrative the contributions and experiences of men and women of all races and ethnicities (Holt, 1990; New York State, 1991).

Through a multicultural approach to the study of United States history, children learn to perceive historical events and experiences from the multiple perspectives of the individuals or groups who participated. For example, older textbooks presented in a positive light nineteenth-century Anglo-American westward migration across what was to become the continental United States. Today, although most historians recognize the benefits of westward expansion for Anglo-American families migrating from the East, they also acknowledge that migration and hunger for land wrought destruction upon Native American and Mexican peoples and cultures (Holt, 1990; Limmerick, 1987). As children mature, they can learn to see past events such as the "westward migration" (or what some have termed the "eastern invasion") from the multiple perspectives of the people involved. In short, the young can learn to respect and appreciate how people from different races, ethnicities, classes, regions, and genders interpret and evaluate historical experiences (New York State, 1991).

In addition to teaching children about the commonality and diversity of the American experience, the study of history also illustrates how people in other times and places lived and interacted. Learning the histories of other societies or civilizations is naturally intriguing to the young (Egan, 1982); it also furnishes a foundation for mitigating ethnocentrism and xenophobia. Because the young live in an increasingly interdependent world, knowledge of how people in other societies have come to interpret and behave in the world is indispensable (Kniep, 1989).

The study of world history also introduces the young to the central themes that characterize civilizations throughout time. Although it may seem an intimidating task to present the complexity of world history to children in comprehensible form, it can be simplified to appeal to the young. The historian William McNeill, for example, writes of the course of human history in terms of "the accumulation of human skills and power over nature and one another" (1989a, p. 1). In the following excerpt, McNeill distills the first thousands of years of human history into two succinct paragraphs:

> Human beings first became the most efficient hunters and moved to the top of the food chain in ancient Africa by learning to use tools—and probably by using language to assure cooperation and to sharpen observation. Next, they learned to use animal skins to keep warm in colder climates, and so spread rapidly round the earth. This was a geographic shift without parallel in biological evolution.
>
> Then in agriculture human beings in different parts of the world began to acquire knowledge of various plants and skills of cultivation. A noticeable series of improvements in agriculture occurred thereafter: from slash and burn to permanent fields with the plow and fallowing. Then there was the diffusion of crops from one part of the earth to the other, including as the most dramatic, the spread of American food crops after 1500. (1989a, 1, 5)

Historical themes not only situate people and societies in and across time; they also situate them in space. Geography is integral to the study of history, for it explains how the environment affected and has been affected by the development of different societies. For example, a study of Native American societies in North and South America before the advent of European contact illustrates the way particular groups of people adapted to their environments. The subsequent study of the English colonization of North America in the seventeenth and eighteenth centuries provides a basis for comparing and contrasting the English settlers' and Native Americans' uses of land and resources. The study of geography in history reveals the extent to which human agency has influenced and been influenced by geographic conditions (Gagnon, 1990; Joint Committee, 1984).

Finally, knowledge of world history is indispensable for understanding both the United States and the world today. Contemporary economic conditions and political alliances and conflicts are based on historical developments. To understand the present, and to retain some hope of improving relations between people or countries today, Americans young and old need to know how particular alliances or conflicts have come about. Again, only by understanding the history of a people's or society's past can individuals or governments hope to propose and implement reasonable compromises over age-old conflicts (McNeill, 1989b).

As important as history is in understanding the world today and in instilling in the young a sense of civic responsibility, adults always have noted the personal satisfactions they and children derive from delving into the past (Freeman and Levstik, 1988). History as a humanistic discipline satisfies a person's natural curiosity about a sense of time and place, a conception of change and continuity, an explanation of how and why things are the way they are today. The history of one's family, community, racial or ethnic group, gender, region, or country situates an individual within a broader context spatially and temporally. History, in short, provides a means for feeling connected to the lives and times of those who lived before (Craig, 1989).

The study of history can be approached from many angles, each with its own set of benefits. Teachers who use a biographical approach can instruct children that individuals great and small have made a difference. In recent years, historians have incorporated into the main historical narrative the actions and reactions of common people. This approach illustrates how ordinary people had become extraordinary as they rose to meet a challenge and thereby influenced the course of events (Nash, 1989). Harriet Tubman and Rosa Parks are but two examples of women who have displayed remarkable courage in the face of difficult and dangerous circumstances. In short, historical biography is a way to personalize history, to illustrate both the effects individuals have had on the course of events and the effects the course of events have had on individuals (Crabtree, 1989; Freeman and Levstik, 1988).

For young children, biographies also can serve as lessons in morality, in which the actions of historical actors are compared and evaluated. Through biography, children learn that evil as well as good resides within the human character and that individuals often have choices in their actions. Biography also enables children to enter vicariously into the lives and times of others and to discover the causes and consequences of decisions and actions. And finally, biography enables children to learn that heroines and heroes come from all races, all religions, all walks of life (Crabtree, 1989; Freeman and Levstik, 1988; Levstik, 1990).

As the articles in this volume make clear, biography is but one of the more meaningful and memorable ways of teaching and learning about the past. Personal narratives, historical fiction, and other literary forms bring history to life. Such sources invite an engaged reader to enter into other times and places by creating images of and feelings for the historical experiences of others. In short, historical literature and literary forms enable students to develop a sense of empathy with the people portrayed (Eisner, 1991; Freeman and Levstik, 1988; Levstik, 1990).

Finally, history is well taught and well learned when students can assess the past with a critical as well as creative eye. Young people learn from historical heroes and heroines whose acts of political or moral courage inspire young and old alike. The young also need to recognize human frailty and failure. No society or group of people has a lock on human virtue, and wise judgment develops as much from lessons about human failure as from stories of success. History, like life itself, reveals the range of human experience in all its complexity and all its capacity for beauty and brutality. History holds many lessons, but only for those who can evaluate critically the meaning of events from many perspectives.

History speaks to our individual and collective humanity. It keeps us connected to our ancestors and enables us to understand and appreciate the minds, mores, and experiences of others. History provides a sense of common heritage at the same time that it presents the origins and development of our diversity. History promotes a conscious and critical sense of citizenship in national and global communities. And in its lessons about the ordinary, the extraordinary, and the extreme, history divulges the depth and breadth of human experience.

In an essay entitled, "A Talk to Teachers," written in 1962 yet still relevant today, the writer James Baldwin expressed his beliefs about the significance of teaching history to the young:

> I would try to make him [young person] know that just as American history is longer, larger, more various, more beautiful, and more terrible than anything anyone has ever said about it, so is the world larger, more daring, more beautiful and more terrible, but principally larger—and that it belongs to him. I would teach him that he doesn't have to be bound by the expediencies of any given administration, any given policy, any given morality; that he has the right and the necessity to examine everything. (1988, 11–12)

In these sentiments, the hope in the power of history resides.

REFERENCES

Baldwin, J. (1988). A talk to teachers. In R. Simonson and S. Walker (Eds.), *Multicultural literacy*. (pp. 3–12). Saint Paul, Minn.: Graywolf Press.

Bradley Commission on History in Schools. (1988). *Building a history curriculum: Guidelines for teaching history in the schools*. Washington, D.C.: Educational Excellence Network.

Crabtree, C. (1989). Returning history to the elementary school. In P. A. Gagnon (Ed.), *Historical literacy* (pp. 173–87). New York: Macmillan.

Craig, G. A. (1989). History as a humanistic discipline. In P. A. Gagnon (Ed.), *Historical literacy* (pp. 119–37). New York: Macmillan.

Egan, K. (1982). Teaching history to young children. *Phi Delta Kappan, 61*, 439–41.

Eisner, E. W. (1991). *The enlightened eye*. New York: Macmillan.

Freeman, E. B., & Levstik, L. S. (1988). Recreating the past: Historical fiction in the social studies curriculum. *Elementary School Journal, 88*, 329–37.

Gagnon, P. A. (1988, November). Why study history? *The Atlantic*, pp. 43–66.

Gagnon, P. A. (1990, January). Human interaction with the environment. *History Matters!* 2, 1:5.

Hertzberg, H. W. (1981). *Social studies reform: 1880–1980*. Boulder, Colorado: Social Science Education Consortium.

History-Social Science Curriculum Framework & Criteria Committee. (1988). *History-social science framework for California public schools*. Sacramento: California State Department of Education.

Holt, T. (1990). American history. In National Commission on Social Studies in the Schools, *Charting a course: Social studies for the twenty-first century* (pp. 49–52). Washington, D.C.: National Commission on Social Studies in the Schools.

Joint Committee on Geographic Education. (1984). *Guidelines for geographic education*. Washington, D. C.: Association of American Geographers and National Council for Geographic Education.

Kniep, W. M. (1989). Social studies within a global education. *Social Education, 53*, 399–403.

Levstik, L. S. (1990). Mediating content through literary texts. *Language Arts, 67*, 848–53.

Limmerick, P. N. (1987). *The legacy of conquest*. New York: Norton.

Lomax, A. (1975). *The folk songs of North America*. New York: Doubleday.

McNeill, W. H. (1989a, August). Civilization, cultural diffusion and innovation. *History Matters!* 2, 1:5.

McNeill, W. H. (1989b). How history helps us to understand current affairs. In P. A. Gagnon (Ed.), *Historical literacy* (pp. 157–72). New York: Macmillan.

Nash, G. B. (1989). History for a democratic society: The work of all the people. In P. A. Gagnon and The Bradley Commission on history in schools (Eds.), *Historical literacy: the case for history in American education* (pp. 234–50). New York: Macmillan.

National Commission for Social Studies in the Schools. (1989). *Charting a course: Social studies for the twenty-first century.* Washington, D.C.: National Commission for Social Studies in the Schools.

New York State Social Studies & Review Committee. (1991). *One nation, many peoples.* Albany, N.Y.: State Department of Education.

Ravitch, D. (1990, Summer). Multiculturalism e pluribus plures. *American Scholar,* 337–54.

PART ONE

The Creative Process

Joan W. Blos, author of several award-winning picture books for children, taught children's literature at the Bank Street College of Education in New York City and at the University of Michigan. She won the 1980 Newbery Medal and the American Book Award for her historical novel, *A Gathering of Days.*

* * *

Why write and read historical fiction? What are the contributions of historical fiction? Is fiction a valid way to present facts? What are the pitfalls of historical fiction that can trap writers and mislead readers? In this chapter, Joan Blos not only examines the qualities and functions of historical fiction, but also pinpoints some of the elements that may strengthen or weaken books with historical themes.

Perspectives on Historical Fiction

Joan W. Blos

"Can Movies Teach History?" asked Richard Bernstein in the *New York Times* (1989, p. 1). Can books? Can we?

History, it is easy to agree, is the formal study of the collective past. But ideas as to how it can best be taught tend to be much more varied and have shifted over time. In the past, for example, traditional emphases on names, dates, facts, and treaties had so deadly an effect on curriculum, textbooks, and students that a pedagogical change of heart became as predictable as it was necessary. But just as memorizing facts without context was of limited value, so studying qualities of human experience with no supportive framework of factual material is not very useful either.

Although brutal in its imagery, throwing out the baby with the bathwater is a fairly accurate metaphor for curriculum revision that is more thorough than thoughtful. We will do well to keep this in mind even as we proceed with understandable enthusiasm to new modes of instruction, including those promoting the inclusion of trade books into integrated programs using literature. It's the either/or mentality that gets us every time as an anecdote from my own school experience may, perhaps, demonstrate.

The high school I attended many years ago was known as a progressive school, taking guidance from John Dewey's philosophies of education and his experimental approach. When a new student with a very different educational background joined the class, the discrepancies between her view of social studies and ours showed up very clearly. Succinctly

This contribution is based on talks on historical fiction presented in 1986–1989, and some portions of it derive from previously published statements.

expressing them she said, "I know *when* Columbus discovered America. But you know *why.*"

In offering this perspective on historical fiction I am hopefully imagining that this time around, with the lessons of the past available to guide us (and is that not what history is about?), we shall do a little better. I also want to say that knowing that trade books have come to be seen as a valuable classroom asset both pleases and encourages me as a writer of historical fiction.

Historical fiction is generally considered to have made its appearance in the early nineteenth century. And just as Edgar Allan Poe is said to have invented the mystery story, so Sir Walter Scott is credited with historical fiction. *Waverly*, published in 1810 or 1814 depending on which authority one cites, is considered the first example of the genre, and Scott went on to contribute many other titles, including his especially well known *Ivanhoe*, *Heart of Midlothian*, and *Kenilworth*.

Historical fiction seems to have become quickly successful and, with titles such as *The Scarlet Pimpernel* and *Kidnapped*, was popular with adult and young readers alike. It ran unabashedly to the adventure story and, as was typical of nineteenth-century fiction, engaged in lengthy descriptive passages, as a representative fragment of Scott's *Ivanhoe* illustrates:

> . . . the thieves guided him straight forward to the little eminence, whence he could see, spread beneath him in the moonlight, the palisades of the lists [and] the glimmering pavilions pitched at either end . . .

The very Sir Arthur Conan Doyle who also gave us Sherlock Holmes was a prolific contributor of historical fiction. And so were Robert Louis Stevenson, Alexander Dumas, and Howard Pyle in this country. These writers helped to identify the genre with thoroughly masculine, somewhat stereotypic heroes distinguished by Victorian virtues. The complementary role of the heroines was to necessitate rescue by these heroes and then to be suitably grateful: "I knew you would come," she said.

When the critics first looked at historical fiction (Drinkwater, 1924), they chided its authors for their many inaccuracies and casual approach to facts. Not long afterward, however, historical fiction was discovered by persons who saw it as a means of instilling masses of historical information in young and feckless readers. As anyone knows who has tried to read the historical fiction of the 1930s and 1940s, incorporating too many facts into a narrative has the same dismal effect as that of the stones sewn into Ophelia's dress. By 1953 Lillian Smith felt compelled to observe that "the idea behind the writing of a historical story is not to present the facts of history . . . but in going beyond historical data to give a way of looking at the past" (p. 165).

Fortunately, most persons writing historical fiction today are not attempting to slip facts into their stories for instructional purposes. Facts may indeed be cited and actual events referred to within the frame of the story, but only to the extent that these references help to locate the story in historical time or give it dimension and veridicality. It is important that teachers who intend to use trade books in conjunction with social studies and history curricula recognize this and find other and appropriate means of acquainting their students with historical information. In historical fiction worthy of the name, facts will *serve* the stories and the stories, if valid as fiction, will establish human and social circumstances in which the interaction of historical forces may be known, felt, and observed. Discussing the stories with students is an important part of the process, helping them to know what it is they know as a result of their reading. Historical fiction should be accurate in its portrayals of individuals and environments. But it is emphatically *not* the job of historical fiction to teach factual material.

There are two answers to the question, Why write historical fiction or hope that others will read it? Both may help to clarify historical fiction's potential contribution to the teaching and learning of history and social studies.

First and most apparent is that historical fiction gives a sense of life as it was lived, or might have been lived, at an earlier time. People are fond of describing historical fiction as bringing the past to life. How close it comes to *accuracy* in its representations depends on the kind and amount of information available to the writer, the writer's relationship to the material, and the writer's intentions. These factors operate interactively as a moment's thought makes clear. Not only are postliterate cultures more accessibly documented, but some writers (Patricia MacLachlan in writing *Sarah, Plain and Tall*) have access to pieces of family history while others (Rosemary Sutcliff in writing about Ancient Britain) are necessarily dependent on historical research. And, of course, a writer's relationship to his or her material is going to make a difference in how it is presented and what receives most stress.

In a larger version of this same phenomenon, writers are seen inescapably to interpret historical periods in the light cast on them by their own times. Thus, Esther Forbes, writing *Johnny Tremain* at the start of World War II, saw the War of Independence differently than did Avi, writing *The Fighting Ground* in the 1980s. This tendency to a sociocultural bias affects academic historians as well as writers of historical fiction and representatives of both groups will do better if they acknowledge the existence of the dilemma. But they should certainly not feel ashamed. As Eric Haugaard has pointed out:

> The true historians . . . know that at best all they can achieve is a partial resurrecting of the events which make up history. . . . History is not an exact science and never will be; it deals with material which is often suspect, if not actually false. . . . Not only must the historian suspect his material, but he must be aware that he is not unprejudiced, that he is viewing the past from a certain position. And just as the past casts its shadow into the future, so does the present bear upon the historian's study of the past. History is what we choose to recall. If this were not true, all history books would be alike, and the difference between them would be the latest discovery of some ancient facts. (1979, pp. 698–706)

Second only to its capacity to animate the past, a main function of historical fiction is to help us consider the present, and even to look ahead. Asked, one day, why I write historical fiction, I heard myself spontaneously reply, "Because I am interested in the future." And I meant it, too. Especially when we are speaking of books for young people, I think there is particular value in examining both social and personal issues in the context of the past. Sometimes it is simply easier to do so. A *Gathering of Days'* nineteenth-century New England setting allows, for example, the exploration of a number of topics that we associate with the twentieth century. These include parent loss, death and remarriage, teacher accountability, community control, civil rights, and moral responsibility vs. personal loyalty. But, in the sense of allowing a young protagonist to take an active part in the proceedings, it would be much more difficult to deal with these issues in a novel set in the present time.

Depending on the criteria used, historical fiction is (a) a work of fiction in which the story takes place twenty-five or more years before its publication date, or (b) a work of fiction set two or more generations before that of the author so that the author may be presumed not to have had any direct knowledge of it. Alas the latter definition excludes some of the best loved examples of historical fiction in children's literature, beginning with *The Little House in the Big Woods*; the former seems a bit abrupt, especially to those of us for whom twenty-five years is barely yesterday. Few definitions are perfect. In this instance it doesn't seem to matter very much, so long as persons charged with the selection of books are aware, as has already been mentioned above, that an author's relationship to the material and the means of obtaining it are two factors that will substantially influence the nature of the work.

Brief mention should also be made here of the seldom recognized tradition whereby at least three fundamentally different kinds of books will be found catalogued together as historical fiction. These are (1) the fictionalized memoir, such as the Laura Ingalls Wilder books and Ruth

Sawyer's *Roller Skates*; (2) fictionalized family history, such as Carol Ryrie Brink's *Caddie Woodlawn* and *Sarah, Plain and Tall*, already mentioned; and (3) fiction based on research such as the books I write.

Elsewhere I have written somewhat differently about historical fiction, emphasizing means for its assessment and identifying "certain characteristic flaws that often signal unchecked flaws of concept or execution" (1985, pp. 38–39). Another way of saying this is that errors appearing on the surface of a work tend, like a measles patient's rash, to be symptomatic of a systemic ailment. I named three diagnostic signs. These were "The Overstuffed Sentence," "The Privy Observed," and "Bunches of Hessians."

In errors of the first kind the author didactically includes bits of information irrelevant to the story. In mild cases it merely slows down the reading. In more severe instances it causes the reader to suspect that the author's intention was to teach a lesson and not to tell a story. The second category of errors refers to those made by authors who, like intrusive tour guides, busy themselves with pointing out the quaint details of the region and the natives' unusual habits. As a matter of principle, authors should not describe things that a story's characters would simply take for granted. (One of the reasons that the device of time travel works so well is that it provides the author with a character as new to the situation as the reader is, thereby legitimizing certain kinds of descriptions and explanations.) The third heading, "Bunches of Hessians," simply refers to inappropriately used contemporary language. It derives from an improvised example: "Peering out of her bedroom window, Deeney saw bunches of Hessians heading for the green." For an utterly egregious example combining all three errors one might propose something on the order of the following: "Deeney, who had often overheard her father talking of General Lafayette, now hurried to her twelve paned bedroom window with the delicate fluted trim that had taken a craftsman many a long day's labor to create, in hopes of seeing the youthful Frenchman who had been born in 1757. She was disappointed, however. All she saw below her on the roughly cobbled street were several bunches of Hessians heading for the green."

It was Helen Gardner, a British scholar and critic, who noted in the essays collected under the title *In Defense of the Imagination* that

> . . . literature, of all the arts, has the power to take us back into what it felt like to live in past ages, and discover certain constancies in human experience . . . (1982, p. 45)

In this way literature participates in the overarching goal of all of the humanities, which is to answer that deceptively simple question: what does it mean to be human? It is important to recognize what a powerful ally we have when we enlist literature in our educative attempts. On its own strengths, and because of its own merits, literature can and does lead us to an improved understanding of the world and our place in it. This, and not meeting the superficial requirements of escapism, is the true work of literature.

But Dame Helen, when she spoke of the power of literature to take us back into past ages, was speaking of adult readers and works that were contemporaneous with those long-ago times. No matter how pertinent the content, what would the "younge fresshe folkes" of today make of "The Love Unfeigned" (Chaucer), which begins:

> O younge fresshe folkes, he or she,
> In which that love up groweth with your age,
> Repeyreth hoom from worldly vanitee . . .

Would they be patient with works such as *Silas Marner*, once a staple item of high school English classes? Eliot was ahead of her time but hardly in step with ours when she wrote paragraphs such as the one commencing as follows and inserted them into her fiction:

> Even people whose lives have been made various by learning sometimes find it hard to keep a fast hold on their habitual views of life, on the faith in the Invisible,—nay, on the sense that their past joys and sorrows are a real experience, when they are suddenly transported . . . (Eliot, p. 16)

Historical fiction provides, I believe, an imperfect but ready answer to the question: how may we offer students incapable of reading outmoded or archaic works (or unready or not willing to do so) the immediacy of historical experience that literature provides?

In this context, qualities that sometimes appear as historical fiction's deficiencies become its virtues. That is to say, if it is selective in what it tells of other eras, the way it does so will at least be congruent with contemporary tastes, values, and modes of expression. In short, it can mediate between the two periods—the one of which it tells and the one in which it is read—because it is its very nature to do so. If we add the proviso that we are not only speaking of historical fiction in general but principally of books written for young readers, I think a strong argument may be made for the case of historical fiction and its place in the classroom. As a valid literary genre, it comes as close as possible to the authentic works of other eras in its capacity to evoke past times while yet being likely to succeed with school-age students today.

REFERENCES

Bernstein, R. (1989, November 26). Can movies teach history? *New York Times*, sec. 2, p. 1.

Blos, J. W. (1985, November). The overstuffed sentence and other means of assessing historical fiction for children. *School Library Journal*, pp. 38–39.

Drinkwater, J. (1924). *Outline of literature*. New York: Putnam.

Eliot, G. (1960). *Silas Marner*. New York: New American Library.

Gardner, H. (1982). *In defense of the imagination*. Cambridge, Mass: Harvard UP.

Haugaard, E. (1979, December). Before I was born: History and the child. *The Horn Book*, pp. 698–706.

Smith, L. (1953). *The unreluctant years*. New York: Viking.

Leonard Everett Fisher has illustrated or written and illustrated well over two hundred books for young readers. In 1991 he received both the Regina Medal and the Kerlan Award for his body of work. Among his numerous other honors is the 1950 Pulitzer painting award. Many of Leonard Everett Fisher's works have historical themes.

*   *   *

What is the artist's responsibility when interpreting historical events? How does the artist bring to life historical personalities? In this chapter Leonard Everett Fisher begins by decrying our society's apathy toward history and then tells how the artist of historical books for young readers works to combat this indifference.

Historical Nonfiction for Young Readers: An Artist's Perspective

Leonard Everett Fisher

History is more than written or pictorialized accounts and remembrances of the tides of human thoughts and events. It is not, as some would have it, beyond recall, behind us, and of no practical use.

With that broad view in mind, history is survival bracketed by life and death since the beginning of human presence. History resides in the happenings of that presence. We—all of us—derive from that past our behavior, our character, our responses to the obstacles and challenges heaved at us by life. And we never seem to learn anything from our mistakes. Our ignorance before that fact says little for our collective progress as human beings. To know history is to know a good deal about oneself, let alone the other fellow. To forsake historical knowledge is to invite the continuing cycle of mistakes that burden the human race.

Recently, I heard a college student challenge a query about the Industrial Revolution while fingering some designer jeans in a fashionable clothing store. "What do I need to know that for? It's old stuff. Will knowing who invented the steam engine get me a good job?" The retort surprised me. I thought that such irreverence for the remembrances of things past went out with the '60s. But here it was in the '90s, a generation later. This perception of history's irrelevance brings into focus questions about the objectives of higher education, which today seems "later" rather than "higher."

That young person could never work for me. There would be no interest in utilizing my discipline's history to feed my present and future artistry (such as it is)—an essential road to creativity. Moreover, "higher," or as I now prefer to call it, "later" education in that young person's view was very narrowly defined—a job. Nothing in that definition suggests a broader, more humane purpose as it relates to the world-at-large.

"I am into relevant issues. I am today. The past is past. Dead!" We hear a troublesome perspective if that is the limit of interest. Never once is there realized that one must have an obligation to the past if society is to have pride and excellence in its performance today. Today is the sum of all the yesterdays. And today is the anticipation of all the tomorrows. In a sense there is no "today," only yesterday and tomorrow.

"Those who cannot remember the past," wrote George Santayana, "are condemned to repeat it." How this heroic and monumental view of history relates to one's work as a creator of books for young readers is at the core of my desire to elevate historical memory in the young. And historical memory in the young is an essential ingredient in the search for a more perfect place on our tortured planet.

History has to be made more meaningful and memorable for young readers. They cannot know where they (and the rest of us) are going if none of us knows where we are. And to understand where we are in the light of our changing world we must all know where we have been. The artist and the author of books for young readers, chiefly nonfiction literature, have an obligation toward this end.

Surely, artists and authors have the power to make visible the invisible. But the visibility of whatever event is chosen from history's grab bag by those of us whose books are published with some regularity must be implanted in the young reader's or viewer's memory, let alone in his or her line of sight.

Take, for example, my reference in *The Wailing Wall* (New York: Macmillan, 1989) to "a ferocious Assyrian army" that swept out of the East to destroy the Kingdom of Israel and its ten tribes. Those "Lost Tribes of Israel" disappeared from history but not from memory. Now tie this to our most immediate world. The warring Assyrians of 2700 years ago came out of Mesopotamia—out of the Tigris-Euphrates valley—and are the direct antecedents of the modern Iraqis determined by their own admission to repeat the event of their predecessors. This idea has festered for 2700 years. To understand today's Middle East mind-set, which has not changed for 2700 years or more, it is necessary to understand the currents of that history that now repeat themselves over and over again paralyzing an entire world that no longer desires to be paralyzed by tribal autocracies, hatreds, and vacancies.

Obviously, the artist/author must communicate given historical events as near as they can be factually reconstructed. The 1620 Massachusetts Pilgrims have to be dressed as the pilgrims: the men must not have buckles on their "sugar loaf" hats. It was the 1636 Massachusetts Puritans who had buckles on their hats.

However, beyond the surface, beyond the facts of costuming, accessories, architecture, and more, there are restrictions that underwrite the

From *Pyramid of the Sun Pyramid of the Moon* by Leonard Everett Fisher.

images in the book. Full color as opposed to one, two, or three colors; page size; page space; halftone or line; color separation or painting for laser scanning; and so on. All this is linked to the cost of the book, its shelf price, and targeted market. For these reasons, 600 years of British behavior (1066–1666) had to be limited to 22 pages of a 32-page picture book in one color (except for the full color coats-of-arms indicating the changing reigns) in my book *The Tower of London* (New York: Macmillan, 1987).

I might add, too, that one-color "realistic" images (i.e., black and white) or two- and three-color "realistic" images, for that matter, are in the realm of the abstract, since nature itself does not exist in such a limited palette. Nevertheless, those 32 pages and the pictorial specifications were the restraints within which the tumult of six centuries of English history had to be conveyed and their reality understood—likewise for the professional life and accomplishments of Portugal's Prince Henry (*Prince Henry the Navigator*, New York: Macmillan, 1990).

The same limitations were imposed on *The Wailing Wall*. Except this time, instead of putting 600 years into a very slim format, 4,000 years of history had to be communicated on 22 illustrated pages.

Given the mechanical boundaries and historical facts of the work, the author/artist's first priority is to express a sense of life's drama and energy and make them memorable. Such expressiveness might require foregoing eye-stopping details of costume and environment in favor of a facial expression or the look of an eye. Of what use is the solitary portrait of a cleaned and pressed soldier of the Continental Army aiming his rifle at no discernible target in the conveyance of the idea of revolution and independence when there is not a clue of complaint on his figure or face?

Considering the formidable challenge of a book's prerequisites and physical limitations, illustrations that depict every detail of an historic event with lifeless antiseptic rendering without a sense of time and humanity are forgettable. We exist in an atmosphere charged with our own energies and the dynamics of every moment. It is just that energy that gives life to art and literature. Without it there can be no memory, no past, historical or otherwise. People without a past have no pride; and people without a knowledge of the past have no sense of purpose and should not be called upon to solve whatever social, political, or economic dilemma is current. The pursuit of artistic and literary expressiveness in the interest of history, in the interest of what was, is as valid for the truth of nonfiction as it is for imaginative flights of fiction.

I readily admit to the joy of manipulating words and colors without burdening my audience or myself with a message; of creating form, rhythm, and atmosphere for the sake of themselves. These are basic artistic compulsions—the engines of artistic communication. These are the impulses of a driven artistic soul needed to deliver nonfiction information (as well as fiction) with aesthetic excitement, and make it matter in the mind of the young reader or viewer. These are the spiritual essences that give us a more compassionate art, historical purpose, pride, and a quality of mind without which our humanity cannot take root. And that should be the target of our aspirations, that is what should matter—our humanity.

How I do this? The technique, so to speak—the language of pictorial communication—is something of a mystery since instinct plays a major part in the rendition or execution. Frankly, if I could explain how I do what I do and why my images look like they do I would not have to create visual images. Visual imagery is, in effect, my speech. Also, my social, artistic, and historical interests are so fused after a lifetime of practice that I am not aware how automatically I perform. I have particular beliefs that have given rise to the techniques that I use. Or, to put it another way, my techniques, whatever they are, evolved through the currents of my beliefs. If I believe strongly in something, my visual expression of that "something" will be unwavering. If my belief falters, so will my visual expression falter.

Obviously, I have professional knowledge and long-practiced skills. But knowledge and skill are worthless without a vision. I must have a vision in my head—a vision that emerges from the manuscript—to make the art succeed. And I cannot explain how that vision gets there except to say that it is a combination of interests, desire, expectation, and a manuscript that comes together simultaneously and affects me in some way. If that chemistry is absent and I deal with the manuscript neverthe-less, as has happened on occasion, I fail.

In any event, I pursue my vision with those techniques with which I am now most comfortable. The only thing I carefully plot is the general design—where and how an illustration will appear on a given page, its size, and its relationship to what came before it and what will come after. I do not plot, plan, and calculate every illustration with respect to the interior artistic elements. These things, the aesthetics, as it were—light sources, cast shadows, the interaction of shape, form, color, and so on—all flow out of my educated subconscious. The light source will usually be to my left, up and forward of the picture plane. Everything follows from there as a matter of experience (i.e., the anatomy of objects), logic, and instinct. Often I will respond subconsciously to the design elements. And this response will have an effect on the appearance of the picture. Broadly speaking, the artistic nature of my work emerges without my having to think about it. If I had to think about it, there would be no art. And, once again, if I could explain how art happens, I would not have to do it.

My interests, visions, and the techniques that communicate them—black and white soft engraving (i.e., scratchboard) for form, light, and drama; black and gray acrylic paint for form, volume in space, and drama; color acrylic paint for all of the above plus an additional element of decoration; and various other means—all combine to effect an imagery *in toto* that I trust evokes the response from the viewer that I intend and that the viewer will remember.

No artist or illustrator of books for young readers can be just a picture maker or decorator. There should be some compelling reason that moves such an individual to communicate ideas pictorially that will by force move the rest of us. Sometimes that compelling reason is nothing

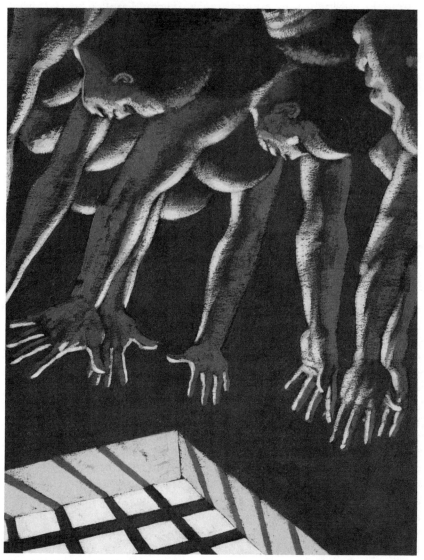

From *Prince Henry the Navigator* by Leonard Everett Fisher.

more than the image itself, the lonely grandeur of which works on our souls and softens our barbarous natures. Sometimes the image is more evident in its story-telling implications to improve our social or historical understanding. I do both. But in either case, I lean toward the dramatic presentation—of severe contrasts in black and white, of powerful form in grays, of bright power in color—to make my point and implant it in the memory of the viewer.

Where it concerns our youth, nonfiction has taken on an increasingly important role in a world exercised by the literature and lyrics of entertainment and escape (be it in a book, on tape, or on television). The management of daily realities has become a problem of bearing responsibility. There is a seeming preference not to bear responsibility for one's neighborly obligations and to escape from a world that few seem willing or able to manage. Moreover, there seems to be such an interchange between reality and surreality that reality now defies recognition.

Consider the astonishing number of young Americans who have reached adulthood since the 1960s without historical perspective, with poor language capability, and with no idea where they are geographically. This creeping indifference to history, language, and geography can and will diminish us, the freest nation on earth. Our narrow, if not vacant, educational vision has spawned bewildering priorities that tear at our character, craftsmanship, and quality.

We delude ourselves if we think that our society can endure if we continue to place cosmetics and appearances over content and substance. It is unsettling to contemplate a strong American Future where today's vision is a stenciled T-shirt, where today's reach is the value of a baseball card, where a successful educational agenda is measured by cartoon puppetry, and where the ultimate goal is to cover us all with a blanket of entertainment. The truth of the matter is that we have put so much currency and faith in our pleasure domes that we are failing to confront our problems with serious resolve. We are too busy with nonsense and silliness to think—the sign of a mindless civilization.

"Why is America wallowing in piffle?" asks columnist and author Russell Baker (*New York Times*, March 10, 1990). "The answer is that the country is nearly brain dead . . . more comfortable to let the mind go soggy. . . ."

In this, our push-button age of information, designer arrogance, power seekers, the addict, the homeless, uncertain world nationalism, terrorism, unrelenting violence, the arena, the roar of the crowd, and the pleasuring of America, among the things we have most to fear is ignorance . . . Ignorance, the Fifth Horseman of the Apocalypse. Ignorance stalks the planet while we at home cheerfully and fearlessly drift along on an adolescent sea of greed, self, and mediocrity.

If there is such a thing as a mission to create books for young readers, it must be more than mere entertainment or the nudging of their fantasies. It must banish ignorance. Artistic toil as such—and here I am not addressing the day-to-day mechanics, but rather the struggle to pursue and maintain an aesthetic raison d'etre—is too compelling not to have one's instincts lurking between fact and reader, image and viewer. And that compulsion starts early in the creative life and process.

Milton Meltzer has written over eighty books dealing with history, biography, and social issues. Most of his books examine how the forces of change have affected not only leaders but ordinary people throughout history. He has received many awards for his writing, including five nominations for the National Book Award.

* * *

How might an author help young readers establish common bonds with the people from history? What place do values have in shaping an author's perspective on social change? Whether Meltzer writes history or biography, he tries to let people tell their story in their own words to help provide a new perspective on the world around us.

4

Voices from the Past

Milton Meltzer

Almost everything I write has to do with social change—how it comes about, the forces that advance it, and the forces that resist it, the moral issues that beset men and women seeking to realize their humanity. I don't pretend to be objective or neutral in my books. I start with what I am. The direction my work takes comes out of the values I am committed to. No writer is ever disinterested, no matter how much he or she may claim to be. It's a question of what interests the work will serve. If you believe in certain values—peace, equality, economic security, freedom of expression—then implicit in your work is the urge to contribute to the realization of those values.

There are many ways to approach the writing of history. My own work began to take a certain form many years ago. It combines two aspects of historical writing: the straight narrative account of what happened (as I see it and interpret it), and the documentation of it. Traditionally these two are published separately. There are books that provide a collection of documentary sources and other books that tell the story derived from a study of these sources. My purpose is to meld the eyewitness accounts with my narrative to create a dramatic history that will illuminate fundamental issues and bring to life the people who shaped them. I have found that pattern effective no matter what the scope of the subject. In *The American Revolutionaries* (Crowell, 1987) or in *Voices from the Civil War* (Crowell, 1989) it is the story of the people who fought in those great upheavals, as well as the people back home. In *Bread—and Roses* (Mentor, 1977) it is those fifty tumultuous years when workers battled for a living wage and to establish unions; in *Brother, Can You Spare a Dime?* (Knopf, 1969) it is the first few years of the Great Depression; in *Bound for the Rio Grande* (Knopf, 1974) it is the internal uproar caused by our war against Mexico. In *Never to Forget* (Harper, 1976) it is the ancient seeding of anti-Semitism and the twelve years of Hitler's rule that brought on the Holocaust; and in *Rescue* (Harper, 1988) it is the deeds of gentle men and women who cared enough to try to save the lives of Jews in Nazi-occupied Europe.

In preparing to write such a history I read as widely as possible in the available sources, both primary and secondary, making notes on what I think I may want to use. At the same time I hunt everywhere for the documentary material that will let people speak in their own words. I don't mean only the kings and generals—the Lords of Creation—I mean the anonymous ones upon whom society rests and without whom the superstructure would collapse. Their words are found in letters, journals, diaries, autobiographies, in songs and poems, in speeches, in court testimony and in legislative hearings, in newspaper reports, in eyewitness accounts, and, more recently, in oral history interviews. I want the reader to discover how it felt to be alive at that time, I want the reader to share directly in that experience, to know the doubts, the hopes, the fears, the anger and the joy of the men, women, and children who were the blood and bone of that history.

Some of you, as teachers, have probably had the experience of working in a town where a major event occurred in the past—let's say a strike—in a time before the students in your school were born. Yet the boys and girls know nothing about it. It is not discussed or even mentioned in their schools. That part of the community's life has been hidden from history.

Why? Because the history of so-called "ordinary people" is not thought to be important. And because many of the books used in the schools downplay actions of working people or the poor when they challenge social injustice. It is that neglect which has led many scholars in recent years to search the "history from below." For workers, women, ethnic and racial minorities, immigrants—all have a history that should be uncovered, and made known.

For it isn't only historians who are interested in the past. What boys or girls in your classroom are not interested in who they are and where they came from? Interested in the story of their families, their community, their organizations? They need only to be shown examples of how fascinating and how significant their personal and family histories are to change the all-too-common impression that history is a bore and a waste of time.

After all, what is history but the coherent story of the lives of people of the past? And not just of the empire builders, but people very much like themselves. And thus in the kind of history I try to write, young readers find those timeless constants which all persons and societies share: sorrow and happiness, success and defeat, effort and reward, effort and failure, love and hatred, guilt, shame, pride, compassion, cruelty, justice, injustice, birth, death. Everywhere you look, no matter what the time or place, you find these great fixed elements. We cannot imagine that life in the future will ever be without them.

When young people, or adults for that matter, read this kind of history—the original documents left behind by the people of the time, which are then woven into a narrative—they are helped to locate their individual lives in the chain of generations. They can find common bonds with people far off in time and space, recognizing in them our common humanity, while understanding the differences that may separate us.

Such history provides a way of understanding one's background, of finding roots that grow not only out of the family, but out of the workplace, the community, the region, the nation.

To examine the past by reading what people said of it in their own words is to gain a new perspective on the world around us. Exposed to such living testimony, readers find out not only what people did, but how they felt and thought about what they lived through. They see how things have changed; they develop a sense of perspective that makes their world of today more understandable.

I think too that this kind of history helps students to see they are not outsiders, living on the fringe of great events, just looking on as the world turns and changes. History written on the grand scale, sweeping over great issues and crises, dealing only with the powerful few, can make students feel insignificant. What do they have to do with all that?

But reading the personal record, told in their own words, returns readers to the face-to-face world of everyday life. It connects them to life as people experienced it *then*—whether in their own parents' generation, or a hundred, or five hundred years ago.

My emphasis on the experience of ordinary people does not mean that I think power and power-holders should not be investigated in the telling of the story. The grave abuses of power the nation suffered from in the 1960s, 1970s, and 1980s—Vietnam, Watergate, the Iran Contra scandal, the savings and loan disaster, and other events I will not stop to list—fill us with disgust. The best defense against their continuing to occur is to acquire an understanding of the institutions and the actors in whom power is invested and through whom power operates. Our best values make us feel concern for the people without power. But they cannot act in their own defense unless they understand the powerful and learn how they seek to control affairs.

Young people, says the Stanford University historian David M. Kennedy,

> should be growing into a consciousness of their efficacy, not
> prematurely resigning themselves to a status as mere flotsam
> on the great tides of history. As a society we rely on the young

to agitate and churn and push forward. In fact, however, the young too often either take the world for granted, or scorn it as a contemptible inheritance of folly and injustice.

But history, Professor Kennedy goes on, properly taught or written,

can transmit two important lessons. The first is that despite all the evident stupidity and oppression in the world, mankind has in fact won at least some victories over at least some of these follies and injustices; that those victories have been hard-won, and are even now in jeopardy; that eternal vigilance—and historically informed vigilance—is indeed the price of liberty.

The second philosophical lesson that history can impart is that the world, as William James said, is not a finished place. There is much work to be done, and the young—especially the young—can help to do it.

The history I've tried to write gives us examples of real men and women trying to meet the issues of their day, just as we here and now are called upon to solve the issues of our own time. Honest writing will point to the value, and to the necessity as well, of human efforts to make the world move closer to our highest ideas.

A last word about the art of writing history. And here I turn to one of our most respected historians, C. Vann Woodward. Recently he said:

All history that the historian writes—with the rare exception of that part of which he was an eyewitness—has to be imagined before it can be written. Documents and other sources help, but unless he is present at them, events have to be reconstructed by the imagination. To say that good history "reads like fiction" always struck me as a dubious and presumptuous compliment. It should read better than fiction for being about the real instead of the invented. To catch and convey in words the color and texture and tone and meaning of an infinite variety of events, their interrelations and their participants, demands no less of the historian than of the novelist, and may well demand more.

Pam Conrad is an author of historical fiction, contemporary realistic fiction, and picture books for young readers. Her historical novel *Prairie Songs* (Harper, 1985) won the International Reading Association Children's Book Award. She has written other books about the prairie, including *My Daniel* (Harper, 1989) and *Prairie Visions: The Life and Times of Solomon Butcher* (Harper, 1991). Pam Conrad has also won the Edgar Allan Poe Award for *Stonewords* (Harper, 1990).

*   *   *

How does the author of historical fiction meld fiction and fact? Is the universal human experience as important as the historical details? Pam Conrad addresses the risks and rewards of writing fiction placed in historical settings.

5

Finding Ourselves in History

Pam Conrad

I'm always a little intimidated when I speak to or write for the academic community, people with high and impressive degrees who are involved in education. I myself was the daughter of a gas station mechanic until I was in junior high. Then he went to college to become a teacher. The vocabulary in my house changed. I was no longer overhearing talk about slipping fan belts, bonking transmissions, and bald tires, but now I was hearing new words: motivation, evaluation, syllabus, pedagogy. I didn't like it. I had been perfectly comfortable waiting on a pile of tires after dancing class for my father to take me home. But things were changing. Soon he wore jackets with leather elbow patches. He got a pair of glasses. His hands grew clean. My mother typed a lot. I didn't like it, and while I'd been a pretty good daughter most of my life, I was kind of ornery.

So no one was surprised when I dropped out of a teachers college after one semester to get married. The academic life was not for me. But in many ways I followed my father's footsteps. Twenty years later I got my B.A. the hard way, part time while raising children and handling a divorce.

So I have never been the great student. I am helpless and hopeless at history. I cannot remember the dates of my daughter's dentist appointments and I can't remember when the Civil War ended. I hate to play Trivial Pursuit because I know sooner or later I will see those shocked expressions of disbelief when my friends discover how dumb I am. I am totally in the dark when it comes to telling teachers how to bring history to young readers, how to reveal their heritage to them through my own books or those of others, or what age levels are best for approaching what topics. I am not an expert on anything. So my cards are on the table.

Now after that major disclaimer, I can tell you what I *truly* am, and what exactly it is that I *can* share with you. I am a storyteller, a spinner of tales and adventures, and sometimes when I am very lucky my imagination takes me not only to a different place but also to a different time, and then my work is called "historical." A nonfiction writer friend of mine once said, he was a writer of "truth," and I was a writer of "nontruth." So historical fiction is a little tricky; it's a truthful setting for an illusion of nontruths.

I have seen teachers cringe when I tell kids I wrote *Prairie Songs* (Harper, 1985) without doing any initial research. I didn't have to. I had been reading pioneer stories and old journals all my life from Laura Ingalls Wilder to Mari Sandoz, so when I sat down to write *Prairie Songs*, I knew the place and the time as if I had been born and raised there myself. I truly experience this sense of immediacy with my writing. It wasn't until I was done with *Prairie Songs* that I finally did my research, not to gather facts, but to check my information, and my information, I am pleased to tell you, was accurate.

All this reminds me of Lois Lowry's Newbery speech. She said:

> I would be a terrible newspaper reporter because I can't write well about huge events. They use the verb "cover" in newsrooms. They send reporters out to "cover" things. But if they sent me out to cover some catastrophe, I would stand there watching while flood water carried away houses, and flames spurted into the sky, and buildings toppled, and victims were extricated by the hundreds. I would watch it all, and I would see it all. But I would write about a broken lunch box lying shattered in a puddle. (1990, p. 416)

I think Lois Lowry is speaking of truths and nontruths here. The truths are all there to be recorded, facts, as they happen, but it is the tiny mystery lying in a puddle that grips the fiction writer, the storyteller. Because it's here that we sift truths through the filter of our own personal histories and make a new history. Maybe to make sense of our own lives.

My Daniel (Harper, 1989) is one of my historical books. In it an old woman tells the story about her childhood and her older brother who'd found dinosaur bones on their Nebraska farm in the nineteenth century. The brother dies suddenly, leaving the responsibility of getting the dinosaur to the right museum in the hands of his sister, the narrator. Before I began writing this novel I found myself living in the dream house of my marriage when my husband abruptly left, leaving the responsibility of the house in my hands. I didn't even know I was beginning to write the book when one morning, I jumped out of the shower three or four times to jot down words that were pouring into my mind. This is from the book:

> I loved my brother, Daniel, loved him with a white fire. And like a burnt-out buffalo chip will crumble into dust if you stomp your foot beside it, that's what I was like once Daniel

was gone. I never loved anyone like that again. And I always knew that one good jolt would've robbed me of my form and I'd have been nothing more than dust in a prairie wind.

That's how much I loved my brother, and yet, even now, these years later, I have forgotten his face, and there's no photoprint, no sketch to bring him back to me. Only my memories and in these he is faceless—his shoulder disappearing behind the rump of the cow, his legs churning up the side of the soddy roof, or his hands, that day, limp and lifeless in the brown grass, up by the graveyard of dragons. (1989, pp. 24–25)

I see today it was history starting to leak through the filter of my own life.

With *Prairie Songs* as well, I had been reading for years about grim living conditions on the prairies, about women going mad, some growing to hate their farmer husbands, and many watching their children die. In *Prairie Songs* there are two children whose little sister Delilah had died. One night their mother returns after being at the birth and death of a neighbor's baby. I cannot imagine that the death of a baby in the nineteenth century was any different than the death of a baby in the twentieth, and because I had had my own baby die, history filtered through me again:

I could see Poppa put his arms around her and pull her to him. "It's over now, Clara," he murmured. "It's done."

Momma's sobs filled the room, and Poppa patted her and shushed her like a child. "How is Emmeline?" he asked. "Is she all right now?"

"She's alive. Barely. Half alive, knowing her baby's dead. Doc couldn't do anything. All that doctoring know-how and there was just nothing he could do that I couldn't have done all by myself. It just went on and on." She collapsed into the chair, and I heard Lester move next to me. He was awake, too.

"And then when the baby came, a tiny boy, Doc took one look at the gray little child, and I guess he knew there was just no hope. He worked and worked on Emmeline. She was bleeding so." Momma grew upset. "Oh, J.T., I'm sorry to be going on like this."

Poppa pulled a chair alongside her. "It's over now, Clara."

"But I held that baby, J.T., and he wouldn't breathe. You have no idea. He just jerked a little, and I tried to keep him warm, give him life, but I couldn't. I couldn't do it." She began to cry.

"Shhhh, now," Poppa said. "You did all you could."

"Momma?" Lester's whisper seemed to shatter the air in the room, as if he had given away the secret that we were listening.

"Momma? The baby died?"

"Yes, sweetheart." She walked slowly to our beds and sat down near Lester. Her hair was down her back, and her face was all swollen. "The baby died. He was just too weak and little to live. Come," she said, drawing back the blankets. "Come let me feel how alive you are."

I sprang up too, and both Lester and me went into her arms. She was trembling and began to rock us. I felt Poppa gather the blanket up around the three of us, and I closed my eyes. We rocked slowly in big rocking movements, back and forth, as vast as the Milky Way, as wide and as far as the prairie.

"Momma?" Lester asked.

"What, honey?"

"Am I gonna die, Momma?"

"Oh, no, Lester, no."

"Are you gonna die, Momma?"

"No, no, sweetie, not me."

"Just Delilah, Momma? That's all?"

"Just Delilah," she answered. "Just Delilah, that's all."

And then Momma began to cry, a sad mournful lament that I had never heard before and I have never heard since. I must have fallen asleep in Momma's arm that night. (1985, pp. 101–4)

It's always my hope that this story will transport the reader to another time and another place, but is this history? Can I claim that this is anyone's heritage? In my heart I know it is only my own personal truth.

I've had another experience with historical fiction that, gratefully, has been a much more humorous one. Kent Brown from Boyds Mills Press contacted me awhile ago and asked if I would write captions for a book that would be supposedly the sketch book of the ship's boy on the Santa Maria in Columbus's first voyage to America. Well, I've told you already that I was not a wonderful student, and the thought of Columbus really gagged me. All I could think of was third-grade bulletin board art projects with those three awful boats and sailors in tights with big buckles on their shoes. And crosses. Big wooden crosses thrust into the sand. It was with a certain ornery reluctance that I picked up and read Columbus's log for his first journey.

I was astounded. The log spoke to me, and what had started out as a job of writing captions became the working out of a full young adult novel. Not because the fifteenth century intrigued me, and not because the politics and nonsense of the day were so thrilling, but because I discovered I was so much like the ship's boy.

Now I had never learned of this particular incident in school, and certainly such an event was never illustrated with construction paper and glue on any bulletin board I'd ever seen, but the ship's boy, this twelve-year-old kid, *sank* the Santa Maria when they got to the islands. Imagine! And it turned out he sank it on Christmas Eve because the whole crew had partied and drunk and fallen into a drunken stupor, leaving the boy at the helm. Doing his best, he sailed the ship right onto a coral reef. Imagine how that rattled me. My own father was an active alcoholic when I was twelve, and there were certainly experiences I'd had that translated, that filtered.

In addition to this experience that Pedro and I shared, the other thing that drew me to this story and this historical point was that within the last two years I had bought my own sailboat and had attempted to sail it to Block Island. Now I know there is absolutely no comparison between the first transatlantic sail and a jaunt across Gardner's Bay, but the fear and exhilaration I felt could not have been much less that the ship's boy's. I discovered that every time I went on my own boat, the Sarah Moon, my experiences began translating into fifteenth century Santa Maria adventures. For instance, one day I was with someone who was encouraging me to jump off the side of the boat. I am not a good swimmer—that's putting it mildly—fact is, I'm a sinker. But this friend jumped in ahead and patiently bobbed near the side of the boat while I worked up my courage. I finally did slide off the edge, only to find that my bathing suit was hooked to a cleat and I dangled over the edge frantically laughing, until I could fling myself back into the cockpit. All this, incredibly translated into Columbus material. This is an entry from Pedro's journal that I wrote myself:

September 25, 1492

We have come to clear waters at last. So clear and so calm that once again I had a chance to swim with the crew. This time a few promised to toss me over, claiming that was the only way to learn, but luckily Diego threatened to teach a lesson to whoever tried such a thing. He went ahead of me and called to me as I sat for a long while on the gunwale. Out in the sun with my shirt off, I was surprised to see how brown my hands had gotten from the wrist down.

"Leap, Pedro. I am here," Diego called.

"I'm frightened," I answered and the others laughed, trying to splash me from the water. The Admiral was behind me, his arms crossed, his face serious.

"Can you swim, sir?" I asked him.

"Like a porpoise," he answered. "And I have come to observe over the years, that those who take easily to the written word—scribes, readers—they are the best swimmers."

It was what I needed. I looked down into the calm water. And at the men who couldn't read and yet were floating before me like so many corks. I thought of my letters, my journal, the Admiral's heavy log, and keeping my eyes on Diego, I slid myself to the very edge and went over. But I am ashamed to say I was not sea wet within the next instant. I was suddenly dangling over the side by a cleat that had hooked onto my pants. Screaming and kicking, I hung above the water and the crew's hooting. Even Diego, I could hear him laughing. Until suddenly behind me, a hand clasped my arm and I felt my pants eased off the cleat and I was free.

I flew straight down like a diving bird, and once smacking the cold wet surface, went down farther and farther. I feared I would never come up, but just continue down away from Diego and my Admiral and the Santa Maria. But soon I was emerging and there were friends around me, their laughing faces transformed by the hair laid flat and wet against their heads. A couple took hold of me and I held on for dear life. Little by little they taught me to tread water, to dive below and open my eyes to an incredible light of green. I guess the Admiral was right. I didn't want to go back on board. I dove deeper and deeper, paddling like mad to catch my breath and find Diego. But after awhile we all climbed back up on board. I was shivering and Sancho told everyone to look at my blue lips. I am sorry I waited so long to try this.

In conclusion, I have to admit that the making up of any story is like levitating. I find that the act of writing contemporary fiction lets me levitate about eight inches off the ground. Whereas the act of writing historical fiction forces me to levitate two miles over the earth.

Both are very difficult, very satisfying, very extraordinary achievements, as you well know if you've ever levitated. However, sometimes I think historical fiction has taken the greatest amount of personal courage, partially because of the risks and the daring, but mostly because there are so many Truth people out there, people like you who are watching me.

REFERENCES

Conrad, P. (1986). *Prairie songs*. New York: Harper.

Conrad, P. (1989). *My Daniel*. New York: Harper.

Conrad, P. (1991). *Pedro's journal: A voyage with Christopher Columbus*, April 3, 1492–February 14, 1493. Honesdale, Pa.: Caroline House.

Lowry, L. (1990). Newbery Medal acceptance. *The Horn Book*, 66 (4), 412–21.

Russell Freedman is the author of more than thirty-five nonfiction books, most of which were written for young readers. Many of his works are biographies or about historical topics, and he has become noted for his fresh writing style and his masterful use of archival photographs to enliven his subjects further. Russell Freedman lives in New York City but travels extensively to gather information for his books. He won the 1988 Newbery Medal for *Lincoln: A Photobiography* (Clarion, 1987) and the 1990 Orbis Pictus Award for *Franklin Delano Roosevelt* (Clarion, 1990).

* * *

How does a biographer writing for younger readers bring to life his subjects? Can the dramatic elements of story telling strengthen nonfiction? Russell Freedman discusses the goals and responsibilities of an author who chooses to write nonfiction accounts about historical figures and events.

6

Bring 'Em Back Alive

Russell Freedman

Not long ago I received a letter from a boy in Indiana who wrote: "Dear Mr. Freedman, I read your biography of Abraham Lincoln and liked it very much. Did you take the photographs yourself?"

Then he added: "I'm a photographer too!"

I value that letter because of its humor, and because of what the humor implies. Did you take the pictures yourself? he asks. That youngster came away from my book with the feeling that Abraham Lincoln was a real person who must have lived the day before yesterday. That's exactly the response I'm aiming for. After all, the goal of any biographer, any historian, is to make the past seem real, to breathe life and meaning into people and events that are dead and gone.

This is a special responsibility if you're writing for an audience of impressionable young readers. Your book may be the first they've ever read on the subject. They will come to it with great expectations—with high hopes and open hearts.

I sometimes hear that children today aren't really interested in history. It's one of their least favorite subjects. They look upon history as a kind of castor oil that one has to take—something that's good for you, maybe, but repulsive.

If that attitude exists, then it can only result from the way history is taught. I believe that history can be far more exciting than any imaginary adventure story because truth is so much stranger than fiction. Rather than castor oil, history should be thought of as a tonic. It should wake us up, because it is the story of ourselves.

The word *history*, remember, is made up mostly of the word *story*. Historians traditionally have been storytellers. Going all the way back to Homer and beyond, historians have been people who were telling, singing, reciting epic poems. They were storytellers sitting around

41

the fire inside the cave, holding their audience spellbound on a winter's night.

When I begin a new book, I like to remember that tradition. I think of myself first of all as a storyteller, and I do my best to give dramatic shape to my subject, whatever it is. I always feel that I have a story to tell that is worth telling, and I want to tell it as clearly, as simply, and as forcefully as I can.

By story telling, I do not mean making things up, of course. I don't mean invented scenes or manufactured dialogue or imaginary characters. As a writer of nonfiction, I have a pact with the reader to stick to the facts, to be as factually accurate as human frailty will allow. What I write is based on research, on the documented historical record. And yet there are certain story-telling techniques that I can use without straying from the straight and narrow path of factual accuracy. Facts in a literal sense do not rule out art or imagination.

There's a story to almost everything, and the task of the nonfiction writer is to find the story—the narrative line—that exists in nearly every subject. Jean Fritz puts it succinctly and well when she speaks of giving dramatic shape to her books. "Nonfiction can be told in a narrative voice and still maintain its integrity," she says. "The art of fiction is making up facts; the art of nonfiction is using facts to make up a form." ("Biography: Readability Plus Responsibility." *The Horn Book*, November/December 1988, pp. 759–760.)

Recently in *The New York Times* (*The New York Times Book Review*, January 27, 1991) I read a review of the current crop of children's dictionaries. It was written by Betsy Hearne, editor of *The Bulletin of the Center for Children's Books*. Choosing the dictionary she liked best, Betsy Hearne said: "I was immediately drawn to the *Lincoln Writing Dictionary for Children* (Harcourt Brace Jovanovich) because of its storytelling quality. Definitions are frequently accompanied by quotations that not only clarify words but use them imaginatively ('"Come near me while I *sing* the ancient ways" (William Butler Yeats)') or by evocative explanations ('There are many stories about Robin Hood's *accuracy* with a bow and arrow')."

So, if a dictionary can have a story-telling quality, certainly a book of history or biography can. Betsy Hearne, I think, is using the word *story* in the sense of igniting the reader's imagination, evoking pictures and scenes in the reader's mind. Story telling means creating vivid and believable people, places, and events—creating a convincing, meaningful, and memorable world. It means pulling the reader into that world. And it means using a narrative framework, a story-telling voice, that will keep that reader turning the pages with a mounting sense of anticipation and discovery.

Nonfiction can and does make use of traditional story-telling techniques. One of the most effective techniques, for example, is to create a vivid, detailed scene that the reader can visualize—like a scene from a movie, if you will. In my book *Children of the Wild West* (Clarion, 1983), I use that device to help establish the setting and the mood, and to pull the reader into the story. After a short introduction, the book's opening chapter begins like this:

> It was a typical wagon train of the 1840s. The swaying wagons, plodding animals, and walking people stretched out along the trail for almost a mile.
>
> Near the end of the train, a boy holding a hickory stick moved slowly through the dust. He used the stick to poke and prod the cows that trudged beside him, mooing and complaining.
>
> "Get along!" he shouted. "Hey! Hey! Get along!"
>
> Dust floated in the air. It clogged the boy's nose, parched his throat, and coated his face. His cheeks were smeared where he had brushed away the big mosquitoes that buzzed about everywhere.
>
> Up ahead, his family's wagon bounced down the trail. He would hear the *crack* of his father's whip above the heads of the oxen that pulled the wagon. The animals coughed and snorted. The chains on their yokes rattled with every step they took. (13)

Now, that is nonfiction. The scene is dramatized in order to make it visual, and in order to convey the texture and flavor of the event and the time. But it is entirely factual. And it introduces the story line—the narrative framework—of the book. *Children of the Wild West* is the story of children who accompanied their parents on the great westward journey, and the story of what happened to them after they arrived in the West.

Another familiar story-telling device is to develop character, to create vivid word pictures of people. One way to do that is to point out the telling personal details that help characterize a person. There are plenty of personal details that provide glimpses of Abraham Lincoln's life in the White House, for example. He said "Howdy" to visitors and invited them to "stay a spell." He greeted diplomats while wearing carpet slippers, called his wife "Mother" at receptions, and told bawdy jokes at cabinet meetings. He mended his gold-rimmed spectacles with a string. One passage in my Lincoln biography (*Lincoln*: A *Photobiography*, Clarion: 1987) that people often seem to remember and comment on is the simple inventory of the President's pockets after he was assassinated—spectacles folded in a silver case, a small velvet eyeglass cleaner, a large linen handkerchief with "A. Lincoln" stitched in red, an ivory pocketknife trimmed with silver, a brown leather wallet lined with purple silk, and inside that wallet, a Confederate five-dollar bill and eight newspaper clippings praising the President, clippings that Lincoln had cut out and saved.

It's important for the reader to picture people and events, and it's also important to hear those people talking. In real life, the way we get to know people is by observing them and also by *listening* to what they say. In a nonfiction book, quotations from diaries, journals, letters, and memoirs can take the place of dialogue in a fictional story. Quotations help give a book a sense of immediacy, of reality.

One of my favorite quotes about Lincoln, and one of the most revealing, comes from his law partner, William Herndon. Lincoln adored his sons, denied them nothing, and seemed incapable of disciplining them. He liked to take Willie and Tad to the office when he worked on Sundays, and their wild behavior just about drove Herndon mad. "The boys were absolutely unrestrained in their amusement," he complained. "If they pulled down all the books from the shelves, bent the points of all the pens, overturned the spittoon, it never disturbed the serenity of their father's good nature. I have felt many and many a time that I wanted to wring the necks of those little brats and pitch them out of the windows" (p. 41).

As far as Lincoln was concerned, his boys could do no wrong. His wife, Mary, remarked: "Mr. Lincoln was very exceedingly indulgent to his children. He always said: 'It is my pleasure that my children are free, happy, and unrestrained by parental tyranny. Love is the chain whereby to bind a child to its parents' " (p. 43).

Another essential story-telling device is the use of anecdote. My desk dictionary gives two definitions of anecdote: (1) a short account of some interesting or humorous incident, and (2) secret or hitherto undivulged particulars of history or biography. The word comes from the Greek word *anekdota*, meaning "things unpublished," which gives us some idea of why anecdotes are so appealing—because they're closely related to gossip. A good anecdote can do wonders to reveal character and bring a subject to life. The best anecdotes are the ones that conjure up a vivid picture while throwing an illuminating spotlight on the subject.

For example, a couple of anecdotes from the boyhood of Franklin Roosevelt provide insight into his developing character and into the political and diplomatic skills that he would display so masterfully as an adult. Here's a passage from my recent Roosevelt biography (*Franklin Delano Roosevelt*, Clarion: 1990):

> His mother often said that she would never try to influence Franklin against his own wishes, but in her heart, she was quite sure she knew what was best for her darling boy. Franklin learned to agree cheerfully with his mother on most things big and small, but he knew how to get around her, how to have his

own way. When he wanted to skip a piano lesson, he told his governess that his hand hurt. When he didn't want to attend church services on Sunday, he complained of a headache that always seemed to clear up by early afternoon. His parents called it "Franklin's Sunday headache."

He never rebelled openly, but now and again he would do something to show his spirit. At Campobello one summer, he got in trouble with some other boys for releasing all the horses in the hotel stable in the middle of the night. Another time, when he was about nine, he climbed to the top of one of his father's giant oaks at Springwood. He sat there while darkness fell, watching in gleeful silence as the servants and his worried mother called for him from far below. (pp. 12–13)

One of the themes I wanted to convey in this biography was a sense of the complex, evolving, intense relationship between Franklin and Eleanor. Here's a passage where I combine a couple of revealing anecdotes with quotes from Eleanor, from FDR, and from their son James:

Franklin and Eleanor were both exceptionally strong-willed people. And while they led independent lives, they were also close. "We are really very dependent on each other though we do see so little of each other," Eleanor wrote from one of her trips. "I miss you and hate to feel you so far away."

Franklin sometimes teased his wife about her reputation as a "do-gooder," but he was enormously proud of her and would not allow anyone to criticize her in his presence. A portrait of Eleanor hung over the door of his White House study. It had been painted long before, when she was very young. Once, when Frances Perkins was leaving the president's study, she paused in front of the portrait and looked at it carefully.

"I always liked that portrait of Eleanor," FDR said. "That's just the way Eleanor looks, you know—lovely hair, pretty eyes."

Roosevelt could be warm and affectionate. Yet even with those close to him, he seldom talked about personal matters or discussed his deepest feelings. Eleanor felt there was a part of himself that her husband allowed no one to see. "He had no real confidants," she once said. "I don't think I was ever his confidante, either."

And yet Roosevelt could express his feelings in deeds. His son James recalled the day the family learned that Eleanor's brother Hall had died: "Father struggled to her side and put his arm around her. 'Sit down,' he said, so tenderly. I can still hear it. And he sank down beside her and hugged her and kissed her and held her head on his chest. . . ." (p. 118)

Another of my recent books is about the Wright brothers (*The Wright Brothers: How They Invented the Airplane*, Holiday House, 1991) and their invention of the airplane. A key theme here is the close partnership and trust between the brothers, which made it possible for them to function so effectively as a team. As the book opens, I focus on their close relationship by combining a quote from Wilbur with a brief but telling anecdote:

> "From the time we were little children," Wilbur Wright once said, "my brother Orville and myself lived together, played together, worked together, and in fact, thought together."
>
> As the brothers worked side by side in their bicycle shop, they would sometimes start whistling or humming the same tune at exactly the same moment. Their voices were so much alike, a listener in another room had a hard time telling them apart. (p. 3)

There are any number of incidents from the Wright brothers' boyhood and youth that illustrate their mechanical aptitude and their ingenuity. Once, when Orville was still in high school, they built a printing press using scrap parts scrounged from a local junkyard. Orville planned to use this press to turn out a weekly newspaper that he was starting. To make even copies, they had to devise a way of putting the exact amount of pressure required on the type each time. Orville found an old family buggy with a folding top. The hinged bars that supported the top were exactly what they needed, and so the buggy frame was mated to the press bed. While the press looked makeshift, it could print a thousand pages an hour.

Some time later, a visiting printer from Chicago dropped by to see the homemade press. He went into the press room, stood by the machine, looked at it, then sat down beside it, and finally crawled underneath it. After he had been under the machine for quite a while, he crawled back out, stood up, and said: "Well, it works, but I certainly don't see how!"

My favorite quote in this book comes from Orville and refers to the brothers' 1901 wind-tunnel experiments, which provided the scientific data they needed to build their successful gliders and powered airplanes. Nowhere is their persistence and determination more apparent than in the story of this particular series of experiments. For weeks they were absorbed in painstaking and systematic lab work—testing, measuring, and calculating as they tried to unlock the secrets of an aircraft wing. This work was tedious. It was repetitive. From our vantage point today, it doesn't seem nearly as dramatic or glamorous as the Wright brothers' daredevil test flights at Kitty Hawk. And yet Wilbur and Orville knew that with their wind-tunnel tests, they were exploring uncharted territory. Each new bit of data jotted down in their notebooks added to their understanding of how an airfoil works. They would look back on those winter weeks as a time of great excitement and joy, a period when each new day promised discoveries waiting to be made. Here's what Orville remembered about those winter weeks. He said: "Wilbur and I could hardly wait for morning to come, to get at something that interested us. *That's* happiness."

And that's the attitude I wanted to convey in my book about the Wright brothers—their work, and the exultant sense of fulfillment that they found in that work, is what makes their lives meaningful.

But of course, nothing is as simple as it seems. At the end of the book I include another quote from Orville in this passage:

> There were moments when Orville looked back wistfully to those long-ago days when flying was still a dream that he shared with his brother. He once said, "I got more thrill out of flying before I had ever been in the air at all—while lying in bed thinking how exciting it would be to fly." (p. 116)

PART TWO

Research and Other Considerations

Carl Tomlinson has written many journal articles dealing with language arts and children's literature and has specialized in multicultural and international literature. He is the coauthor of *Essentials of Children's Literature,* which is to be published by Allyn and Bacon.

Michael Tunnell has authored a number of articles and books about children's literature, including *The Prydain Companion* (Greenwood, 1989), and he has written three children's picture books (*Chinook!, The Joke's on George,* and *Beauty and the Beastly Children*), all forthcoming from Tambourine Books.

Donald Richgels has written many articles for reading journals and is the coauthor of the book *Literacy's Beginnings* (Allyn and Bacon, 1990).

Tomlinson and Richgels are language arts and/or children's literature professors in the Department of Curriculum and Instruction at Northern Illinois University. Tunnell is a children's literature professor in the Department of Elementary Education at Brigham Young University.

*   *   *

How do history textbooks and history-related trade books compare as tools for teaching history in elementary and middle schools? Tomlinson, Tunnell, and Richgels compare and contrast history textbooks and trade books by examining the content considerations of emphasis and coverage. They also compare features of writing, including form, text structure, style, and "interestingness."

The Content and Writing of History in Textbooks and Trade Books

Carl M. Tomlinson, Michael O. Tunnell,
and Donald J. Richgels

Early in this century, the study of history, once considered a mainstay in any general curriculum, gave way in the elementary and middle school grades to what came to be known as "social studies." In these classes the story of our past was merged with information about current social, economic, and political structures of the world's societies. Sharing limited class time, the study of history languished.

Now, educators are beginning to rediscover the importance of the study of history. They have begun to assert—contrary to notions held for decades—that history is relevant to the non–college-bound student (Gagnon, 1985), that younger children are capable of coping with the time concepts inherent in the study of history (Downey and Levstik, 1988), and that the problems today's students face can be addressed by learning about the past (Ravitch, 1985).

As history becomes a more important part of the elementary and middle school curriculum, it is important to reevaluate the materials used to teach it. Traditionally, history has been taught from one main source, a history textbook. (Social studies/history textbooks will be referred to in this chapter as history textbooks.) But as recently as 1988, studies reported by Sewall indicated that students at all grade levels identified social studies as their most boring class and cited social studies texts as one of the major reasons for this. Clearly, the materials used to teach history are due for an examination.

During the last two decades, the number and variety of children's trade books have increased dramatically, and teachers have reported success using trade books to teach reading, as well as other subjects, by employing whole language teaching methods and an integrated-day approach. These developments have made available to the history teacher a promising new teaching tool, the historical trade book.

The purpose of this chapter is to compare history textbooks with historical fiction and nonfictional trade books as tools for teaching history. Through this comparison, we hope to make a strong case for using trade books in elementary and middle school history classes and to encourage teachers to incorporate these books into their history teaching, either instead of the history text or in concert with it. Our comparison will be organized around the content and writing features generally representative of the two types of books. Figure 7–1 provides an overview of the comparison as well as profiles of the two types of books.

Content of History Textbooks and Trade Books

Emphasis

History texts used in U.S. schools traditionally have been little more than repositories of dates, names, and facts that students have been required to memorize. One must ask whether the learning of such content helps students gain the judgment, perspective, and knowledge of human nature and society that Gagnon (1988) describes as being the dividends of studying history. As early as 1893, the Committee of Ten (an NEA Commission on high school curriculum) noted that memorizing facts was "the most difficult and the least important outcome of historical study. When the facts are chosen with as little discrimination as in many school textbooks, when they are mere lists of lifeless dates, details of military movements . . . [t]hey are repellent" (as reported in Ravitch, 1985, p. 13). The committee suggested that history be taught in a way that promotes judgment and thinking, and that it be taught in conjunction with literature, geography, art, and languages.

In contrast to textbooks' emphasis on facts, historical trade literature emphasizes human motives, human problems, and the consequences of human actions. In historical literature, facts, names, and dates are woven into the story as part of the setting. When facts are an integral part of a compelling story, they are much more interesting and of more immediate consequence to a young reader than when presented in lists and pseudo-prose collections, as in a textbook.

Another important difference in emphasis is in the characters featured in the two types of books. Textbooks take a "top–down" approach to historical events. That is, they emphasize world leaders and famous people who masterminded global events. Trade books, more often than not, use a "bottom–up" approach. They describe how the lives of common people were affected by world or national events or they tell how

Comparison of History Textbooks and Trade Books by Content and Writing

Feature	Textbook	Trade Books
Content		
Emphasis	Facts, names, dates	Human motives, solving human problems, consequences of actions
	World leaders, famous people, big events	Ordinary people, human aspects of famous people, effects of world or national events on the lives of the common person
Coverage	Very broad; consequently, shallow	Single subject treated in depth
	Essential information sometimes omitted; text "cleansed" of controversial issues to comply with state adoption commissions	Include unpopular stances on controversial issues
	Usually one textbook per classroom giving a limited perspective	Many books available on most historical subjects give varying perspectives and more complete information and stimulate critical thought
Writing		
Form	Expository; expository with brief narrative inserts	Narrative in historical fiction; expository in historical nonfiction
Text Structure	Shallow coverage and language restraints result in lack of cohesion and clarity	Connected, sequential ideas, focus on topic, and multi-idea-unit sentences result in clear, cohesive passages
Style	Sentence length and vocabulary limited to comply with readability formulae. Elaboration limited to allow for greater coverage. Omission of essential connectors and little elaboration of ideas reduce clarity	Few stylistic restraints make rich vocabulary and varied styles possible. Space for elaboration of ideas and strong descriptions of people, places, and events yield greater clarity
	People and events portrayed as lifeless; use of past tense verbs lends sense of distance and unreality	People and events presented as living; use of present tense verbs and dialog lends a sense of immediacy and reality
Interestingness	Emphasis on facts, names, dates, lifeless people and events, plus lack of cohesion results in loss of interestingness, hence diminished reader involvement and memorability	Emphasis on human stories well told results in greater degree of interestingness, hence greater reader involvement and memorability

FIGURE 7–1

grass-roots movements brought about large-scale change. When trade books do feature famous people, they include the characters' personality traits as well as their political stances, their weaknesses as well as their strengths, and their formative childhood impressions as well as their important adult decisions. Presented in this way, historical figures are more accessible, "real," and memorable to young readers.

RESPONSE   Emphasis in teaching materials, as described here, is important to young readers of history to the extent that it influences their *response* to what they read. Rosenblatt's (1976) transactional theory of literature and reading offers one way of considering how well a text conveys the story of human experience. She makes an important distinction between reading for pleasure (esthetic) and reading for information (efferent). In esthetic reading, the reader's attention is focused on what he or she is living through *during* the reading event, whereas in efferent reading, the reader's attention is centered on what should be retained *after* the reading event. Rosenblatt contends that any literary transaction between the reader and the text being read will fall somewhere on a continuum between the esthetic and efferent poles. In her opinion an honest, unencumbered, individual *response* to what is read will often help the reader attach meaning "to what otherwise would be . . . merely brute facts" (p. 42). We contend that because of differences in content emphasis, readers are far more likely to encounter opportunities for individual, affective response when they read historical trade books than when they read history textbooks.

EMPATHY   Closely tied to the idea of response to historical text is the idea of *historical empathy*. Historians agree that to understand history, one must be able to perceive past events and issues as they were experienced by the people at the time, or as Reed (1989) put it, "to 'get behind the eyeballs' of someone in history" (p. 305). Empathy includes knowing the facts (the social and political context) that pertained to a certain period of time, knowing the values and beliefs of the various historical agents of the time, and being able and willing to entertain these agents' points of view without necessarily sharing them.

Teachers and historians alike have persistently asked whether it is possible for young children who have not yet grasped the concept of time and chronology to achieve historical empathy. Recent research indicates that, with the help of narrative (story), they can. Downey and Levstik (1988) maintain that the structures of narrative can provide "a temporal scaffolding for historical understanding that is accessible even to quite young children" (p. 338). Crabtree (1989) asserts that "truly revealing accounts of the human story, rendered memorable for children through the organizing power of the narrative, address first things first. By vicariously enlarging children's own experience and deepening their understandings of human experience in general, good and true stories furnish the intellectual foundations upon which subsequent historical analyses may be built" (p. 179).

Coverage

Teachers have always faced difficult decisions about what to teach within a subject. It is impossible to cover any topic completely. Teachers should not be lulled into thinking that they have solved the coverage problem, however, simply by using a textbook. They have only allowed someone else to decide what to cover and what to omit.

LIMITED SPACE   Traditional history curricula and textbooks for the various grades (e.g., American History in grades five, eight, and eleven, and World History in grades six and ten) cover several centuries of events (e.g., Ancient Civilizations, U.S. History, World History). This means that even a rather lengthy textbook must give only shallow treatment to any topic within such a wide scope. It is not uncommon, for example, to find events that essentially changed the course of history summarized in a few sentences, as the following excerpt demonstrates:

> Throughout Europe, Hitler had special prisons built for the Jews and others he was trying to destroy. These prisons were called **concentration camps.** Millions of people died in them. By the time the war ended, the Nazis had murdered 6 million Jews. Hitler also had several million other people who opposed him killed. (Graham, Vuicich, Cherryholmes, and Manson, 1988, p. 329)

No other mention is made of the Holocaust in the current, best-selling fifth-grade American History textbook from which this excerpt was taken. Can such cursory treatment convey to a child any sense of what happened during the Holocaust? Is the significance of the event made clear? Is history served?

CLEANSED TEXTS   Limited space is not the only factor curtailing coverage in textbooks. Since the turn of the century, state commissions on textbook adoption and other agents in the business of "purifying" what children learn have systematically brought pressure on publishers to omit from textbooks controversial topics such as evolution, communism, and human rights injustices within the United States. When subjected to these pressures, such highly respectable publishers as Harper & Row, Holt, Rinehart & Winston, Macmillan, and Houghton Mifflin have compromised the intellectual integrity of their products rather than lose a sale. Such incomplete, even biased, coverage results in generic textbooks. These "damaged goods" (Hentoff, 1984, p. 29) not only discount teachers' and students' abilities to evaluate information and issues, but they are often incomprehensible, especially those that have been "cleansed" for the youngest readers. Sewall (1988) insists that publishers' avoidance of any possible controversy has rendered textbooks devoid of voice, drama, and coherence.

IN-DEPTH STUDY   In contrast, those who write historical trade books have the luxury of time and space to focus on a single historical event, era, or person and to treat that subject in depth. They have the freedom to present both popular and unpopular stands on controversial issues. The best of these authors are able to create for their young readers an actual sense or feel for a historical era through their thoroughly researched and masterfully constructed settings.

Trade book authors help to create a fuller, more accurate portrayal of our past by writing about our past mistakes—those aspects of our history often omitted from textbooks because they do not reflect well on those in power. The regrettable history of discrimination and disen-franchisement of minorities in our country, for example, comes alive in the books of Julius Lester (*To Be a Slave*, Dial, 1968), Mildred Taylor (*Roll of Thunder, Hear My Cry*, Dial, 1976; *Road to Memphis*, Dial, 1990), Yoshiko Uchida (*Journey to Topaz*, Scribner's, 1971; *Journey Home*, Atheneum, 1978), and Scott O'Dell (*Sing Down the Moon*, Houghton Mifflin, 1970). And the stupidity and awful waste of war, rather than its manifest destiny, are revealed in the books of James and Christopher Collier (*My Brother Sam Is Dead*, Four Winds, 1974), Harold Keith (*Rifles for Watie*, Crowell, 1957), Hans Peter Richter (*Friedrich*, Holt, 1970; *I Was There*, Holt, 1972), Toshi Maruki (*Hiroshima No Pika*, Lothrop, 1980), Peter Härtling (*Crutches*, Lothrop, 1988), and Rudolf Frank (*No Hero for the Kaiser*, Lothrop, 1986). In these stories and many more like them, historical events come alive, their import and gravity are experienced and felt, and in this way, history is served.

Obviously, it takes longer to read a novel about a historical event than it does to read the several paragraphs devoted to that event in a history textbook. If literature is to be integrated regularly into history classes, teachers will have to decide between broad, shallow coverage and in-depth investigations of a few key periods of history. Reading and history teachers can cooperate in planning their students' reading materials so that students will have time for literature in the history class. Teachers might, for example, assign independent, at-home reading of works of historical fiction. Teachers will find that periodic, highly condensed lectures and brief summary fact sheets provide students with the historical context and continuity needed to connect the historical periods to be studied in depth.

PERSPECTIVE   The issue of coverage includes the matter of perspective. For the typical elementary or middle school history student in the United States, the sole source of information is a textbook. Given its shallow, often selective coverage, the textbook alone at best can offer the young student of history a limited perspective—the perspective of the author as edited or censored by the various special interest groups and adoption committees whose approval the textbook publisher had to win.

Such a limited point of view is neither healthy nor wise and is not worthy of a student's time. Students can exercise critical thinking only when they are offered varied points of view from varied sources, which sometimes corroborate and at other times contradict each other. Today, it is possible for teachers to find several children's books on most periods of history either to be read aloud by the teacher or read independently by students and then shared with the class. Even if a textbook is used as the primary resource, a variety of trade books used as secondary resources will offer different, and valuable, perspectives.

Writing in History Textbooks and Trade Books

Form

Writing in history textbooks is almost exclusively exposition, that is, presentation and explication of facts. Many recent research studies, however, suggest that *narrative* is a preferable form for presenting history to students. Downey and Levstik (1988) maintain that narrative has a strong relation "to the development of time and causation concepts" (p. 338). Hidi, Baird, and Hildyard (1982) state that "in contrast to other literary forms . . . narratives deal primarily with living beings . . . and we seem to have special sets of strategies to remember the temporally sequential goal-directed actions and causal events that are normally associated with the lives of experiencing and purposive subjects" (p. 63). Armbruster and Anderson (1984), citing Ernst Nagel, concur, making a case that history and psychology are inextricably intertwined, since history is a matter of understanding human motives: "That is, historical events are . . . explainable in terms of goals and actions taken to attain those goals" (1984, p. 183).

This is not to say, however, that there is no place for exposition in the presentation of history. Most good exposition has a story to tell (Otto, 1990), and many of the components of story grammars (for example, consequences of actions, solving of problems, and repetitions of plan-attempt-resolution cycles) have analogues in so-called expository text structures (causation, problem/solution, and sequential listing).

Editors of history textbooks are not unaware of the strength of narrative, as attested by the current trend toward inserting brief narrative episodes in each textbook chapter. Often, however, these attempts to combine exposition and narrative yield poorly structured texts. For one thing, causal links (essential to both story grammar and the traditional expository text structures of causation and problem/solution) are frequently absent (Richgels, Tunnell, & Tomlinson, 1990). The results of a study by Hidi, Baird, and Hilyard (1982) show that children (fifth and seventh grade) were able to recall essential information when the form of discourse was either purely expository or purely narrative (though narratives yielded the best overall results). However, "mixed" texts, which included narrative episodes intermingled with the regular expository presentation, were the most difficult for the subjects. Editors of history textbooks commonly insert narrative material, often boxed and accompanied with colorful illustrations, "not so much to convey essential information as to maintain children's attention and interest" (Hidi et al., p. 64). The story or a coherent introduction of content is overwhelmed and lost as a result (Sewall, 1988, p. 555). Trade books, on the other hand, are almost always what Hidi, Baird, and Hildyard call "genre specific" (1982, p. 64).

Text Structure

Fielding, Wilson, and Anderson (1986) examined basal readers and content area textbooks and concluded that they lack the richness in vocabulary and structure of trade books. To these researchers, many of the currently used history texts are mostly "baskets of facts, little more than loosely connected lists of propositions about a topic," and the structure of chapters is often "murky" (p. 152). In fact, these researchers noted that it is rare to find content area textbooks that employ the basic structures of good expository writing, such as cause/effect, temporal sequence, comparison/contrast, problem/solution, or even simple listing.

These basic structures are instrumental in creating what Armbruster (1984) calls "considerate text." Another aspect of considerateness is textual coherence, both local and global. Global textual coherence facilitates the integration of important ideas and concepts across entire sections, chapters, or books. Local textual coherence links thoughts and ideas at the word and sentence level, by means of pronouns and their referents, nouns substituted for other nouns, conjunctions, causal connectives (e.g., *because, therefore*), and words that clearly establish the order of presentation (e.g., *first, second, then*). Textbook authors often ignore these simple aspects of clear writing. The result is "at its best, straightforward and, at its worst, choppy, monotonic, metallic prose. Deprived of connectors and qualifiers, historical narrative often becomes cryptic and more difficult to understand" (Sewall, 1988, p. 555).

Richgels, Tunnell, and Tomlinson (1990) compared text structure in topic-similar passages from best-selling fifth-grade American history textbooks and trade books, and they found that the textbook passages exhibited structure problems related to readability considerations. These problems included an absence of multi-idea-unit sentences, few words per sentence, and poor local coherence—all of which have been shown to disrupt idea connectedness and decrease comprehensibility. In contrast, the trade book passages were all well structured as narratives. Ideas in these passages were sequential and connected, topic focus was achieved early, and there were multi-idea-unit sentences where appropriate.

Style

In the end, the most important criterion for educators to use in selecting texts for use with children is that the text contain vivid, stylistic prose. What this means is best presented with examples—of a text that measures up and a text that does not. The following excerpts describe Abraham Lincoln. One is from a fifth-grade history textbook, and the other is from a nonfiction trade book.

Textbook excerpt

Lincoln kept up with politics in Illinois and in the nation. He was often called upon to make campaign speeches for men running for office. He was a good political speaker. Though he was a great gangling figure of a man, and wore old clothes, and did not have a good voice, he impressed people when he spoke. Lincoln knew what he was talking about and meant what he said. He could make people listen and take notice. (Gross, Follett, Gabler, Burton, Alschwede, 1980, p. 266)

Trade book excerpt

Abraham Lincoln wasn't the sort of man who could lose himself in a crowd. After all, he stood six feet four inches tall, and to top it off, he wore a high silk hat. His height was mostly in his long, bony legs. When he sat in a chair, he seemed no taller than anyone else. It was only when he stood up that he towered above other men.

At first glance, most people thought he was homely. Lincoln thought so too, referring once to his "poor, lean, lank face." As a young man he was sensitive about his gawky looks, but in time, he learned to laugh at himself. When a rival called him "two-faced" during a political debate, Lincoln replied: "I leave it to my audience. If I had another face, do you think I'd wear this one?" (Freedman, 1987, p. 1)

These passages exemplify what we believe to be true: textbook editors generally place less value on style than do children's trade book authors. In the first excerpt Lincoln remains one of that distant throng of important, but "unreal" historical figures, In the second excerpt, because the author chose to reveal in an amusing anecdote Lincoln's wit and unusual physical features, the man seems alive and, therefore, memorable. Style, in the sense of *what* authors tell, can make history more tangible to young readers, and therefore more engaging.

Style also has to do with *how* authors tell what they tell. The previously noted restraints within which textbook authors must work cannot help but affect how they write. Researchers (e.g., Davison, 1984; Fielding et al., 1986; Sewall, 1988) have noted the propensity of textbook authors to write in short, disjointed sentences and to use limited vocabulary, partly in order to reduce their texts' readability indices which are typically computed from formulae in which sentence length is a major factor. In addition, these authors must limit elaboration of ideas to allow for greater coverage. These practices continue today despite proof that omission of essential connectors and little elaboration of ideas reduces textual clarity and despite the fact that students perceive the characters and events in current history textbooks as remote and lifeless and, therefore, dull.

Trade book authors, working under few, if any, stylistic constraints, are free to use rich vocabulary and varied writing styles. Their more fully elaborated ideas—strong descriptions of people, places, and events; consequences of actions; causal links; and problem resolution—yield greater textual clarity. Perhaps most important for young readers, trade book authors' use of present tense verbs and dialog lends a sense of vitality, reality, and immediacy to the historical events and the people who experienced them.

An important derivative of style is the *interestingness* of text. Whether reading material that is interesting enough to capture and hold students' attention makes a significant difference in their learning has been the topic of both discussion and research. Anderson, Shirey, Wilson, and Fielding (1987, p. 288) reported the results of four experimental studies in which "rated interest accounted for an average of *thirty times* as much variance in sentence recall as readability." They also reviewed and analyzed various other studies on the topic and concluded that "interestingness of children's reading materials has strong and pervasive effects on learning" (p. 299). Yet, they are quick to point out that the so-called "interesting" formats combining exposition and occasional narratives in social studies and science textbooks are disjointed and counterproductive. We believe that the interestingness of text that Anderson and his colleagues are referring to is born not of a clever print format, but of exciting stories well told, empathy for believable characters, and curiosity for what will happen next.

Conclusion

History, the story of human events, has great value for today's children. With it, they inherit the collective experience of mankind; without it, they have an incomplete notion of who they are as humans. We cannot afford to have generations of students reject the study of history because we make it uninteresting or difficult to understand. We contend that history trade books are more considerate, more interesting, better structured, and more coherent than history textbooks. As such, history trade books will be more captivating and more instructive for students than history textbooks.

REFERENCES

Anderson, R. C., Shirey, L., Wilson, P., & Fielding, L. (1987). Interestingness of children's reading material. In Snow, R. E., & Farr, M. J. (Eds.), *Aptitude, learning, and instruction*, Vol. 3. *Conative and affective process analysis*, (pp. 287–99). Hillsdale, N.J.: Erlbaum.

Armbruster, B. B. (1984). The problem of "inconsiderate text." In Duffy, G. G., Roehler, L. R., & Mason, J. (Eds.), *Comprehension instruction: Perspectives and suggestions* (pp. 202–17). New York: Longman.

Armbruster, B. B., & Anderson, T. H. (1984). Structures for explanation in history textbooks, or what if Governor Stanford missed the spike and hit the rail? In Anderson, R. C., Osborn, J., & Tierney, R. J. (Eds.), *Learning to read in American schools* (pp. 181–94). Hillsdale, N.J.: Erlbaum.

Collier, J. L., & Collier, C. (1974). *My brother Sam is dead*. New York: Four Winds.

Crabtree, C. (1989). Returning history to the elementary schools. In P. Gagnon and the Bradley Commission on history in schools (Eds.), *Historical literacy: the case for history in American education* (pp. 173–87). New York: Macmillan.

Davison, A. (1984). Readability formulas and comprehension. In Duffy, G. G., Roehler, L. R., & Mason, J. (Eds.), *Comprehension instruction: Perspectives and suggestions* (pp. 128–143). New York: Longman.

Downey, M. T., & Levstik, L. S. (1988, September). Teaching and learning history: The research base. *Social Education*, 336–42.

Fielding, L. G., Wilson, P. T., & Anderson, R. C. (1986). A new focus on free reading: The role of trade books in reading instruction. In Raphael, T. E. (Ed.), *The contexts of school-based literacy* (pp. 149–60). New York: Random House.

Frank, R. (1986). *No hero for the Kaiser*. New York: Lothrop.

Freedman, R. (1983). *Children of the wild West*. New York: Clarion Books.

Freedman, R. (1987). *Lincoln: A photobiography*. New York: Clarion Books.

Gagnon, P. (1985, Spring). Finding who and where we are: Can American history tell us? *American Educator*, 9(1), 18–21, 44.

Gagnon, P. (1988, November). Why study history? *The Atlantic Monthly*, pp. 43–66.

Graham, A., Vuicich, G., Cherryholmes, C., & Manson, G. (1988). *United States*. New York: McGraw-Hill.

Gross, H. H., Follett, D. W., Gabler, R. E., Burton, W. L., Ahlschwede, B. F. (1980). *Exploring our world: The Americas*, p. 266. Chicago: Follett.

Härtling, P. (1988). *Crutches*. New York: Lothrop.

Hentoff, N. (1984, February). The dumbing of America. *The Progressive*, pp. 29–31.

Hidi, S., Baird, W., & Hildyard, A. (1982). That's important but is it interesting? Two factors in text processing. In Flammer, A., & Kintsch, W. (Eds.), *Discourse processing* (pp. 63–75). Amsterdam: Elsevier-North Holland.

Keith, H. (1957). *Rifles for Watie*. New York: Crowell.

Lester, J. (1968). *To be a slave*. New York: Dial.

Maruki, T. (1980). *Hiroshima no pika*. New York: Lothrop.

O'Dell, S. (1970). *Sing down the moon*. New York: Houghton Mifflin.

Otto, W. (1990). Telling stories out of school. *Journal of Reading*, 33, pp. 450–52.

Ravitch, D. (1985, Spring). The precarious state of history. *American Educator*, 9(4), pp. 11–17.

Reed, E. W. (1989). For better elementary teaching: Methods old and new. In P. Gagnon and the Bradley Commission on history in schools (Eds.), *Historical literacy: The case for history in American education* (pp. 302–19). New York: Macmillan.

Richgels, D. J., Tunnell, M. O., & Tomlinson, C. M. (1990, October). Comparing text structure in children's history trade books and textbooks. Paper presented at the National Reading Conference, Miami, Florida.

Richgels, D. J., Tunnell, M. O., & Tomlinson, C. M. (In press). Elements of structure in children's history textbooks and trade books. *Journal of Educational Research*.

Richter, H. P. (1970). *Friedrich*. New York: Holt.

Richter, H. P. (1972). *I was there*. New York: Holt.

Rosenblatt, L. M. (1976). *Literature as exploration*. New York: Noble and Noble. (Originally published in 1938)

Sewall, G. T. (1988, April). American history textbooks: Where do we go from here? *Phi Delta Kappan*, 553–58.

Taylor, M. (1976). *Roll of thunder, hear my cry*. New York: Dial.

Taylor, M. (1990). *Road to Memphis*. New York: Dial.

Uchida, Y. (1971). *Journey to Topaz*. New York: Scribner's.

Uchida, Y. (1978). *Journey home*. New York: Atheneum.

Linda Levstik is an associate professor of curriculum and instruction at the University of Kentucky. She has served as the editor of *Social Studies Experiences*, has written extensively concerning history education in leading social science education and literacy journals, and is coauthor of the book *An Integrated Language Perspective in the Elementary School* (Longman, 1990).

*   *   *

Levstik grapples with the following critical questions about history education: How does historical narrative affect a child's need to know? What is the effect of imagination in historical fiction? How do children develop historical judgment? And how may teachers mediate children's understanding of history?

8

"I Wanted to Be There": The Impact of Narrative on Children's Historical Thinking

Linda Levstik

A six-year-old boy and his classmates are asked to imagine an island, and a boat rolling on the surrounding sea. The boy harks back to a much earlier study of Columbus, and a more recent foray into an informational book on constellations, and he then lyrically identifies himself as the star-gazing explorer: "I was Columbus, and I saw the night sky, and the moon, and I saw the stars come together and make things." A fifth grader grapples with issues of justice and morality after finishing *My Brother Sam Is Dead* (Collier and Collier, 1974): "I agree with both of them [loyalists and rebels] because both of them had good reasons and this is not like between Puritans and witches where I only agree with one side." A sixth grader's response to a Holocaust book leaves her wishing "to be there to see what was happening and put a stop to it all."

These children are responding to history, but the language they use and the form their responses take reverberate with the power of literature to recreate the past. If literature shapes their historical understanding, so too do particular classroom circumstances influence the depth and scope of that understanding. For each of these children, history is embedded in a web of literary experiences, often shaped by narrative, sometimes by informational literature, always by discussion and time for reflection.

Researchers have long been interested in reading in the content areas (Mathews and Toepher, 1936; McCallister, 1930), but until fairly recently, studies have focused on how teachers use, and students learn (or fail to learn), from content area textbooks (Alvermann, 1989; Graves et al., 1988). Researchers interested in children's responses to trade books, on the other hand, have concentrated primarily on language and literacy development, including how children learn to read through literature, and how their collaborative conversations about literature influence their construction of meaning (Galda,1983; Hickman,1981; Holdaway, 1979). Although this tendency is not surprising, given the emphasis on literacy issues in the early school years, it has meant that less attention has been paid to the impact of literary texts on content learning. Even as some teachers and researchers turned their attention to "whole language" or "integrated language" classrooms, the emphasis on language and literacy continued (cf. Routmann, 1988).

At the same time, influenced by global stage theories of cognition, some researchers began to look for general theories of learning that applied across subjects or to investigate the stages of development in particular domains (Gelman and Baillargeon, 1983). In history, for instance, researchers concentrated on connections between historical understanding and Piagetian stage development. The work of Roy W. Hallam is the best known of this research. Hallam (1979) asked students ages eleven to sixteen to respond to questions based on short historical passages. He found that the students reached concrete and formal operational stages in historical thinking considerably later than had Piaget's students in science and mathematics. When subsequent studies (Lodwick,1972; Stokes,1970) also found that adolescents had difficulty thinking hypothetically and deductively in history, there was concern that history was an inappropriate subject of study for children before the secondary level (Laville and Rosenzweig, 1975).

Two major criticisms have surfaced in response to this body of research. The first argues that these studies were based on an excessively narrow view of historical thinking (Booth, 1980; Kennedy,1983; Laville and Rosenzweig,1975). Of particular interest to a discussion of the connections between narrative and history is Booth's contention that historical thinking is not primarily deductive, as Hallam's work suggests, but relies more on the ability to "recreate in words the most credible account of the world we have lost" (1980, p. 104).

A second criticism arises from more recent research on knowledge restructuring and challenges the assumption that global explanations of thinking and learning such as Piaget's are the best model for studying cognition (Carey, 1985). This body of research suggests that the topic or conceptual domain that a child is involved with more directly influences cognition. According to this interpretation, there may be some general principles of learning to which we all appeal when faced with an area out of our range of experience, but these seem to be the resort of the novice. Keil (1984), for instance, suggests that learners assume—and look for—the presence of underlying causal structures, and that as they become more knowledgeable in a domain, they become increasingly dissatisfied with the notion that meaning (or a concept) is merely a set of characteristic features that happens to be associated with a class of things.

Arguments about the nature of thinking in history and theories of knowledge restructuring have led to increased attention to how (and if) younger children come to learn history. In addition, scholarship on children's response to literature and curricular reform movements calling for more emphasis on narrative history in the elementary curriculum (cf. California's *History-Social Science Framework*; Bradley Commission on History in Schools) have heightened interest in using historical literature to teach history. Any such discussion, however, must address three interrelated concerns: how young learners use literary texts to build historical understanding, how the texts themselves structure history, and how teachers mediate among children, texts, and history. In the following sections of this chapter, I will look more closely at each of these issues.

The Connection Between History and Narrative

It is no accident that history is often described as the story of the past. For centuries, historians have used narrative to order and assign cause and effect to events in the past. Although the use of narrative history has been less common among modern academic historians, there is a body of scholarship relevant to a discussion of the connections between literature and history. Egan (1983; 1989), for instance, suggests that a grounding in stories, with their emphasis on human response to historical events, is the beginning of historical understanding. Narrative does more than allow a reader to look into other lives. It also shapes those lives and embeds them in a culture. Hayden White (1980) describes narrative as a "metacode" transmitting transcultural messages about a shared reality. Narrative, he argues, "solves the problem of how to translate *knowing* into *telling*" (pp. 5–6). Put another way, narrative transforms chronology (a list of events) into history (an interpretation of events). A ten-year-old explains: "The social studies book doesn't give you a lot of detail. You don't imagine yourself there because they're not doing it as if it were a person" (Levstik, 1989). For this child, narrative acts "as if it were a person."

In contrast, a historical text may make lawlike statements: " 'Whenever, within a feudal system, towns and trade begin to grow . . . *then* feudalism gives way to capitalism' " (Megill, 1989, p. 633). Perhaps the emphasis on explanation in historical writing has led to such attempts to "universalize" history. Yet history has aims in addition to explanation. Allan Megill (1989) argues that every work of history includes four intertwined aims: interpretation, description, explanation, and argument or justification. He suggests that description is especially crucial in that it links history to the particular—not generic "immigrants," for instance, but particular people whose families are uprooted by war or famine. This, perhaps, is what the ten-year-old above failed to find in her history textbook.

In a historical novel the author holds a magnifying glass up to a piece of history, providing humanizing details often left out of broad survey history texts. The reader finds out how particular people felt about history, how they lived their daily lives, what they wore, how they spoke. These details are an integral part of the transcultural messages of which Hayden White speaks, but they are not, of course, the whole message. Instead, the author organizes details to further the narrative and, by doing so, both interprets and explains historical incidents. Kermode calls this the "arbitrary imposition of truth" (1980). It both represents history within a particular ethic and attempts to justify the author's historical perspective. This notion of the arbitrary imposition of truth raises three questions crucial to understanding the potential impact of historical narrative on young learners. First, what is the ethical or moral context supported by the narrative? Second, if narrative does, in fact, moralize history, does it also influence the development of historical judgment—the ability to think carefully and critically about issues of morality and interpretation? Finally, how can teachers mediate between child and text, so that children move toward more mature historical understanding?

Moralizing History

In literature, readers encounter the human capacity for both good and evil in a framework that generally invites them to sympathize with, or at least understand, the protagonist's point of view. In a series of studies conducted by the author, children seemed to find this experience of sympathy a compellingly satisfying aspect of literature. Three studies, a case study of a fifth-grade girl (Levstik, 1989), a naturalistic study of a sixth-grade class (Levstik, 1986), and a naturalistic study of a first grade (Levstik, 1990), investigated the impact of literature on interest in and understanding of history. In the two classroom studies, the teachers incorporated a variety of literature into the curriculum; in both, narrative literature was a central part of teaching and learning history. The case study was designed so that, over the course of a year, the fifth grader read and was interviewed about literature selected to match topics in the ongoing school history curriculum.

Older elementary students, in particular, associated themselves very strongly with characters in historical fiction and biography:

When I read Helen Keller it really made me want to be like her because she was so determined. . . . I thought maybe I could do that too. (sixth grade)

I felt I was in Ilse Cohen's place. (sixth grade)

> If I wanted freedom that much I probably would have done the same things, but I think I'd probably rather stay. I might talk about what was right but I wouldn't get involved into the fighting. (fifth grade)

For these older children, there was particular interest in such historical challenges as the Holocaust and the women's movement. On the other hand, younger children's literature was less apt to deal with the more violent aspects of history, and their teacher preferred to emphasize positive aspects of human nature. Her approach included encouraging children to identify themselves with positive aspects of characters in historical literature. A frequent pattern in this first-grade classroom involved discussing the ways in which the children were like historical figures and acting out parts of stories that demonstrated such "positive" traits as caring, learning, or working.

The corollary of this interest in human behavior seems to be the children's expressed "need to know." One of the most striking features of children's response to historical literature in each of these studies was the frequency with which they explained their interest in historical topics in terms of "needing to know" about a topic, of wanting to learn "the truth" or "what really happened." A first grader moves from a story about an aboriginal child in Australia to an encyclopedia, because "I need to know about where this is." A sixth grader willingly reads a difficult biography because he "needs to know" how Hitler turned out the way he did.

This search for "truth" is both an issue of ethics and morality, and of narrative structure. Narrative changes historical data by forming a story that implies certain things to the reader. White (1980) suggests that one of the purposes of narrative is "to moralize the events of which it treats." Thus, narrative holds history up against a social system "that is the source of any morality that we can imagine" (p. 18).

This aspect of narrative operates on several levels. To begin with, narrative conflict and sequencing invite the reader to see history as "caused" (Rabinowitz, 1987). The reader assumes that first events cause subsequent events unless there is a contrary indication. As one child explained, "Even if it weren't all true, it could have been true, and it could have happened like that" (Levstik, 1989). On another level, the conflict at the heart of most narratives implies that at least two versions of the story are possible, even as it enlists the reader's identification with the protagonist's cause. The possibility of alternate points of view raises two issues. First, as the story enlists the reader's identification with a particular perspective, it may also raise moral issues that influence the child reader's search for "truth." Second, the reader may also come to expect history, at least in its narrative forms, to be interpretive and to involve moral issues. After reading several historical novels, a fifth-grade child explains her frustration with the textbook version of American history: "[The textbook] just says that Americans were right but it doesn't tell you exactly why they were right, or why the British fought" (Levstik, 1989, p. 117).

In fact, the textbook does provide reasons for the American Revolution, but they do not appear to be the kinds of reasons that have power for young readers. Two studies of fifth graders' interpretations of American history (Thornton and McCourt-Lewis, 1990; Beck, McKeown, and Sinatra, 1989) found that their subjects generally misinterpreted, misassigned, or ignored textbook explanations for historical incidents. Looked at another way, however, it may be that the textbook misses the point. The fifth grader quoted above drew on her reading in historical fiction to discuss in detail the morality of choosing sides at the time of the American Revolution and the painful complexities of individual choices in the face of historical events. She differentiated between the moral issues involved in witchcraft trials and revolution, and she recognized how an individual might be trapped by fear and ignorance (Levstik, 1989). The textbook's more universal and depersonalized explanations did not have the moral power of the more particularistic and personal narrative description. As a result, the textbook fails to match students' understanding of the object of studying history.

The Object of Studying History:
"Human Behavior" Schemata

In a study of Swedish secondary students' understanding of history, Hallden (1986) concluded that "for [pupils], the object of study in history is persons or personified phenomena. The condition that has to be met if an explanation is to be accepted is that an event must be definable in terms of intentional actions" (pp. 63–64). Students tended to explain history in terms of human reactions and desires, even when that was not the focus of instruction and historical narrative was not a primary reference source. It appears that students tend to impose an ethical or at least purposive frame on historical data well beyond the elementary years, regardless of whether such a frame is called for by text structure or teacher intent.

It is possible that the most readily available schemata students have to bring to bear in understanding history are "human behavior" schemata (Barton, 1990). These schemata are not only readily available, they are also among the most fully developed in young children. It would seem logical, then, to call on these in trying to make sense of historical information. Moreover, these schemata are particularly appropriate in understanding historical fiction, based as it is on the particulars of human, and often child, behavior. They are not, however, equally useful in interpreting historical textbooks in which human particulars, and especially individual human intentions and motivations, are often replaced by political and economic analyses. As a result, students may find it more difficult to identify and recall these more analytical historical accounts without considerable assistance.

The Role of Imagination

Contrary to what children expect to gain from reading history, those who construct history curricula often assume that "*the* way to understand human behavior and societies is to survey, quantify, generalize, hypothesize, and test" (Degenhardt and McKay, 1988, p. 240). Well-written historical narrative, on the other hand, invites the reader to do what Collingwood (1961) describes as the historian's main task: to enter imaginatively the "inside" of events, "to think himself into this action" (p. 213). A well-written narrative that is historically sound also supports *informed* and *disciplined* imaginative entry into events. As Degenhardt and McKay (1988) note, without both information and imagination, a student will not only not do well at entering the perspective of people from other times and places, but will also "not be good at empathizing with the people next door" (p. 244).

Informed, disciplined, and imaginative engagement with moral and ethical issues, it seems to me, is crucial to meaningful historical study for two reasons. First, if history is just chronology, there is little reason to "understand" it. If, on the other hand, it involves the interpretation of vital moral and ethical issues, it is also relevant to the way in which we come to understand ourselves and the world around us. Bardige's (1988) study of adolescent moral development in the context of a literature-based history curriculum points out a second consideration in attending to the moral and ethical dimensions of history. She notes that history instruction that emphasizes greater and greater degrees of abstraction, while trying to maintain a neutral or "objective" stance, can increase children's feelings of impotence and lead to their inability to take action against evil:

> If we are to meet the challenge of educating in ways that help our children ... become more human, then we must attend to and build on the "finely human" aspects of their thinking. As we help them to see and understand the realities, complexities and laws of the world, we must also help them to hang on to their moral sensitivities and impulses. (p. 109)

Developing Historical Judgment

Interpreting history involves more than understanding human motivation or adopting a moral stance. It is also a matter of weighing evidence and holding conclusions to be tentative pending further information. As Bardige (1988) notes, there is a tension here, between helping children to see multiple perspectives and leaving them unable to take any kind of stand, because all perspectives are perceived as equally good. This delicate balance is especially interesting in light of the findings in both the sixth-grade classroom study and the fifth-grade case study. In neither study did historical fiction trigger student questions about an author's correctness of interpretation. Instead, children valued the "truthfulness" of the historical fiction and used it as the standard against which other information was measured. Spontaneous skepticism was evident in the way children viewed their social studies text. They generally recognized that another perspective could have been represented in a particular story, but the teacher had to lead children to consider seriously alternatives to a literary interpretation of history. This response to historical narrative places a double obligation on authors and teachers to create and select historical narratives that are both good literature and careful, supportable history. It also means that special attention must be paid to how teachers mediate texts.

Teacher Mediation

Iser (1978) suggests that meaning lies at the intersection between reader and text. So far, my discussion has concentrated on the possible contributions of narrative historical literature to meaning construction in the domain of history. But there is another aspect to this process, especially as it occurs in classrooms. As Golden (1989) notes, texts are also constructed in particular contexts. When those contexts are classrooms, teachers have the opportunity to mediate some of the ways in which text and reader come together.

Both Bardige (1989) and Levstik (1986; 1990) studied children as they responded to history and historical literature. In Bardige's study, children kept journals in which they recorded personal feelings, observations, opinions, and questions about the material they were encountering. The intent of the journals was to provide a forum for "facing history" and "facing one's self," and was a written conversation between students and teacher (p. 90). In Levstik's (1986) study, the teacher used journals, but she also organized response groups. Because children often read multiple books on a topic, they had several opportunities to reencounter ideas and issues from previous discussions. For instance, children reading Holocaust literature returned several times to a discussion of Hitler's "bravery." One student declared that Hitler was brave for wanting to take on the whole world. Others disagreed, and the discussion moved on. But several children were still concerned. Was he brave? Could an evil man be considered brave? They returned to their reading, to see if they could make sense of the questions raised in discussion. In a later response group, another student shared information from a biography that he was reading. He suggested that Hitler was insane. The first student nodded, perhaps recognizing a way out of her original dilemma: "It was insane bravery." By providing opportunities to encounter and reencounter a topic, the teacher has also provided a context for communal construction of meaning. Students adjust their ideas, not just in response to the text, or to teachers' comments, but on the basis of interactions with their peers.

In addition, the teacher encouraged reference to multiple sources of information. When a dispute over the accuracy of historical information arose, the teacher arbitrated by first having students check each author's credentials, and then sending students to the library to look for confirming or disconfirming information. Eventually, she arranged for the students to contact a professor at a nearby university to help them resolve their dilemma.

The first-grade teacher also emphasized the tentative nature of information. Her students had been studying the history of the Earth and had heard several stories about the end of the dinosaurs. She invited children to speculate about what might have happened to the dinosaurs:

Child 1: The weather changed, and all the flowers died, and the plants got frozen.
Teacher: And do we know this for a fact?
Child 2: No.
Teacher: No, we think that's a very good . . .
Child 1: Idea.

In each case, teachers arranged an environment in which there were opportunities to propose ideas, test them in interaction with peers and/or the teacher, and modify or retain them. Children were expected to begin with a personal response: "It made me sad," or "It made me think that I could do that too." In addition, each teacher extended the literary experience in other ways. In the sixth grade, journals and response groups provided opportunities to ponder historical data before students selected and presented history-related projects. In the first grade, the teacher presented a piece of literature, helped children construct word webs to outline what they thought they knew and wanted to find out, and then provided extension activities culminating in a class discussion and class-produced "story."

This cycle of subjective response followed by more critical analysis of data and then reinforcement through art, writing, and projects was also a feature of the child in the case study. The researcher provided a forum for literary discussions, whereas the child interpreted her historical readings through artistic productions created between interview sessions.

In each of these instances, history was grounded in the behavior of particular individuals and began with their "human behavior" schemata. The fifth grader's perception of the period leading up to the American Revolution hinged on her understanding of the fear specific characters felt when faced with such issues as witchcraft or choosing to be a Tory or Loyalist, rebel or patriot. In the same way, the sixth graders experienced the Holocaust through the eyes of real and fictional characters who had to decide whether to shelter a Jew or acquiesce to Nazi rule, who tried to find ways to survive war, starvation, terror, and ultimately, genocide. The first graders were invited to imagine themselves on a ship with Christopher Columbus, struggling for an education with George Washington Carver, or marching for civil rights with Martin Luther King.

In addition, these children were given a variety of opportunities to reflect on what they were learning. Through journals and art, through discussion and debate, they tried their ideas out, modified them sometimes in the face of new information, and revisited those that disturbed or intrigued them.

It would seem important in the development of any mature historical understanding that learners see history as a human enterprise made up of interpretations and subject to revision. The structure of narrative seems to encourage readers to recognize the human aspects of history and, with some mediation, to develop a better sense of its interpretive and tentative aspects. Perhaps most important, it may help students maintain a balance between the abstractions of history as an intellectual exercise and history as an ongoing, participatory drama. In any case, history is more than narrative. It is also learning to sift evidence before it has been shaped and interpreted. It is coming to understand the interplay of social, economic, political, cultural, and ideological influences that shape individual behavior and our collective history. Ultimately, it is putting one's own time and place into a broader perspective and seeing oneself as making choices that are, cumulatively, historic. As Barton (1990) notes, "Such a transition would undoubtedly involve a 'radical restructuring' of students' schemata . . ." (p. 19). Certainly that is an intellectual and social task worthy of attention in the elementary school day.

REFERENCES

Alvermann, D. E. (1989). Teacher-student mediation of content area texts. *Theory into Practice*, 28, (2), 142–47.

Bardige, B. (1988). Things so finely human: Moral sensibilities at risk in adolescence. In Gilligan, C., Ward, J. V., & Taylor, J. M. (Eds.), *Mapping the Moral Domain*, (pp. 87–110). Cambridge, Mass.: Harvard University Graduate School of Education.

Barton, K. C. (1990). Developmental research in history. Unpublished paper, University of Kentucky.

Beck, I. L., McKeown, M. G., & Sinatra, G. M. (1989). The representations that fifth-graders develop about the American Revolutionary period from reading social studies textbooks. Unpublished manuscript, University of Pittsburgh.

Booth, M. (1980). A modern world history course and the thinking of adolescent pupils. *Educational Review, 32*, 245–257.

Bradley Commission on History in Schools (1988). *Resolutions of the commission: Steps toward excellence in the school history curriculum.* Westlake, Oh.: Bradley Commission on History in the Schools.

California State Department of Education. (1988). *History-Social Science Framework for California Public Schools, Kindergarten through Grade Twelve.* Sacramento, Calif.

Carey, S. (1985). *Conceptual change in childhood.* Cambridge, Mass.: MIT Press.

Collier, J. K., & Collier, C. (1974). *My brother Sam is dead.* New York: Four Winds.

Collingwood, R. G. (1961). *The idea of history.* London: Oxford University Press.

Degenhardt, M., & McKay, E. (1988). Imagination and education for intercultural understanding. In Egan, K., & Nadaner, D. (Eds.), *Imagination and education*, (pp. 237–55). New York: Teacher's College Press.

Egan, K. (1983). Accumulating history. *History and theory: Studies in the philosophy of history* (pp. 66–80). Belkeft 22: Middletown, Conn.: Wesleyan University Press.

Egan, K. (1989). *Teaching as storytelling: An alternative approach to teaching and curriculum in the elementary school.* Chicago: University of Chicago Press.

Galda, L. (1983). Research in response to literature. *Journal of Research and Development in Education, 16*, (3), 1–7.

Gelman, R., & Baillargeon, R. (1983). A review of some Piagetian concepts. In J. H. Flavell & E. M. Markman (Eds.), *Cognitive development, vol. 3* (pp. 167–230) of P. H. Mussen (Gen. Ed.), *Handbook of child psychology.* New York: Wiley.

Golden, J. M. (1989). The literary text event. *Theory into Practice, 28*, (2), 83–87.

Graves, M. F., Slater, W. H., Roen, D., Redd-Boyd, T., Buin, A. H., Furniss, D. W., & Hazeltine, P. (1988). Some characteristics of memorable expository writing. *Research in the Teaching of English, 22*, 242–65.

Hallam, R. N. (1979). Attempting to improve logical thinking in school history. *Research in Education, 21*, 1–24.

Hallden, O. (1986). Learning history. *Oxford Review of Education, 12*, 53–66.

Hickman, J. (1981). A new perspective on response to literature: Research in an elementary school setting. *Research in the Teaching of English, 15*, (4), 343–354.

Holdaway, D. (1979). *Foundations of literacy.* Sydney, Australia: Ashton Scholastic.

Iser, W. (1978). *The act of reading: A theory of aesthetic response.* Baltimore: Johns Hopkins University Press.

Keil, F. C. (1984). Mechanisms of cognitive development and the structure of knowledge. In R.J. Sternberg (Ed.), *Mechanisms of cognitive development* (pp. 81–99). New York: W.H. Freeman.

Kennedy, K.J. (1983). Assessing the relationship between information processing capacity and historical understanding. *Theory and Research in Social Education, 11,* 1–22.

Kermode, F. (1980). Secrets and narrative sequence. *Critical Inquiry, 7,* (1), 83–101.

Laville, C., and Rosenzweig, L. W. (1975). Teaching and learning history: developmental dimensions. In Rosenzweig, L. (Ed.), *Developmental perspectives on the social studies,* (pp. 54–66). Washington, D.C.: National Council for the Social Studies.

Levstik, L. S. (1986). The relationship between historical response and narrative in a sixth-grade classroom. *Theory and Research in Social Education, 14,* 1–15.

Levstik, L. S. (1989). Coming to terms with history: Historical narrativity and the young reader. *Theory Into Practice, 2,* 114–119.

Levstik, L. S. (1990). "I prefer success: Subject specificity in a first grade setting." Paper presented at the 1990 Annual Meeting of the American Educational Research Association, Boston, Massachusetts.

Lodwick, A. R. (1972). The development of children's reasoning in relation to mathematical, scientific and historical problems. Unpublished M.Ed. thesis, University of Manchester.

Mathews, C. O., & Toepher, N. (1936). Comparison of principles and practices of study. *The School Review, 54,* 184–92.

McCallister, J. M. (1930). Reading difficulties in studying content subjects. *Elementary School Journal, 31,* 191–201.

Megill, A. (1989). Recounting the past: "Description," explanation, and narrative in historiography. *American Historical Review, 94,* (3), 627–53.

Rabinowitz, P. J. (1987). *Before reading: Narrative conventions and the politics of interpretation.* Ithaca, N.Y.: Cornell University Press.

Routman, R. (1988). *Transitions: From literature to literacy.* Portsmouth, N.H.: Heinemann.

Stokes, A. B. G. (1970). An investigation into the presence of logical thinking in a group of 18-year-olds in historical and related study. Unpublished M.A. in education dissertation, University of Leeds.

Thornton, S. J., & McCourt-Lewis, A. A. (1990). A question in search of an answer: What do elementary children learn from studying the American Revolution? Paper presented at the College and University Faculty Assembly Symposium, "Making American Citizens," at the annual meeting of the National Council for the Social Studies, Anaheim, California.

Thornton, S. J., & Vukelich, R. (1988). Effects of children's understanding of time concepts on historical understanding. *Theory and Research in Social Education*, 15, 69–82.

Vukelich, R. (1984). Time language for interpreting history collections to children. *Museum Studies Journal*, 4, (1), 43–50.

White, H. (1980). The value of narrativity in the representation of reality. *Critical Inquiry*, 7, (1), 5–27.

Michael O. Tunnell teaches children's literature in the Department of Elementary Education at Brigham Young University. He has authored a number of articles about children's literature in journals such as *The Reading Teacher, Language Arts,* and *The Horn Book.* He has also written professional books, including *The Prydain Companion* (Greenwood, 1989), and three children's picture books, *Chinook!, The Joke's on George,* and *Beauty and the Beastly Children,* to be published by William Morrow (Tambourine Books).

* * *

Have changes in society altered the content and writing style of children's history trade books? Are current historical novels and informational books for children more honest in their presentation of history than books from earlier decades? Do changes benefit teachers who wish to use trade books to help teach history? Michael Tunnell examines the "maturing" of historical trade books written for young readers. He suggests that the changes have been positive because trade books now provide children with a more relevant, balanced, and captivating view of the past.

9

Unmasking the Fiction of History: Children's Historical Literature Begins to Come of Age

Michael O. Tunnell

Geoffrey Trease (1977), British author of historical novels for children, recalls that during the 1930s, when he began his career, the genre of historical fiction was "in the doldrums"—and for good reason. "It was long-winded," says Trease, "its vocabulary unfamiliar and unreal," including an overabundance of words like "varlet" and "quothas" (p. 22). The works of Sir Walter Scott were the school-approved historical works of fiction in Great Britain at that time, but as one student so aptly put it, "Though the details of Scott's novels are not always correct, they give one a very good idea of the period, and though they are painful to read they always give benefit" (Trease, 1977, p. 22). Trease observes that children in England, up through the thirties, mostly read Scott's "third-rate imitators," and the genre was stuck at that level well into the twentieth century: "Those of us who began to write . . . in the nineteen-thirties had to overcome plenty of prejudice among children . . ." (1977, p. 22).

But children were not the only ones authors of historical books (both fiction and nonfiction) have had to please, for it has always been through the sieve of adult sensitivities that books for children have been screened. Certainly John Newbery understood how society defines publishing parameters, especially for children's books. For example, he recognized that books with young characters who denied parental authority appealed to children. And though he published books that hinted at such denial, Newbery was careful not to alarm too many adults.

Two centuries after Newbery, in the mid-1960s, perhaps the most radical changes in the content and style of children's books began to take place—an age of new realism. Long-standing taboos began to fall away and continue to do so even now. The beginning of this "opening up" period is marked by the publication of two nonhistorical pieces: Sendak's picture book *Where the Wild Things Are* (Harper, 1963), and Fitzhugh's novel *Harriet the Spy* (Harper, 1964). Both were mildly controversial at the time of their publication primarily for representing what were considered uncomfortable truths about family relationships and psychological problems faced by young children.

For instance, both books show children at odds with their parents—a situation virtually unheard of in earlier children's books. Max's mother loses her temper at his unruly behavior, and Max is "sent to bed without eating anything." And Harriet's parents are "psychologically absent, being too engrossed in their own affairs to be overly concerned about their daughter's activities" (Huck, Hepler, and Hickman, 1987, p. 133). Max's psychological fantasy, a vent for his frustration, and Harriet's eventual need for psychotherapy were unsettling story elements for some adults.

Historical literature suffered from many of the same growing pains as books from other genres. Taboos in children's literature often adversely affected an honest portrayal of human motivations as related to historical events. For instance, Trease (1983, pp. 153–54) lists a sample of the restrictions that applied to the writing of children's books into the 1950s: no budding love affairs, no liquor, no supernatural phenomenon, no undermining of authority, no parents with serious human weaknesses, no realistic working-class speech (including the mildest cursing). Trease also recalls that his first historical novel, *Bows Against the Barons* (1966), was "unacceptably controversial at the time" and that "only the boldest of teachers dared to take [it] into schools." The reason for the problem was that this retelling of the Robin Hood story was "grimly realistic rather than in romantic terms" (1977, p. 24).

Historical fiction, biography, and informational books about history have long suffered from this sort of romanticism and from a narrow, if not altered, view of human motives. In other words, societies have dictated that their histories be recounted to children in idealistic terms. Children's books about the American Revolution are a perfect example, as illustrated in a study by Joel Taxel. Taxel (1983) analyzed the content of thirty-two recommended children's novels dealing with the American Revolution, books published between 1899 and 1976, "in order to understand how authors explain the Revolution as an historical event" (p. 61). Twenty-one of the books in Taxel's sample were published prior to 1954, and every one of those titles represent the Revolution from the Whig interpretation, which focuses on a divinely inspired, unified struggle for the ideological principles of representative government and individual liberty. "Moralistic and pedantic," says author Christopher Collier, "depicting simple, freedom-loving farmers marching in a crusade . . ." (1976, p. 132). Complex issues concerning the most monumental U. S. historical events are missing from these earlier novels; it is often idealism and, yes, romanticism that governs the writing. Characters are often polarized in terms of good and evil, according to which side of the conflict they support: "good, idealistic Patriots being opposed by calculating, avaricious Tories" (Taxel, 1983, p. 70).

Of course, as Taxel, Collier, and a legion of historians point out, the American Revolution was not so simply defined. For example, Progressive interpretations of the Revolution highlight the economic impetus as being a greater factor than anything ideological. And the Imperialist interpretation examines the conflict from both sides of the Atlantic, drawing attention to the English point of view. The Imperialist historians have had little effect on children's books about the Revolution, but Collier (1976) imagines that it could be intriguing "to see the American Revolution through the eyes of a white teenager in Quebec . . . or a black boy in Bermuda . . . [or] a ten-year-old cotton mill worker thrown out on the streets of Manchester as a result of the American embargo" (p. 134).

Eleven of the books in Taxel's sample were published between 1959 and 1976. During this time period, a shift toward a more open-minded, objective, complex approach to dealing with the Revolution began to appear. According to Taxel, the Consensus interpretation, much like the Whig, appeared in the majority of these eleven books. Still focusing on the unity of the colonists, the Consensus interpretation is nevertheless more refined. For example, good and evil are no longer assigned to sides in the war—Tories are no longer archetypally evil and some Patriots are depicted as "mean and brutish" (1983, p. 72).

It is not until the 1970s, a few years after Sendak and Fitzhugh helped usher in the age of new realism in children's books, that significant changes in fiction dealing with the American Revolution began to appear. A few books that clearly moved away from the Whig or Consensus interpretations were published, providing young readers with at least a few choices written from varying perspectives. Young protagonists in some of these books are indecisive about or uncommitted to the Patriot cause or even go as far as to reject it (My Brother Sam Is Dead [Collier and Collier, 1974], Who Comes to King's Mountain? [Beatty and Beatty, 1975], and When the World's on Fire [Edwards, 1972] are examples of such books.) Also, some of the later novels in Taxel's study no longer represent the Americans as having a corner on virtue and decency, and values and ideals are no longer enough to motivate protagonists. Edwards's novel When the World's on Fire is Taxel's best example of a book that takes several unusual yet valid approaches to presenting the Revolution. First, the story is told by a black protagonist, thus automatically confronting the paradox of a war fought for individual liberties although many leaders themselves held slaves. Also, Edwards does not concentrate on the Whig-Tory division among the colonists, but instead exposes the divisions among the patriots—artisans versus aristocrats for instance. Her book contains viewpoints heretofore unthinkable in children's books about the American Revolution—particularly "the implicit understanding that for significant numbers of Americans, the Revolution had not been won and had actually just begun" (Taxel, 1983, p. 76).

As children's publishing moved into the 1980s, a number of books about the American Revolution were published that contain more realistic characters and that examine a wider range of human motives for and emotions about the conflict. Examples include Avi's (1984) *The Fighting Ground*, wherein the young protagonist, Jonathan, changes from being a flaming Patriot to wondering which side, if any, he is on. It is interesting that the battle in Avi's story is against Hessian mercenaries, who suddenly seem to Jonathan no worse than the American corporal who has directed the execution of a Tory family. *Sarah Bishop* by Scott O'Dell (1980) shows a girl from a Tory family who is brutalized by the war and eventually flees to a place safe from Patriots and the British alike. James Lincoln and Christopher Collier (1981) wrote *Jump Ship to Freedom*, the first in a trilogy (*War Comes to Willy Freeman* [1983], *Who Is Carrie?* [1984]) that also has young black protagonists. Set against the background of the Constitutional Convention, this novel focuses on the futile hope of American blacks, including war veterans, that the new government might actually provide liberty and justice for all.

The metamorphosis beginning to take place in children's fiction about the American Revolution can be generalized to other historical novels, as well as to biography and informational books written about historical figures and topics. This is not to say that historical books for children categorically had little worth in earlier decades. Certainly *Johnny Tremain* (Forbes, 1943) remains an important and moving story of the Revolutionary period. But the changes in historical books for children allow for more reading options—choices that, when read in combination, give a more balanced and relevant view of history.

Margaret Hutchinson (1978, pp. 56–57), in her examination of trends in literature for young adult readers, notes research that indicates that the turbulent 1960s brought about a demand by young readers for relevance in their literature. As Wilmott (1965, p. 143) contends, they were concerned primarily with the following three areas:

1. The individual—his growth, personality, and philosophy . . .
2. . . . social problems and social responsibility, whether it be the great national concern of Civil Rights or the problems of the mentally retarded, the alcoholic, or the juvenile delinquent.
3. [concern] for the world . . . on both the national and the international levels.

Among the earliest books with this sort of "relevance" were the sudden outpouring of books in the 1960s about blacks (Hutchinson, 1978, p. 57). Many were second-rate, but over time issues and characters have been dealt with in more honest and realistic ways, especially as more black authors entered the publishing arena. Of course, historical books were influenced at the same time by these developments, as evidenced by several of the Revolutionary War books mentioned earlier and books by authors such as Mildred Taylor (*Roll of Thunder, Hear My Cry,* 1976), Virginia Hamilton (*Anthony Burns: The Defeat and Triumph of a Fugitive Slave,* 1988), and Julius Lester (*To Be a Slave,* 1969).

Recently, the publication of novels and informational books that deal honestly with the Vietnam War, America's most controversial foreign conflict, is another example of the growth that has occurred in historical books for young readers. Informational books from 1990 such as *Vietnam: Why We Fought* (Hoobler and Hoobler, 1990), *Portrait of a Tragedy: America and the Vietnam War* (Warren, 1990), and *Vietnam: A War on Two Fronts* (Lens, 1990) provide historical perspective and examine varying points of view concerning America's involvement in Vietnam. Painfully honest novels, such as Myers's (1988) *Fallen Angels* and Nelson's (1989) *And One For All,* illuminate the tragedy of war for young readers. War is shocking and ugly. In many ways, no one wins, for the toll of human suffering scars everyone involved. The following excerpt from *Fallen Angels* exemplifies the honesty in some of today's books:

> . . . I thought it was cool when the [Vietnamese] woman stopped just before she reached the dikes and handed one of the kids to a guy from Charlie Company.
>
> The GI's arms and legs flung apart from the impact of the blast. The damn kid had been mined, had exploded in his arms.
>
> Guys not even near him, guys who had just been watching him take the kid into his arms, fell to the ground as if the very idea of a kid exploding in your arms had its own power, its own killing force. (p. 231)

War, often glorified in books and films, is certainly revealed in all its horror in Myers's uncompromising work.

Though television newscasts have been credited with (or accused of) bringing a realistic social awareness into children's lives—such as an awareness of the atrocities of Vietnam or of inner city violence—it easily can be argued that television can and mostly does produce the opposite effect, an effect that books must be able to counteract. Author Kathryn Lasky recalls the misleading influences of TV from her growing-up years in

the 1950s and 1960s when she watched TV westerns like "Gunsmoke."
She did not realize until later in life that she was seeing "the fiction of
history" rather than historical fiction. After all, she asks, "What did Miss
Kitty really do?"

> Prostitutes, perish the thought, were not Miss Kitty! They
> were those women between 23rd Street and 18th Street
> on Meridian in Indianapolis where there were bars with signs
> like NUDE!NUDE!NUDE!GIRLS!GIRLS!GIRLS! These women
> were not like Miss Kitty at all. They did not dress like Can
> Can dancers, work in saloons with swinging doors, and help
> the sheriff solve social problems in towns like Tombstone. . . .
> I later realized as I began my research for *Beyond the Divide*
> that of all the crimes they used to focus on weekly in those
> TV westerns, the one crime they assiduously avoided was the
> West's consistent and appalling history of violence against
> women. In the Old West rape was not random, and there
> were more prostitutes than school marms. Nevertheless . . . it
> was still rape if it was an action against [a woman's] will.
> Women were often murdered and they did not only fall victim
> to Indians; they fell victim to white men as well and as often.
> (1990, p. 159)

Lasky continues by explaining that an author, therefore, has the
responsibility to preserve what she calls "the fabric of the time." This is
the only way to represent the human story honestly, to understand the
struggle for freedom from abuse and fear, to develop a clear view of
where we are going by knowing where we have been. Television more
often than not distorts the picture of human experience, as can dishon-
est books.

In times not too distant, it was the overriding opinion that an
author of books for young readers had a responsibility to withhold or
soften information about the unsavory sides of our history, to camouflage
the story of, say, American wrongs needing to be righted, such as the
internment of Japanese Americans during World War II or the human
suffering of African slaves. There are likely many adults who still feel this
way. George Santayana is often quoted as saying, "Those who cannot
remember the past are condemned to repeat it." Yet, it is even worse for
our children to have never really known the past—much less to forget it.
Children need to know not so much the events and dates of history as the
people—the big names and the little ones—who *are* our history. They
need to face in books what Brozo and Tomlinson (1986) call the "salient
concepts" of history. These salient concepts deal with the human condition, and Brozo and Tomlinson define them by asking three questions:

1. What are the driving human forces behind the events?
2. What phenomena . . . have affected ordinary people . . . ?
3. What universal patterns of behavior . . . should be explained?
   (p. 289)

Prejudice, man's inhumanity to man, and man's driving need for freedom are but a few examples of salient history concepts that are only hinted at or ignored in history textbooks. Indeed, as Lasky points out, women have been victims throughout history—another salient concept that needs to be understood by children so the world today can be changed.

We are fortunate today that the intellectual freedom exists to make possible historical books for children that help us better understand ourselves in light of what has happened before us. Many of today's historical books for young readers do grapple with the sad truth that the motivations for events in history were not always (or often) of glorious nature. The opening of our great American West is another prime example of how propaganda in textbooks, films, and juvenile fiction and nonfiction have over the years clouded important historical issues. Take "Spanish greed," for instance. According to Lasky (1990) textbooks make it seem as if Spaniards invented greed, as evidenced by their almost maniacal lust for gold: "But the word 'greed' was rarely, if ever, mentioned in references to Americans in my textbooks. Greed does not go well in textbook versions of America's concept of itself. But, of course, greed was really what the westward expansion, the Gold Rush, and Manifest Destiny were all about" (p. 160). Lasky's books of historical fiction (such as *Beyond the Divide* [1983] and *The Bone Wars* [1988]) examine the western movement with less ripping of "the fabric of time." *Beyond the Divide* is a carefully researched and boldly honest picture of the westward migration over the Rockies to California and is strengthened by its historically accurate portrayals of both the dark and the bright sides of human nature. Pam Conrad's (1985) *Prairie Songs* is another gritty and compelling novel of America's Westward Expansion, which paints a candid portrait of the hardships (especially for the women who had no choice in the matter) of settling the Nebraska wilderness. *Beyond the Divide* and *Prairie Songs* provide a much needed contrast to lighthearted accounts of frontier life and the Westward Movement found in books like *Caddie Woodlawn* (Brink, 1935) or to books that are primarily adventure stories like *On to Oregon* (Morrow, 1926).

Trade books today do come closer to offering our young readers a balanced view of history, and nonfiction trade books are no exception. Better designed, written, and illustrated than ever before, nonfiction has experienced phenomenal growth in the last two decades that has been one of the noteworthy trends in children's publishing, as noted by Barbara Elleman of the American Library Association: "A fictionalized, saccharine, often dull approach was prevalent in early series of nonfiction books that were formulaic and usually written on consignment. . . . subjects today are approached seriously and without condescension: perceptive, in-depth writing has placed informational books solidly in the category of quality literature" (1987, p. 422). Nonfiction children's books often not only provide information but also evoke emotion. Now, more than ever before, promoting an understanding of the human experience seems to be a principal thrust of good nonfiction authors, and this is accomplished through stylistic writing. Of nonfiction writing today, E. L. Doctorow says, "There is no more fiction or nonfiction—only narrative" (quoted in Donelson and Nilsen, 1989, p. 252). Doctorow's observation seems confirmed by the writing of contemporary authors like Milton Meltzer, one of our most prolific nonfiction writers for young readers. Of his own work Meltzer says:

> During the many years of writing nonfiction about social issues, I've often used the devices of fiction to multiply the power of facts by evoking from readers their sense of concern, even of constructive anger. I've wanted to help them see the weaknesses of our world, its inequality, its injustice, that leave so many poor, so many ignored, abused, betrayed. . . . I think I've used almost every technique fiction writers call on (except to invent the facts) in order to draw readers in, deepen their feeling for people whose lives may be remote from their own, and enrich their understanding of forces that shape the outcome of all our lives. (quoted in Donelson and Nilsen, 1989, p. 259)

Meltzer's (1990) *Christopher Columbus and the World Around Him* is a fine example of the newer brand of historical nonfiction for young readers. Meltzer places Columbus within the context of his own time by showing readers how Columbus was at least in part defined by a European world moving out of the Middle Ages and into the Renaissance. In perhaps the most insightful biography ever written for young readers about Columbus, the author has given children a way to truly understand the motivations and actions of the famed explorer by creating for them a well-structured frame of reference. In an effort to present a balanced view of history, Meltzer is extremely honest about Columbus's weaknesses as well as his strengths, noting not only that he was tenacious and possessed uncanny skills at limited elements of seamanship, but also that he actually was not a great sailor, was not a visionary (in fact, he was given to reworking the truth to satisfy himself), and was exceedingly cruel to the Native Americans. In fact, Meltzer (1990, p. 144) is daring enough to say that, in light of Columbus's systematic annihilation of the Native Americans, Columbus Day perhaps should be mourned rather than celebrated.

Newer informational books are giving young readers a fresh, forthright look at historical topics often gone stale in the pages of a school textbook. For example, the Civil War can be the most deadly of classroom topics, but these recent titles offer students and teachers varying and fascinating perspectives: *The Boys' War* (Murphy, 1990), *A Nation Torn: The Story of How the Civil War Began* (Ray, 1990), and *Voices from the Civil War* (Meltzer, 1989). Also, the biographies of Jean Fritz and Russell Freedman have helped to set a new standard for the genre in children's publishing and to breathe life into famous and seemingly stodgy names from history. Fritz was one of the first of the children's biographers to treat Columbus as something less than a demigod. Her fresh and saucy simplified biography titled *Where Do You Think You're Going, Christopher Columbus?* (1980) presents an egotistical, bullheaded Columbus who was, however, talented and determined. Of course, Fritz's biography incensed some adults who saw it as unpatriotic.

Freedman's masterful use of archival photographs adds an extra dimension to his subjects, "bringing them back alive." But Freedman can also write with style and verve. Note these lines from the opening of the Newbery Award–winning *Lincoln: A Photobiography*:

> At first glance, most people thought he was homely. Lincoln thought so too, referring once to his "poor, lean, lank face." As a young man he was sensitive about his gawky looks, but in time, he learned to laugh at himself. When a rival called him "two-faced" during a political debate, Lincoln replied: "I leave it to my audience. If I had another face, do you think I'd wear this one?" (1987, p. 1)

Freedman takes care not to glorify his subjects and works to give young readers a balanced view of both their public and private lives. He shows us the Lincoln who fought with serious bouts of depression, whose law office was notoriously dirty and cluttered, and whose marriage with Mary was sometimes stormy, as well as the Lincoln of the Gettysburg Address and the Emancipation Proclamation (both of which were, by the way, quite unpopular in their day). Freedman also represents the arguments of his subjects' detractors as well as their proponents. For instance, in Freedman's *Franklin Delano Roosevelt* (1990) he makes it clear that during Roosevelt's administration the national debt and taxes skyrocketed, and that many began calling the New Deal the "Raw Deal." "No president since Abraham Lincoln had aroused such intense antagonism and angry debate" says Freedman (p. 102). Freedman even reveals to young readers the affair Roosevelt had with Lucy Mercer—an event that, no matter how Roosevelt might have tried to make amends, seriously affected his relationship with Eleanor for the remainder of their lives. Freedman has revealed the real human being, the genuine Roosevelt—a man who changed American politics forever, who made many a daring and controversial decision, who set aside the class distinctions of his upbringing to reach out to the common man, who was indeed far less than perfect.

"But where are the heroes, the models, for today's children?" is the cry of many who fear such honest portrayals in children's books and prefer that our Lincolns and Washingtons be mythologized as virtually infallible beings. Yet, it seems a better lesson to know that the famous men and women from history had flaws, the human weaknesses we all share, but were able to rise above them to accomplish important things. Or, conversely, to know that a villain from history was at one time a mother's innocent child, raising the question, for example, of what events changed the boy Hitler into the murderous tyrant (see Albert Marrin's [1987] *Hitler: Portrait of a Tyrant*).

As the 1990s begin, the outlook for historical trade books for children continues to be reasonably bright. Elleman (1987, p. 418) reports a resurgence of historical fiction in the 1980s and a new and bountiful selection of top-notch nonfiction. Educators and scholars (Fielding, Wilson, and Anderson, 1984; Brozo and Tomlinson, 1986; Holmes and Ammon, 1985; Sewall, 1988; Ravitch, 1985; Downey and Levstik, 1988) are promoting the use of trade books rather than textbooks to help children learn history, because children's literature is better written, provides clearer historical context, offers varying perspectives, and puts "real people" back into the study of history. Authors have taken advantage of a changing social climate that has promoted increased intellectual freedom in children's publishing.

But what has brought about this age of increased openness? The progress in civil rights and women's rights? The disillusionment of Vietnam? Global awareness brought about by advances in technology? Certainly all of these are factors. Undoubtedly, children are more informed about society than ever before because of television. They see the effects of war, injustice, and hatred in living color and stereo sound right in their own living rooms. Maybe adults are beginning to realize that children must face and cope with the truth about the human experience because it is less possible to hide them from it. And perhaps each generation of adults, especially since Vietnam, has come to understand and accept this realization a little more. Speaking of these changes in our society, Christopher Collier (1976) says that books like his Revolutionary War novel, *My Brother Sam Is Dead*, benefit "from the revolution of our own times in that publishers are ready now to present teenagers with some complex issues and some raw reality to chew on" (p. 138). Undoubtedly, publishers are ready because we, the adults, are ready. So, perhaps one can dare speculate that it is we who are slowly coming of age, that change in historical literature for children is merely a by-product of our incomplete but continuing growth toward social maturity.

REFERENCES

Avi. (1984). *The Fighting Ground*. New York: Lippincott.

Beatty, J., & Beatty, P. (1975). *Who comes to King's Mountain?* New York: Morrow.

Brink, C. R. (1935). *Caddie Woodlawn*. New York: Macmillan.

Brozo, W. G., & Tomlinson, C. M. (1986, December). Literature: The key to lively content courses. *The Reading Teacher*, 40 (3), 288–93.

Collier, C. (1976, April). Johnny and Sam: Old and new approaches to the American Revolution. *The Horn Book*, 52 (2), 132–38.

Collier, J. L., & Collier, C. (1974). *My brother Sam is dead*. New York: Four Winds Press.

Collier, J. L., & Collier, C. (1981). *Jump ship to freedom*. New York: Delacorte.

Collier, J. L., & Collier, C. (1983). *War comes to Willy Freeman*. New York: Delacorte.

Collier, J. L., & Collier, C. (1984). *Who is Carrie?* New York: Delacorte.

Conrad, P. (1985). *Prairie songs*. New York: Harper & Row.

Donelson, K. L., & Nilsen, A. P. (1989). *Literature for today's young adults*. Glenview, Ill.: Scott, Foresman.

Downey, M. T., & Levstik, L. S. (1988, September). Teaching and learning history: The research base. *Social Education*, 52 (5), 336–42.

Edwards, S. (1972). *When the world's on fire*. New York: Coward, McCann & Geoghegan.

Elleman, B. (1987, Winter). Current trends in literature for children, *Library Trends*, 35 (3), 413–26.

Fielding, L. G., Wilson, P. T., & Anderson, R. C. (1986). A new focus on free reading: The role of trade books in reading instruction. In T. E. Raphael (Ed.), *The contexts of school-based literacy*, (pp. 149–160). New York: Random House.

Fitzhugh, L. (1964). *Harriet the Spy*. New York: Harper & Row.

Forbes, E. (1943). *Johnny Tremain*. Boston: Houghton Mifflin.

Freedman, R. (1987). *Lincoln: A photobiography*. New York: Clarion.

Freedman, R. (1990). *Franklin Delano Roosevelt*. New York: Clarion.

Fritz, J. (1980). *Where do you think you're going, Christopher Columbus?* New York: G. P. Putnam's.

Hamilton, V. (1988). *Anthony Burns: The defeat and triumph of a fugitive slave*. New York: Knopf.

Holmes, B. C., & Ammon, R. I. (1985, May/June). Teaching content with trade books: A strategy. *Childhood Education*, 61, 366–70.

Hoobler, D., & Hoobler, T. (1990). *Vietnam: Why we fought*. New York: Knopf.

Huck, C. S., Hepler, S., & Hickman, J. (1987). *Children's literature in the elementary school.* 4th ed. New York: Holt, Rinehart & Winston.

Hutchinson, M. (1978). Fifty years of young adult reading, 1921–1971. In J. Varlejs (Ed.), *Young adult literature in the seventies.* Metuchen, N.J.: Scarecrow Press.

Lasky, K. (1983). *Beyond the divide.* New York: Macmillan.

Lasky, K. (1988). *The bone wars.* New York: Morrow.

Lasky, K. (1990, Summer). The fiction of history: Or, what did Miss Kitty really do? *The New Advocate,* 3 (3), 157–66.

Lens, S. (1990). *Vietnam: A war on two fronts.* New York: Dutton, Lodestar.

Lester, J. (1969). *To be a slave.* New York: Dial.

Marrin, A. (1987). *Hitler: Portrait of a tyrant.* New York: Viking, Kestrel.

Meltzer, M. (1989). *Voices from the Civil War.* New York: Crowell.

Meltzer, M. (1990). *Christopher Columbus and the world around him.* New York: Watts.

Murphy, J. (1990). *The boys' war.* New York: Clarion.

Morrow, H. (1926). *On to Oregon.* New York: Morrow.

Myers, W. D. (1988). *Fallen angels.* New York: Scholastic.

Nelson, T. (1989). *And one for all.* New York: Orchard.

O'Dell, S. (1980). *Sarah Bishop.* Boston: Houghton Mifflin.

Ravitch, D. (1985, Spring). The precarious state of history. *American Educator,* 9 (4), 11–17.

Ray, D. (1990). *A nation torn: The story of how the Civil War began.* New York: Dutton, Lodestar.

Sendak, M. (1963). *Where the wild things are.* New York: Harper & Row.

Sewall, G. T. (1988, April). American history textbooks: Where do we go from here? *Phi Delta Kappan,* 553–58.

Taylor, M. (1976). *Roll of thunder, hear my cry.* New York: Dial.

Taxel, J. (1983, February). The American Revolution in children's fiction. *Research in the Teaching of English,* 17 (1), 61–83.

Trease, G. (1966). *Bows against the baron.* London: Lawrence; New York: Meredith. (Originally published in 1934)

Trease, G. (1977, February). The historical story: Is it relevant today? *The Horn Book,* 53 (1), 21–28.

Trease, G. (1983, Autumn). Fifty years on: a writer looks back. *Children's Literature in Education,* 14 (3), 149–59.

Warren, J. A. (1990). *Portrait of a tragedy: America and the Vietnam War.* New York: Lothrop.

Wilmott, H. (1965, January). YASD asks the young adult. *Top of the News,* 21, 143–47.

PART THREE

Practical Applications

Richard Ammon teaches children's literature at The Pennsylvania State University at Harrisburg. Among numerous articles in leading journals, he coauthored "Teaching Content with Trade Books" (*Childhood Education,* 1985). He has also written two children's nonfiction books—*The Kid's Book of Chocolate* (1987) and *Growing Up Amish* (1989) (both Atheneum).

Diane Weigard teaches first grade in Hershey, Pennsylvania, where she practices what she preaches—engaging first graders in hands-on social studies activities and encouraging them to read many early reader trade books about historical events.

* * *

Does learning history need to be passive? Is nonfiction the only genre suitable for teaching history? Does the teaching of American history have to center around the Revolutionary and Civil Wars? Or could history be built around other themes? Drawing from their teaching experiences, Ammon and Weigard suggest an active process approach to teaching history, discuss how various genres can enhance a history or social studies curriculum, and propose a unit that looks at American history from a different perspective than one marked by wars.

A Look at Other Trade Book Topics and Genres

Richard Ammon and Diane Weigard

In her autobiographical novel, Homesick (1982), Jean Fritz tells of her first day in school in America after having lived all her life in China:

> Miss Crofts put a bunch of history books on the first desk of each row so they could be passed back, student to student. I was glad to see that we'd be studying the history of Pennsylvania. Since both my mother's and father's families had helped settle Washington County, I was interested to know how they and other pioneers had fared. Opening the book to the first chapter, "From Forest to Farmland," I skimmed through the pages but I couldn't find any mention of people at all. There was talk about dates and square miles and cultivation and population growth and immigration and the Western movement, but it was as if the forest had lain down and given way to farmland without anyone being brave or scared or tired or sad, without babies being born, without people dying. Well, I thought, maybe that would come later. (p. 153)

Unfortunately, social studies texts haven't changed that much since Jean Fritz first opened an American history book. In an effort to make texts palatable to each vocal special interest group, publishers have leached these books of the humanness, detail, and differing voices that enliven the study of history (Hentoff, 1984; Sewall, 1988; Gagnon, 1989). Therefore, it should come as no surprise to learn that students read very little in their truncated texts. Unfortunately, they read little from other sources as well (Downey and Levstik, 1988, p. 337).

93

Moreover, the methodology in most social studies classrooms is teacher directed (Mehlinger, 1988, 204). Mehlinger reported that "nearly everywhere it is the same: directed discussion is *the* method for teaching social studies" (p. 204).

Process Teaching and Learning

Happily, teachers are now rallying around some exciting curricular trends. Today's students are engaged in the process of learning. They are encouraged to formulate their own historical questions and conduct authentic research, using library skills and reading a wide range of trade books. Students take control of their own learning and choose their own reading material (Olson, 1959; Holdaway, 1980). Not only does process teaching emphasize much writing (Graves, 1983) and critical thinking (Beyer, 1988) but it is also characterized through cooperative learning and interdisciplinary teaching. Process teaching makes sense as states and local districts move away from traditional content curricula toward learning outcomes, such as critical thinking, library research, process writing, and purposeful reading skills.

Instead of a pell-mell dash to cover a curriculum by treating topics superficially, process teaching requires time for in-depth study. Jackson (1988) asks, "Has the notion that 'less is more' been considered, as themes, topics, and questions are selected?" (p. 22). Downey and Levstik (1988) have advocated "courses that devote sufficient time to a particular topic or period to establish an adequate context for historical learning" (p. 340). For example, rather than having students read the two paragraphs about the Holocaust from a social studies textbook, teachers might devote a full marking period to this topic, as described in chapter 12.

Discovering the Past Through History Projects

To many students, history is something distant and illusive. But the past doesn't have to be so inaccessible. An excellent way for children to learn about the process of history is to trace the history of their own families. Children's books can help students develop such projects. For instance, in *The Great Ancestor Hunt* (1989), Lila Perl tells children how to create their own family trees by conducting family interviews and researching family memorabilia and public records. Not only will students have fun learning, but they will also discover the process of history.

David Weitzman designed *My Backyard History Book* (1975) as a handbook or field guide with an accessible format that enables students to become history detectives. One chapter shows students how to glean information from cemeteries, whereas another chapter tells of history that may be found in old obituary pages as well as the yellow pages. In the section titled "Hanging Around Old Town," students can learn how to gather information about their town by going to a realtor's office, taking rubbings from various markers, and exploring old junkyards. Weitzman reminds students that there is no such thing as an empty backyard.

In addition to providing questions about a student's family history, Weitzman includes a Personal History Test that asks questions such as, How did the town you live in happen to get its name? Who and what lived there before it became a town or a city? and Why does your town happen to be where it is?

Weitzman also gives instructions for developing a personal time line, making a birthday time capsule, and creating a family map—a map that might show great-grandparents arriving in New York City, for example, and the family later moving from city to city.

Told from a grandfather's perspective, *My Block* (1988) by Richard Rosenblum, captures the energy and activity of one block in Brooklyn three generations ago. This small picture book may evoke inspiration for intergenerational teaching and learning. Taking suggestions from *My Backyard History Book*, teachers may arrange for elderly persons to help children reconstruct certain blocks in their town.

Studying History Through Literary Genres

Whether the topic to be studied is part of a mandated curriculum or has evolved from classroom activities, students will have no trouble generating an array of questions and will need to gather background information. In the library, the teacher and librarian should guide children to read not just those necessary reference and nonfiction titles but also other less obvious literary genres.

Many scholars have argued for the benefits of using historical novels to study history. Levstik (1990), for example, reported the frustrations of a fifth-grade girl who, after reading several historical novels, said that the textbook "just says that Americans were right but it doesn't tell you exactly why they were right, or why the British fought" (p. 850).

Adolescent literature specialists Gallo and Barksdale (1983) write that

> in contrast to the usually passive style of history texts, historical novels allow readers to participate vicariously in the historical period, seeing the sights, feeling the emotions, being part of the events as they occur. And when the novel has a teenager as the main character, especially if the narration is done in first person, the adolescent reader is even more likely to feel an involvement with the emotions and the events of the book. In effect, the historical novel makes history come alive. (p. 286)

In chapter 8 of this book, Levstik reminds students that history is the product of human emotion and decision and that, as young scholars, they should realize that history, especially their own, is subject to revision.

Students need to understand that historical novels, like all novels, are often told from the point of view of the protagonist. One way of expanding perspectives is by reading novels with more than one point of view, such as Harold Keith's *Rifles for Watie* (1957), Irene Hunt's *Across Five Aprils* (1964), or the Colliers' *My Brother Sam Is Dead* (1974). Of course, reading a number of titles on a particular topic also broadens perspectives. Lehman and Hayes (1985) add that "critical reading of several sources will spark discussions of various issues or controversies, which can be both a motivator for reading and a better alternative to censorship" (p. 168).

Teachers and students of history should not stop with historical fiction, however; other genres not usually associated with history can provide unique and often dramatic interpretations.

Who could imagine fantasy having anything to do with the study of history? Yet in attempting to make history come alive, writers have drawn upon devices of fantasy.

In *The Devil's Arithmetic* (1988), Jane Yolen uses a time warp to propel her contemporary protagonist, who doesn't appreciate her grandfather's stories of the Holocaust, back into the Nazi-controlled Poland of the 1940s. Then, just as she walks "through the door into endless night," (p. 160) she falls back into her grandfather's dining room where, with all her relatives gathered around, she joins in on the family's stories about the camps.

Instead of taking the protagonist back in time, Elaine Marie Alphin creates a ghost of a Civil War soldier who leaps forward to the present to visit Benjy Stark, who is not happy about having to spend his spring vacation with his grandmother in Virginia. Grounded in thorough research, *The Ghost Cadet* (1991) tells the Battle of New Market from a Southern perspective.

Naturally, great numbers of picture books are designed for elementary school children. Unfortunately, middle school students often dismiss this genre, believing these books are intended only for primary grade children. When these books are presented by thoughtful teachers and librarians, however, early adolescents will respond favorably to the concise stories and inspiring illustrations (Chatton, 1990; Odland, 1980; DuBois and McIntosh, 1986). In fact, many picture books possess a level of sophistication especially suited for middle school readers. Tunnell and Ammon begin their literature unit on the Holocaust by reading aloud Eve Bunting's picture book allegory, *Terrible Things* (1989). *Shaker Lane* (1987) by Alice and Martin Provensen can spark a discussion on the price of progress. And David Macaulay's nonfiction title *The Mill* (1983) shows the history and evolution of a manufacturing mill from the early nineteenth century to the present.

Each year, *Notable Children's Trade Books in the Field of Social Studies,*[*] prepared jointly by the Children's Book Council and the National Council for the Social Studies, includes a section on folktales and legends. This genre can enhance understanding of many social studies topics because, evolving from the great oral tradition of common folk, these stories carry a sense of values of the culture (Musser and Freeman, 1989; Odland, 1980). Consequently, folktales can become minilessons in cultural diversity.

For example, in the Chinese tale *The Fourth Question*, retold by Rosalind C. Wang, the protagonist, Yee-Lee, sets off to ask the wise man a question. Along the way, he meets three other people who give him their questions to ask. Unfortunately, the wise man allows Yee-Lee only three questions. So, Yee-Lee asks the strangers' questions, but not his own. In the end, he finds happiness helping others. Characteristic of many Chinese tales, this unselfish ending contrasts sharply with Western tales in which the protagonist finds a mate or riches and rides off to the castle to "live happily ever after."

Folktales can also point up differences in values from one culture to another as seen in Paul Goble's *Death of the Iron Horse* (1987). When the Cheyennes raid a train and break open a boxcar, they use the American flag as a blanket and scatter paper money to the wind.

No matter what region, ethnic group, or time period students are studying, there are bound to be folktales representing those cultures.

At first thought, poetry may not seem to link with social studies or history teaching. Yet, a number of books of poetry have direct connections.

In the Caldecott Medal picture book *Ox-Cart Man* (1979), Donald Hall's verse and Barbara Cooney's lush paintings characterize early New England. The poems of Claudia Lewis in *Long Ago in Oregon* (1987) tell of a young girl living in a small town during World War I. In *Heartland* (1989), Diane Siebert's lyrical words and Wendell Minor's stunning paintings celebrate America's Midwest.

One creative teacher near Hershey, Pennsylvania, developed a social studies unit on the history and economics of chocolate, topping it off with *Chocolate Dreams* (1989), poems by Arnold Adoff.

[*]Teachers and librarians can keep abreast of new books by sending a self-addressed, stamped envelope to the Children's Book Council, 568 Broadway, NY, NY 10012, and requesting "Notable Children's Trade Books in the Field of Social Studies." This joint publication by the Children's Book Council and the National Council for the Social Studies is reprinted in the April/May issues of *Social Education*.

Unique Units

Finally, when teachers think about their history curricula—that is, what to teach and how to organize it—they might consider presenting history from different perspectives. Too often, the content of history curricula is marked by wars. Consequently, many people think of history only in terms of dates, battles, generals, and politicians. But what if American history were taught from another angle? For example, what different concepts might students develop if they looked at America from the point of view of immigrants, since all of us are immigrants or descendants of immigrants?

You may want to introduce such a unit with *Before Columbus* (1981). In this picture book, author/illustrator Muriel Batherman tells of the trek made by early Native Americans across the land bridge that connected Asia and North America and describes several of their early civilizations.

Reading selections from *In the Trail of the Wind: American Indian Poems and Ritual Orations* (1987) edited by John Bierhorst and *Dancing Teepees: Poems of American Indian Youth* (1989) by Virginia Driving Hawk Sneve, teachers can present Native American thought from a time before white man to a time of hope for today.

Told in seventeenth-century English, Marcia Sewall gives a glimpse of life in the early Massachusetts colony in her picture book *The Pilgrims of Plimouth* (1986), whereas Edna Barth debunks a number of popular myths in *Turkeys, Pilgrims, and Indian Corn: The Story of the Thanksgiving Symbols* (1975). For example, did you know that "the only pies the Pilgrims knew were meat pies" (p. 85), but they did turn pumpkins into beer!

Two contemporary Thanksgiving stories give special meaning to this traditional holiday. In *Molly's Pilgrim* (1983) by Barbara Cohen, a teacher tells her class to make Pilgrim dolls for a model of Plymouth village. When an immigrant girl takes to school a doll dressed in Eastern European costume, rather than Pilgrim clothing, she is teased by her schoolmates. This sensitive teacher helps the class understand that Molly is a modern-day Pilgrim.

In a controversial story, Eve Bunting tells about a Latin American family who escapes from a war-ravaged country in *How Many Days to America?* (1988). After an arduous voyage, they land in America on Thanksgiving Day. Students might be challenged to compare similarities between the Pilgrims and these illegal aliens.

Most black Americans immigrated to America against their own will. In *The Black Americans: A History in Their Own Words 1619–1983* (1984), Milton Meltzer reports firsthand descriptions of the horrific conditions on slave ships as well as accounts of very recent struggles for equality. The inhumanity aboard those slave ships is also brought to life in Paula Fox's *The Slave Dancer* (1973).

The study of black history may also be enhanced through the reading of tales from Virginia Hamilton's *The People Could Fly* (1985), a collection of African American folktales, many of which deal with hopeful flight from slavery.

Because most American music can be traced to African-American origins, history teachers might encourage students to read James Haskins's history, *Black Music in America* (1987). At the same time, music teachers may lead students in singing black American spirituals from Ashley Bryan's three books, *Walk Together Children* (1976), *I'm Going to Sing* (1982), and *All Night, All Day* (1991).

Chronicling the great wave of European immigration, Milton Meltzer describes in his memoir, *Starting from Home* (1988), what it was like aboard the ship that brought his grandfather to America.

> He slept in a compartment way below deck that held 300 immigrants. The berths, in two tiers, were six feet, two inches long, with a two-and-a-half-foot space above each berth. His blanket was so flimsy that he had to sleep in his clothing to keep warm.

> There were no waste barrels or sickness cans; the steerage floor was always damp and filthy and the air stank sickeningly.

Joan Sandin begins her remarkable "I Can Read" book *The Long Way to a New Land* (1981) in Sweden, where young Carl Erik's father feels despair over the drought. Brief, crisp sentences and fresh evocative watercolors tell the story of how Carl Erik's father decides to take his family to America. After surviving a frightening three-day storm at sea, the immigrants are allowed on deck for fresh air: "A man sat down beside Papa. 'It was much worse before steamships,' he said. 'It took months then'" (p. 50). Happily, Carl Erik's family does set foot on Ellis Island.

Riki Levinson has a grandmother narrate the story of her voyage to America in *Watch the Stars Come Out* (1985), a picture book illustrated in warm, lucid colors by Diane Goode. The grandmother recalls the crowded conditions aboard ship, with people getting sick and dying. But she also tells young readers how spirits lifted when, through a shroud of fog, they see a small bright torch light, the symbol of their hope.

Leonard Fisher's *Ellis Island* (1986) describes the first stop for most new arrivals. In scratchboard, Fisher illustrates the fire that burned down the new buildings a day after they were completed on June 15, 1897. This tragedy destroyed the records of millions of immigrants.

Brett Harvey begins *Immigrant Girl* (1987) soon after Becky Moscowitz arrives in America. Sitting on her stoop on the Lower East Side of New York, she tells what it's like to be a new immigrant:

I am learning English fast because I don't want to be a "greenie." That's what they call you when you're new in America. I still have trouble mixing up v's and w's.

The heart-warming juvenile novel In the Year of the Boar and Jackie Robinson (1984) by Bette Bao Lord tells the story of Shirley Temple Wong, who emigrates from China speaking only two English words. But living in Brooklyn in the summer of 1947, she listens to Red Barber broadcasting Dodger games and not only learns English but also comes to idolize Jackie Robinson. When her hero visits P.S. 8, Shirley's dream comes true as she is elected to present him with a key to the school.

Under the general series title Coming to America, Delacorte published a collection of books that focus upon emigration from various regions: Immigrants from Eastern Europe (1981) by Shirley Blumental, Immigrants from the British Isles (1981) by Shirley Blumental and Jerome S. Ozer, Immigrants from the Far East (1981) by Linda Pervin, Immigrants from Northern Europe (1981) by Albert Robbins, and Immigrants from Southern Europe (1981) by Gladys Nadler Rips.

Linda Crew tells of the struggles of a young Cambodian girl adjusting to life in Oregon in Children of the River (1989), whereas Brent Ashabranner relates cultural experiences of Arab-Americans in An Ancient Heritage (1991).

Two photographic picture books, Hector Lives in the United States Now: The Story of a Mexican-American Child (1990) by Joan Hewett and Hello Amigos! (1986) by Tricia Brown with photographs by Fran Ortiz, tell of the everyday lives of contemporary Mexican-American children.

A celebration of cultural diversity may serve as a culmination of this unit. As students present their reports and projects, the class may enjoy sampling ethnic foods, listening to music of different cultures, and viewing ethnic art and artifacts.

Other possible units might include Peace, Technology, Transportation, or even Music and Art. Regardless of what topics are selected, teachers need to know that librarians can be most helpful, especially by putting together classroom collections and conducting special library sessions to help students locate materials.

Clearly, the teaching of social studies holds more interesting and exciting possibilities than the ponderous, all-too-prevalent lecture-discussion method. Active learning occurs in classrooms in which students are vital participants in the learning process, in which several teachers representing a variety of disciplines use different approaches to studying the same content, and in which fiction and nonfiction trade books replace the textbooks as primary reading materials. In those classrooms, students may actually look forward to social studies.

REFERENCES

Beyer, Barry K. *Developing a Thinking Skills Program*. Allyn and Bacon 1988.

Chatton, Barbara A., "Picture Books for Young Adults," *The ALAN Review*, 1990, 17, 16–18.

Downey, Matthew T. and Linda S. Levstik. "Teaching and Learning History: The Research Base," *Social Education*, 1988, 52, 336–342.

DuBois, De Lin, and Margaret E. McIntosh. "Reading Aloud to Students in Secondary History Classes," *The Social Studies*. 1986, 77, 210–213.

Gagnon, Paul. *Democracy's Half Told Story*. Washington, D. C.: American Federation of Teachers, 1989.

Gallo, Donald R. and Ellie Barksdale. "Using Fiction in American History," *Social Education*, 1983, 47, 286–287.

Graves, Donald. *Writing: Teachers and Children at Work*. Portsmouth, New Hampshire: Heinemann, 1983.

Hentoff, Nat. "The Dumbing of America," *The Progressive*, 1984, 48, 29–31.

Holdaway, Don. *Independence in Reading*. Portsmouth, New Hampshire: Heinemann, 1980.

Jackson, Kenneth, chair. "Building a History Curriculum," *Bradley Commission on History in Schools*. Washington: Educational Excellence Network. 1988.

Lehman, Barbara, and David Hayes. "Advancing Critical Reading through Historical Fiction and Biography," *The Social Studies*, 1985, 165–169.

Levstik, Linda S. "Research Directions: Mediating Content Through Literary Texts," *Language Arts*, 1990, 67, 848–853.

Mehlinger, Howard D. "The Reform of Social Studies and the Role of the National Commission for the Social Studies," *The History Teacher*, 1988, 21, 195–206.

Musser, Louise and Evelyn Freeman. "Teach Young Students about Native Americans: Use Myths, Legends and Folktales," *The Social Studies*, 1989, 5–8.

Odland, Norine. "American History in Fact and Fiction: Literature for Young Readers," *Social Education*, 1980, 44, 474–481

Olson, Willard. "Seeking, Self-Selection, and Pacing in the Use of Books by Children" as found in *Individualizing Your Reading Program* by Jeannette Veatch. Putnam 1959, pp. 89–98.

Sewall, Gilbert. "American History Textbooks: Where Do We Go from Here?" *Phi Delta Kappan*, 1988, 69, 553–558.

CHILDREN'S AND YOUNG ADULT LITERATURE

Adoff, Arnold. *Chocolate Dreams*, illustrated by Turi MacCombie. New York: Lothrop, Lee & Shepard, 1989.

Alphin, Elaine Marie. *The Ghost Cadet*. New York: Henry Holt, 1991.

Ashabranner, Brent. *An Ancient Heritage*, photographs by Paul S. Conklin. New York: HarperCollins, 1991.

Barth, Edna. *Turkeys, Pilgrims, and Indian Corn: The Story of the Thanksgiving Symbols*, illustrated by Ursula Arndt. New York: Clarion, 1975.

Batherman, Muriel. *Before Columbus*. Boston: Houghton Mifflin, 1981.

Bierhorst, John. *In the Trail of the Wind: American Indian Poems and Ritual Orations*. New York: Farrar Straus & Giroux, 1987.

Blumenthal, Shirley. *Coming to America: Immigrants from Eastern Europe*. New York: Delacorte, 1981.

Blumenthal, Shirley and Jerome S. Ozer. *Coming to America: Immigrants from the British Isles*. New York: Delacorte, 1981.

Brown, Tricia. *Hello Amigos!*, photographs by Fran Ortiz. New York: Henry Holt, 1986.

Bryan, Ashley. *Walk Together Children*. New York: Atheneum, 1974.

Bryan, Ashley. *I'm Going to Sing*. New York: Atheneum, 1982.

Bryan, Ashley. *All Night, All Day*. New York: Atheneum, 1991.

Bunting, Eve. *How many Days to America?*, illustrated by Beth Peck. New York: Clarion, 1988.

Bunting, Eve. *Terrible Things*, illustrated by Stephen Gammell. New York: The Jewish Publication Society, 5749.

Cohen, Barbara. *Molly's Pilgrim*, illustrated by Michael J. Deraney. New York: Lothrop, 1983.

Collier, James and Christopher Collier. *My Brother Sam Is Dead*. New York: Macmillan, 1974.

Crew, Linda. *Children of the River*. New York: Delacorte, 1989.

Fisher, Leonard Everett. *Ellis Island*. New York: Holiday House, 1986.

Fox, Paula. *The Slave Dancer*. New York: Dell, 1973.

Fritz, Jean. *Homesick*. New York: Putnam, 1982.

Goble, Paul. *Death of the Iron Horse*. New York: Bradbury 1987.

Hall, Donald. *Ox-Cart Man*. New York: Viking, 1979.

Hamilton, Virginia. *The People Could Fly: American Black Folktales*, illustrated by Leo and Diane Dillon. New York: Alfred A. Knopf, 1985.

Harvey, Brett. *Immigrant Girl*, illustrated by Deborah Kogan Ray. New York: Holiday House, 1987.

Haskins, James. *Black Music in America*. New York: T.Y. Crowell, 1987.

Hewett, Joan. *Hector Lives in the United States Now: The Story of a Mexican-American Child*. New York: Lippincott, 1990.

Hunt, Irene. *Across Five Aprils*. Chicago: Follett, 1964.

Keith, Harold. *Rifles for Watie*. New York: T.Y. Crowell, 1957.

Levinson, Riki. *Watch the Stars Come Out*, illustrated by Diane Goode. New York: Dutton, 1985.

Lewis, Claudia. *Long Ago in Oregon*, illustrated by Joel Fontaine. New York: Harper & Row, 1987.

Lord, Bette Bao. *In the Year of the Boar and Jackie Robinson*. New York: Harper & Row, 1984.

Macaulay, David. *The Mill*. Boston: Houghton Mifflin, 1983.

Meltzer, Milton. *The Black Americans: A History in Their Own Words 1619–1983*. New York: T.Y. Crowell, 1984.

Meltzer, Milton. *Starting From Home*. New York: Viking, 1988.

Murphy, Jim. *The Boys' War*. New York: Clarion, 1990.

Perl, Lila. *The Great Ancestor Hunt*. New York: Clarion, 1989.

Pervin, Linda. *Coming to America: Immigrants from the Far East*. New York: Delacorte, 1981.

Provensen, Alice and Martin. *Shaker Lane*. New York: Viking, 1987.

Rips, Gladys Nadler. *Coming to America: Immigrants from Southern Europe*. New York: Delacorte, 1981.

Robbins, Albert. *Coming to America: Immigrants from Northern Europe*. New York: Delacorte, 1981.

Rosenblum, Richard. *My Block*. New York: Atheneum, 1988.

Sandin, Joan. *The Long Way to a New Land*. New York: Harper & Row, 1981.

Sewall, Marcia. *The Pilgrims of Plimouth*. New York: Atheneum, 1986.

Siebert, Diane. *Heartland*, illustrated by Wendell Minor. New York: T.Y. Crowell, 1989.

Sneve, Virginia Driving Hawk. *Dancing Teepees: Poems of American Indian Youth*, illustrated by Stephen Gammell. New York: Holiday House, 1989.

Wang, Rosalind C. *The Fourth Question*, illustrated by Ju-Hong Chen. New York: Holiday House, 1991.

Weitzman, David. *My Backyard History Book*, illustrated by James Robertson. Boston: Little, Brown, 1975.

Yolen, Jane. *The Devil's Arithmetic*. New York: Viking, 1988.

Judith S. Wooster has served as an elementary classroom teacher, a state social studies specialist, and a director of curriculum activities at Stanford University and the Three Village Central School District in Setauket, New York. She has reviewed social studies materials for many groups including the National Council for the Social Studies/Children's Book Council Notable Trade Books in Social Studies Committee, and she serves as a consultant for those interested in linking literature and social studies to teach concepts, develop understanding, and foster student interest and motivation.

* * *

How can a teacher develop activities that help students learn history through trade books? How can a teacher avoid destroying the impact of a book by asking too many knowledge-level questions? In this chapter, Judith Wooster demonstrates a number of approaches that help children to think critically about the history-related trade books they read.

11

Approaches for Using Children's Literature to Teach Social Studies

Judith S. Wooster

"Pooh looked at his two paws. He knew that one of them was the right, and that when you had decided which one of them was the right, then the other was the left, but he could never remember how to begin."

Children's literature is a natural resource for teaching social studies. Trade books are treasured by teachers. However, like Milne's beloved Pooh, the challenge lies in deciding how to begin. In the world of schools and classrooms, curricular mandates frame what must be taught. These mandates frequently form the basis for student testing. Even when this is not the case, good teachers such as Gail Tunnell and Jeannie Ammon (see chapter 12) recognize the need to help students gain a deeper understanding of a book's context as well as an appreciation of the literature itself. In this chapter, I give examples of an approach to teaching history and social science using children's literature.

The first question to ask yourself when planning to use literature in the classroom is of course, What books should I use? The task is more complex than simply selecting all available books on a topic. To motivate, engage, and excite students, books must be of high literary and artistic quality. Scholarly integrity is also an essential attribute. Do selections accurately portray peoples and places in the present and past? Do our choices help students appreciate different perspectives on events? Taken as a whole, do the selections help students grow in their understanding of an appropriate range of times, places, and cultures, and appreciate relationships as they construct knowledge?

A children's librarian can be an invaluable help in selecting children's books. Periodical resources such as the *School Library Journal*, *The Horn Book*, and the *New York Times Book Review* are also useful. A list of approximately one hundred *Notable Children's Trade Books in Social Studies* is compiled annually by the Children's Book Council in cooperation with the National Council for the Social Studies.* Since excellent new books are written each year, it is important to keep up-to-date with sources.

After identifying an appropriate book for the classroom, ask yourself, What key ideas from this book should be the focus of instruction? By building learning activities around important ideas and concepts, you will ensure that your instruction reinforces curricular goals. Consider the following three examples.

The Founding of the Republic (1985c), one of a series of American history books written by Richard B. Morris and illustrated by Leonard Everett Fisher, is an excellent source for helping students understand how the American political heritage is built on conflict and compromise over ideals such as unity, trust, rights, and justice. In *The Wailing Wall* (1989), author and illustrator Leonard Everett Fisher conveys the continuity and commitment of the Jewish people to their beliefs, in the face of enormous adversity and violent conflict. *A Gathering of Days: A New England Girl's Journal, 1830–1832* by Joan Blos (1979) offers an opportunity to develop the geographic theme of place, through rich description of a New England farming community in the nineteenth century. Each of these key ideas develops and reinforces important social studies understandings.

The next step in the planning process involves asking, What skills should be the focus of activities built around this book? Literature offers a rich opportunity to help students develop skills that enable them to understand people and cultures across time and space. They must, for example, develop an understanding of *before* and *after*, which they will later use on a more sophisticated level to locate events in specific times, order multiple events, and create simple and multilayered time lines.

Students must develop skills that enable them to identify big ideas, to see relationships between ideas, and to apply understandings to new learning. They must learn to process information, distinguish between relevant and irrelevant facts, and recognize and analyze differing points of view. And, perhaps most important, students need to learn to value historical ideas and be motivated to a lifelong interest in learning more about people and cultures. Through purposeful instructional planning, literature can help develop these and other important abilities.

After you decide which book to use and identify the concepts and skills that will be the focus of instruction, the next question to consider is,

---

*See the April/May issue of *Social Education*.

What instructional strategies will best complement this work and build toward concept and skill goals? For the Richard B. Morris book *The Founding of the Republic* (1985c), having pairs of students acting as founders engage in role-playing or write dialogues is effective in conveying the American political heritage of conflict resolved through compromise. Through such activities, students develop analytic skills and gain practice in framing an argument around a point of view.

Using pastels or watercolors to illustrate selected days from the life of thirteen-year-old Catherine Cabot Hall from Joan Blos's A *Gathering of Days: A New England Girl's Journal, 1830–1832* (1979) helps students focus on the geographic setting of nineteenth-century New Hampshire, as well as identify relevant details from a story. Creating a classroom or hall time line based on the details from *The Wailing Wall* by Leonard Everett Fisher (1989) helps students understand continuity and conflict in Jewish history and also develop an understanding of time and chronology.

The remainder of this chapter is devoted to examples of classroom lessons designed using the planning process described above. In each case, high quality children's books were selected to address important concepts and skills in social studies. Students' activities reinforced these goals and related the literature to curricular expectations.

Sample Classroom Lessons

Cause and Effect Relationships: Nineteenth-Century America Series

Leonard Everett Fisher's Nineteenth-Century America series helps students understand that events in history are interrelated, and offers great potential for developing skills in discovering cause and effect relationships. To reinforce these goals, students could do the following activity: Have students work as partners or in groups of four. Give each group or pair a book from the series and two packs of index cards, one blue and one yellow. Ask students to create yellow "cause" cards and corresponding blue "effect" cards based on their books. These cause and effect cards can be shared with other groups, as a part of student presentations. The cards can also be used in card games such as Concentration and Go Fish, thereby reinforcing these relationships. (See Figure 11–1.)

A connections web offers another way to explore the effects of an event, such as the impact of the transcontinental railroad. (See Figure 11–2.)

Technology and Change: Colonial American Craftsmen

Another excellent Fisher series is Colonial American Craftsmen. This set of nineteen books can be used to illustrate technology and help students consider how ways of work have changed over time. By working in pairs to

Cause and effect cards show
that events in history are
interrelated.

Blue index cards

Because unskilled workers could work at machines...

Yellow index cards

children could work in factories to produce goods formerly made by skilled workers

Content based on The Unions
by Leonard Everett Fisher

FIGURE 11-1

Connections web shows cause
and effect relationships.

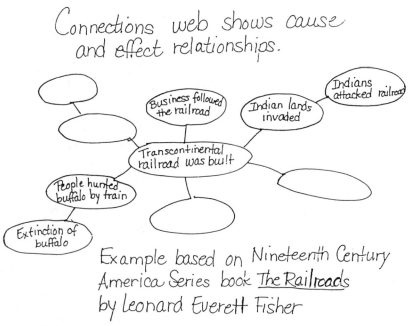

Business followed the railroad

Indian lands invaded

Indians attacked railroad

Transcontinental railroad was built

People hunted buffalo by train

Extinction of buffalo

Example based on Nineteenth Century
America Series book The Railroads
by Leonard Everett Fisher

FIGURE 11-2

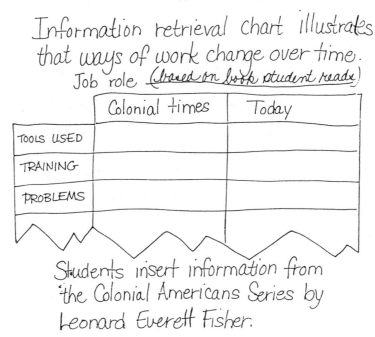

Information retrieval chart illustrates that ways of work change over time.

Job role (based on book student reads)

	Colonial times	Today
TOOLS USED		
TRAINING		
PROBLEMS		

Students insert information from the Colonial Americans Series by Leonard Everett Fisher.

FIGURE 11–3

complete an information retrieval chart such as the one in Figure 11–3, students can enhance their skills of comparing and contrasting. This chart serves as an effective prewriting activity from which students can create a news article showing how a craft in colonial times is similar to or different from that craft today.

Chronology Through Primary Source Collections: In Their Own Words

Milton Meltzer's primary source collections (including *The American Revolutionaries: A History in Their Own Words 1750–1800* [1987], *The Black Americans: A History in Their Own Words* [1984], and *The Jewish Americans: A History in Their Own Words* [1982]) offer an excellent opportunity for students to develop an understanding of chronology and skills of asking questions. Students can create a living time line by reading aloud excerpts of their choice from Meltzer's collections. Students in the audience can generate questions about the times, people, or events, which can be sources for future research.

Decision-Making Skills: Brothers of the Heart

Literature can help students understand that throughout history people have been faced with difficult decisions. By analyzing the decisions of

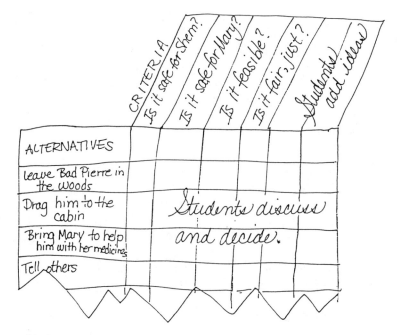

CRITERIA
Is it safe for Shem?
Is it safe for Mary?
Is it feasible?
Is it fair, just?
Students add ideas

ALTERNATIVES

Leave Bad Pierre in the woods

Drag him to the cabin

Bring Mary to help him with her medicine

Tell others

Students discuss and decide.

FIGURE 11–4

characters in literature, students can hone their own decision-making skills. In *Brothers of the Heart* by Joan Blos (1985), Shem Perkins, a lame boy struggling to survive a bitter winter in the Michigan wilderness, comes upon Bad Pierre, unconscious but not dead, in the woods. Shem fears Bad Pierre and knows the trapper to be a thief. What should Shem do? On a decision grid, students can list possible decisions and criteria. They can then work in small groups to weigh and code the criteria (see Figure 11–4).

Another useful strategy is the decision tree, on which students describe the situation, consider alternatives and their possible positive and negative consequences, identify values at stake, and ultimately arrive at a decision. In *Brothers of the Heart*, Shem must decide whether to leave his dying Indian friend, Mary Goodhue, and return to his parents' home to assure them that he is alive. Students can use a decision tree to analyze Shem's choices (see Figure 11–5).

Challenges to Immigrants: Collections on Immigration

Many books on immigration are available, among them Leonard Everett Fisher's *A Russian Farewell* (1980), *Across the Sea from Galway* (1975), and *Letters from Italy* (1977). The student contract shown in Figure 11–6 was developed to highlight the idea that immigrants faced challenges in

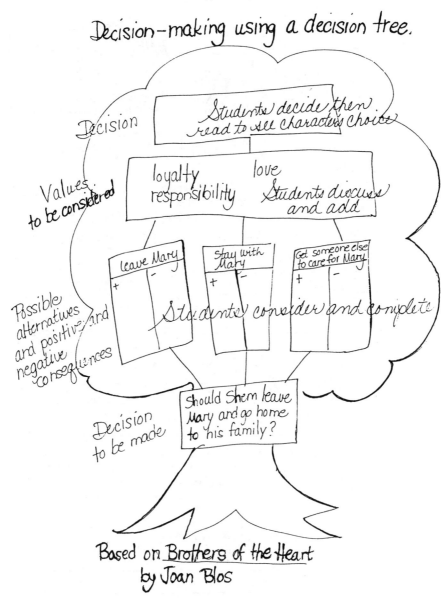

Decision-making using a decision tree.

Decision — Students decide then read to see character's choice

Values to be considered — loyalty, responsibility, love · Students discuss and add

leave Mary (+ / −) · stay with Mary (+ / −) · Get someone else to care for Mary (+ / −)

Possible alternatives and positive and negative consequences — Students consider and complete

Decision to be made — Should Shem leave Mary and go home to his family?

Based on <u>Brothers of the Heart</u> by Joan Blos

FIGURE 11–5

adjusting to a new land. Students can choose fiction and nonfiction books on the migration theme and complete the contract with information from their books. Small group and class discussions can help students develop generalizations about the immigrants' experiences, challenges they faced, and solutions they devised. Such generalizations are of critical importance in our increasingly multicultural nation.

IMMIGRATION INSIGHTS
through books

Both fiction and non-fiction books can help you learn more about the people who have come to America throughout our history. As you read your book, record details to help you share ideas with others in our new social studies unit.

YOUR NAME: _____   BOOK TITLE: _____

DATE STARTED: _____   AUTHOR: _____
TARGET COMPLETION DATE: _____   PUBLISHER: _____
PAGES PER DAY (approx): _____   DATE OF PUBLICATION: _____

1. As you read your book, think about parts you'd like to read to others. You might choose sections of a few pages or even an entire chapter. Try to select parts that would help your listener understand more about immigration or an immigrant group.

Section:	Pages:

2. Some BASIC 'W' questions .... using your book....
. Who immigrated? _____
. When? _____
. Where did they arrive? _____
            did they settle? _____
. Why did they come? _____

3. Describe living conditions of the immigrants: _____

4. Use the chart below (and other paper if needed) to record any problems the immigrants encounter:

PROBLEM:	HOW HANDLED	PAGES:

5. On separate paper, keep a list of questions you have as a result of reading this book.
6. On separate paper, keep a list of interesting facts you learned while reading this book.

FIGURE 11–6

There is strong support in the research community and the classroom for the power of literature-based social studies to motivate and engage students and teach them essential concepts and skills. We can harness that power more effectively through careful instructional planning.

REFERENCES

Blos, J. W. (1979). *A gathering of days: A New England girl's journal, 1830–1832*. New York: Scribner's.

Blos, J. W. (1985). *Brothers of the heart*. New York: Scribner's.

Fisher, L. E. (1975). *Across the sea from Galway*. New York: Four Winds Press.

Fisher, L. E. The Colonial Americans series. New York: Franklin Watts, Inc.

Fisher, L. E. (1977). *Letters from Italy*. New York: Four Winds Press.

Fisher, L. E. Nineteenth Century America series. New York: Holiday House.

Fisher, L. E. (1980). *A Russian farewell*. New York: Four Winds Press.

Fisher, L. E. (1989). *The Wailing Wall*. New York: Macmillan.

Meltzer, M. (Ed.) (1982). *The Jewish Americans: A history in their own words*. New York: Crowell.

Meltzer, M. (Ed). (1984). *The Black Americans: A history in their own words*. New York: Crowell.

Meltzer, M. (Ed.) (1987). *The American revolutionaries: A history in their own words 1750–1800*. New York: Crowell.

Morris, R. B. (1985a). *The American Revolution*. Minneapolis, Minn.: Lerner Publications.

Morris, R. B. (1985b). *The Constitution*. Minneapolis, Minn.: Lerner Publications.

Morris, R. B. (1985c). *The founding of the Republic*. Minneapolis, Minn.: Lerner Publications.

Morris, R. B. (1985d). *The Indian Wars*. Minneapolis, Minn.: Lerner Publications.

Morris, R. B. (1985e). *The War of 1812*. Minneapolis, Minn.: Lerner Publications.

Gail Tunnell teaches eighth-grade English at the Feaser Middle School in Middle-town, Pennsylvania. Throughout each school year her students are actively engaged in projects that demand a great deal of reading and writing.

Jeannie Ammon is the librarian at the Feaser Middle School. She teaches library skills by assisting students in finding answers to their own historical research questions.

* * *

What would you do if you wanted students to read the play *The Diary of Anne Frank,* but you discovered that they did not have the necessary background to understand the lesson? This is what Gail Tunnell experienced. In this chapter, an English teacher and a librarian chronicle their development of this important unit, examining changes in themselves that prompted them to expand the scope of the unit, and to consider including other topics and genres.

Teaching the Holocaust Through Trade Books

12

Gail Tunnell and Jeannie Ammon

The play *The Diary of Anne Frank* (Goodrich, 1989) had been a part of our eighth-grade language arts curriculum for many years. Heretofore, students read parts of the play aloud in class, focusing on the elements of drama. The social studies curricula did not cover World War II. As a result, students studied the play out of its historical context and without discussing its impact on their lives and on society today.

The challenge was clear—the entire unit had to be restructured so that the necessary historical background could be provided and understood. Our students needed not only to appreciate *The Diary of Anne Frank* as a piece of literature, but also to make the connection between Anne's world and their world. These needs led to the evolution of our Anne Frank unit.

Initially, we attempted to provide our students with background information by assigning research reports. With our help and limited reference materials, each student found a topic and wrote a report that was shared with the class. This strategy was not very effective. We found that the students were too isolated from each other and that their discoveries were limited and without focus. Of course, at this time our resources were also limited. As our resources increased to include many trade books so did our own knowledge of the Holocaust. We grew with the unit and were able to guide our students to expanded topics that helped them understand the plight of Jews during World War II.

We discovered the key to revising our strategy in the picture book *Terrible Things*, written by Eve Bunting (1989). This allegory, illustrated with Steven Gammell's powerful black-and-white drawings, tells the story of animals who live in a peaceful clearing. One day the Terrible Things come and take away every creature with feathers on its back. None of the other animals do anything to save the birds. Little Rabbit is the only one to question why the Terrible Things want the feathered creatures. Big Rabbit tells him, "Just be glad it wasn't us they wanted."

The Terrible Things return again and again, each time taking a different group of animals until only the White Rabbits remain. Little Rabbit suggests the rabbits move, but Big Rabbit says, "Why should we move? This has always been our home. And the Terrible Things won't come back. We are the White Rabbits. It couldn't happen to us." Of course, the Terrible Things do return and this time they take the White Rabbits leaving behind only Little Rabbit who is small enough to hide behind a pile of rocks. When everyone is gone, he leaves the clearing hoping to warn others about the Terrible Things before it is too late.

After listening to this story, our students offered possible interpretations. We encouraged them to examine the relationships of the different animals and the effect of the Terrible Things on their lives in the clearing. Immediately, students drew from their own personal experiences similar events or circumstances. One student, appalled at his own inaction when another student was being bullied in the school cafeteria, said, "I just stood there and watched." At this point, the other students realized that they themselves were guilty if they failed to act when they saw bigotry and cruelty. This discussion triggered an awakening within many of our students that caused them to reevaluate their actions and way of thinking toward others.

With the discovery of *Terrible Things* came the realization that other trade books could be equally valuable. The search for and subsequent discovery of many young adult trade books about the Holocaust helped define the unit's objectives. Strategies needed to implement those objectives grew directly from finding new books and materials.

Remember Not to Forget: A Memory of the Holocaust written by Norman H. Finkelstein (1985) and illustrated with bold black-and-white wood cuts by Lois and Lors Hokanson provided an excellent definition of the terms *anti-Semitism* and *Holocaust*. When we read this brief overview of the development of anti-Semitism and how it led to the Holocaust, our students were stunned by facts such as that two-thirds of Europe's Jews died as the result of the Holocaust. The book reminded them that events such as this should never be forgotten. We then shared excerpts from A *Nightmare in History* by Miriam Chaikin (1987), because the first chapter also provides excellent background not only into the history of anti-Semitism but also into Hitler's cultivation of anti-Semitism. We explained to students that they would soon be reading the play *The Diary of Anne Frank* and that Anne lived in a time when anti-Semitism was rampant.

In the library we explained that they would be assigned to one of six different research groups. We scheduled five days in the library for research and five days in the classroom during which they finalized the preparations for their presentation. The five days in the classroom were very important, not only because the students needed time to organize and analyze their materials but also because this classroom time enabled us to spend a few minutes reading or showing them pictures from sources that would enrich their understanding.

Because of the nature of the topic and the powerful subject matter contained in some of the books, we set the tone for the unit by stressing how seriously we, as teachers, felt about the topic. We told them that they would see many horrific pictures and read disturbing descriptions, but that we expected them to handle the material in a mature manner.

Research Groups

We assigned students to six research groups that were mixed academically and socially. Because of the sensitive nature of the subject and material and to foster maximum on-task behavior, we determined the makeup of the groups. Each group was assigned a different topic. We tried to create topics that not only were essential to helping our students understand the play but that would also draw on the special abilities of students within the group. We included such varied activities as map making, drawing, and creating time lines on the computer, as well as giving oral presentations.

The topics changed over the years as new books were discovered. For example, one group investigated people who helped save the Jews during the Holocaust. This topic grew from Milton Meltzer's book *Rescue: The Story of How Gentiles Saved Jews in the Holocaust* (1988) and the need for our students to be made aware that there were people willing to risk everything to help Hitler's victims. Changes in the topics also occurred when we felt the need to define a topic more clearly. For instance, when our students were not locating enough information for a complete understanding of the background of World War II, we added specific events such as Kristallnacht, D Day, and the passage of the Nuremberg Laws for them to research.

Students in group I researched historical background. They documented the major causes of World War II, emphasizing the Treaty of Versailles. They drew a color-coded map showing the countries involved and a key identifying the Allied Countries, Axis Countries, and Occupied Countries. The students in this group also found important dates and events of World War II, including Nuremberg Laws, Kristallnacht, and D Day. They used the computer program *Timeliner* to create a time line, which they illustrated and displayed.

General reference books helped, but we encouraged them to get out of the encyclopedias and into other books. Milton Meltzer's *Never to Forget: The Jews of the Holocaust* (1976) has a chronology of events that directly affected the Jews. The students compared this chronology with others and included important events into their own time line.

Group 2 students researched the lives of World War II personalities and presented character sketches using a creative format emphasizing the roles these figures played in World War II. The group researched Hitler, Himmler, Göring, and Eichmann and also chose to report on any of the following: Mussolini, Goebbels, Churchill, Eisenhower, Hess, and Roosevelt.

The students needed to have enough information to be able to give their classmates insight into the personality of the person they investigated. Again, reference books were useful for finding basic biographical information, but students were encouraged to read trade books like Albert Marrin's *Hitler* (1987). This biography of Hitler tells the students about Hitler's life—his tyrannical father, loving mother, and his early disappointments, such as his rejections from art school. Such in-depth information is not usually available in an encyclopedia or social studies text.

Group 3 studied the concentration camps. Students drew a map showing the location of the major camps, researched medical experiments, camp conditions, discipline, and camp facilities such as gas chambers and ovens. They were required to include information about major camps, such as Bergen-Belsen, Auschwitz, and Dachau.

Because this group was looking not only for data but also for descriptions of life, such as it was, within the camps, Meltzer's book *Never to Forget: The Jews of the Holocaust* (1976) was particularly useful. It gave the students an opportunity to read personal experiences in the forms of letters, diaries, poems, and songs. We introduced this book by reading the personal account of Viktor Frankl, a Viennese physician, who recalled the drama of selection upon arrival at Auschwitz:

> It was my turn. Somebody whispered to me that to be sent to the right would mean work, the way to the left being for the sick and those incapable of work, who would be sent to a special camp. I just waited for things to take their course, the first of many such times to come. . . . The SS man looked me over, appeared to hesitate, then put both his hands on my shoulders, I tried very hard to look smart, and he turned my shoulders very slowly until I faced right, and I moved over to that side. (p. 120)

Other trade books that supported this group's research included Barbara Rogasky's *Smoke and Ashes: The Story of the Holocaust* (1988) and Miriam Chaikin's book *A Nightmare in History: The Holocaust 1933–1945* (1987). These books discuss death camps and work camps, with sections on daily life, selection, medical experiments, and resistance within the camps.

Group 4 students investigated the Nuremberg Trials. Students researched background information and recent developments. They found out which war criminals had recently been found and which were still fugitives.

Barbara Rogasky's book *Smoke and Ashes: The Story of the Holocaust* (1988) has a detailed chapter dealing with the Nuremberg Trials. There, students found a list of Nazi war criminals, their crimes, and punishments.

In Robert Goldston's *The Life and Death of Nazi Germany* (1967), the students read Sir Hearley Shawcross's summation of the case against the Nazi war criminals when he read into the record an eyewitness account of a mass murder by one of Himmler's Special Action Units in the East. The account told how the witness watched as a family of eight waited their turn at an execution pit. "Turning to the French, British, American, and Russian judges, but speaking beyond them in words addressed to all civilized men, Sir Hartley declared: 'You will remember this story when you come to give your decision, but not in vengeance—in determination that these things shall not occur again' " (p. 168).

Burton H. Wolfe's book *Hitler and the Nazis* (1970) discusses crimes committed by the Nazis and gives information about the Nuremberg Trials.

A recently published book, *Nazi War Criminals* by Elaine Landau (1990), assisted this group in locating information about war criminals who went into hiding following World War II.

Group 5 was called "The Rescuers." We found that by emphasizing only the cruel and inhuman side of the Holocaust, we left the students believing no one cared about the Jews, and the question of how could people let this tragedy happen remained unanswered. Milton Meltzer's book *Rescue: The Story of How Gentiles Saved Jews in the Holocaust* (1988) became the cornerstone for this topic. We read from it when introducing this topic:

> To hide a Jew required courage, for you risked your own family's life. But it required even more than courage. You had to find the right place to hide someone and be able to conceal it . . . And if the hideaway didn't have inside toilets (and many did not), how did you dispose of wastes? What could you do if a pregnant woman was about to give birth? How did you get a doctor for a sick Jew? How did you bury one who died in hiding? What if little children cried when an unknowing neighbor dropped in or the SS came to snoop? (p. 16)

In this book, students read about the people who risked their own lives to rescue some of Hitler's victims. Students also found in Chaikin's book *A Nightmare in History* (1987) the heroic and tragic story of Raoul Wallenberg. Students described major rescuers in their presentation, telling of the risks they took and their methods of helping. Because more than one group used some of these books, it became necessary to purchase multiple copies of them.

Group 6 defined the term *neo-Nazi* and studied the history, purpose, and activities of this and other hate groups. They investigated possible dangers these groups present to our way of life, and they formulated a proposal suggesting how to deal with this movement in the United States.

In *The Terrorist* (1983), Meltzer discusses American terrorism and gives background on the Ku Klux Klan. In *The Truth About the Ku Klux Klan* (1982), he traces the history of the Klan from its beginnings during Reconstruction to the 1980s. Meltzer looks at what types of people join racist organizations like the Klan and what can be done to minimize their influence in society. Meltzer also discusses the tactics used by the Klan, especially in the 1980s, to recruit young people.

Other books that were helpful to this group include *Hate Groups in America: A Record of Bigotry and Violence* published by the Anti-Defamation League of B'nai B'rith (1988), *Bigotry* by Kathlyn Gay (1989), and *Taking a Stand Against Racism and Racial Discrimination* by Patricia and Frederick McKissack (1990). These books serve as a source of information on the major anti-Semitic and racist organizations that have a record of violence. Each book suggests ways society can counter the effects of racist groups.

Minilessons

We taught and reviewed library and organizational skills to facilitate students' research. Because we did not want the impact of the Holocaust to be lost in skill activities, we developed a series of minilessons, which we taught at the beginning of each research period.

Using transparencies of a paragraph on Auschwitz and a data sheet (See Figure 12–1), we modeled a method for organizing, locating, and recording data. Following the demonstration and working in their groups, our students filled out their own data sheets with main topics and subtopics.

Another minilesson helped our students organize their groups. They decided what needed to be done and assigned tasks so that each member of the group was responsible for some aspect of the research and presentation.

In yet another minilesson, we modeled the structure for the final presentation. This outline not only guided our students in their search for material but also gave them a means to begin organizing their final presentation.

Research

The five library days were very busy. Students could be found assigning group roles, searching for sources, taking notes, making maps, using the

DATA SHEETS

SUBJECT: AUSCHWITZ CONCENTRATION CAMP   NAME_____

NOTES

HISTORY AND PURPOSE	Opened June 9, 1940 Auschwitz, Poland Extermination center /w 4 gas chambers Rudolf Hess, director 2½ million executed
DESCRIPTION OF CAMP LIFE	People were starved to death
DECRIPTION OF VICTIMS	Most of people were Jews

FIGURE 12-1

opaque projector, using the computer, or reading quietly. The students
began to collect enough materials to make decisions about the type of
presentation they wanted to create.

Initially, the focus of the unit was information gathering. In their
search for information, the students largely ignored historical fiction and
biographies, which personalized the people and events they were investi-
gating. We decided that we needed to incorporate these stories into the

unit. Once again the unit changed. In conjunction with their research, students read other Holocaust stories besides *The Diary of Anne Frank*. One class period in the library was devoted to book talks on the Holocaust. They listened to stories about protagonists such as the Jewish girl Chaya in Jane Yolen's novel *Devil's Arithmetic* (1988); Piri and her family in Aranka Siegal's biography, *Upon the Head of a Goat* (1981); young Elie Wiesel in his book *Night* (1982); and Rosemarie in the novel I Am *Rosemarie* (Moskin, 1972). These young people and their families struggled to survive in the nightmare of Nazi-occupied Europe. Some stories tell of those who risked their lives to help their fellow human beings, as did Annemarie Johansen and her family in the Newbery Award–winning novel *Number the Stars*, by Lois Lowry (1989), or sixteen-year-old Jens Hansen in Nathaniel Benchley's *Bright Candles* (1974). Other stories focus upon the hardships faced by German teenagers during the war as told in Barbara Gehrts's novel, *Don't Say a Word* (1975) and Hans Peter Richter's day-to-day account of life in the Third Reich in I *Was There* (1972). Contemporary protagonists still struggle with the challenges of anti-Semitism, as in Fran Arrick's novel *Chernowitz* (1981). One of the research topics was Nazi war criminals. The story *Gentlehands* (Kerr, 1978) tells about a boy from New Jersey who discovers that his grandfather was a cruel SS officer in a Nazi concentration camp during World War II.

Time did not allow the sharing of all the books on the Holocaust, so we created a bibliography of Holocaust stories for our students. Books rotated quickly so that as many students as possible could be reading while the unit was in progress.

After our students listened to book talks on these and other titles, they chose their own books, which they read in and out of school. Their reading was tracked through our reading lab program, which is based upon Nancy Atwell's reading workshop described in *In the Middle: Writing and Reading and Learning with Adolescents* (1987, pp. 151–197). In this program our students selected novels and read them during a reading lab period. As part of the reading lab requirement students kept journals and wrote weekly letters to other students responding to what they had read.

Presentations

In the classroom our students continued to plan their presentations and practiced their roles. Along with their independent work during this class time, we continued to share several books that we found very moving. *The Children We Remember* by Chana Byers Abells (1986) is a book of photographs from the Yad Vashem Archives in Jerusalem. The pictures tell the story of children who lived and died during the time of the Nazis. The captions beneath the pictures reveal the horror that these children experienced. The most moving part of the book is the section with the caption:

"These children were killed by the Nazis." Photographs follow of a girl named Chana, her brother, Willie, and children whose names are unknown.

In *My Brother's Keeper: The Holocaust Through the Eyes of an Artist* by Israel Bernbaum (1985), the artist uses his own illustrations to portray the suffering and inhumanity. Our students were fascinated by his illustrations of the Warsaw Ghetto, the deportations, and of course, his one picture with Anne Frank.

We also used this class time to show the film *The Wave* (1981), which dramatizes a high school social studies teacher's powerful lesson to his students on the tyranny of extreme social conformity. After discussing the film, the students further understood Hitler's control over the German people.

Following five days' preparation time in the classroom, the students shared their presentations with their classmates. They performed skits, game and talk shows, courtroom trials, and one group conducted a seance in which Hitler, Himmler, and Göring came back from the dead to talk to the class. A student even came to class dressed as Hitler for his presentation.

These presentations brought the research to life for our students as they shared their feelings and knowledge of the tragic and heroic events of the Holocaust. Although our students have never experienced the sustained fear of an Anne Frank, they were encouraged to draw parallels to events today. They discussed the activity of modern-day hate groups in this context as well as the extraordinary response to the persecuted by rescue networks. They analyzed the viciousness of the skinheads and followed the pursuit of Nazi war criminals after Nuremberg. Through it all, their awareness of man's inhumanity to man developed on their own terms. They became sensitive to the plight of youth during this time of turmoil and related it to their own existence.

The presentations aren't the only indication of the students' emotional and intellectual growth. Their responses to an evaluation survey also revealed how the experience of the unit had matured them.

Evaluating the Unit

In their evaluations a majority of our students commented on their earlier lack of knowledge about the Holocaust. One even admitted, "Before the Holocaust unit I thought Hanukkah and Holocaust were the same." The following was typical of many other comments: "Before this unit I knew nothing about the Holocaust, nothing about the millions of Jews tortured, and nothing of Hitler and his cruel army."

Some students expressed a fear of future holocausts. "We could possibly live through another holocaust and . . . next time I could be one of the victims." Another concluded, "If the Holocaust is not remembered, it might happen again."

Several students commented on their own past behaviors. One girl said, "I am able to look back and realize all the prejudiced things I have done in the past, whether it be about popularity, clothes, or anything else and I realize how serious something like prejudice can be." Commenting on racist jokes another student said, "They are not funny anymore and we should not abuse any one group because of their background."

Some students suggested that we bring in speakers who had firsthand knowledge of the Holocaust. We are considering this for the future, because there are survivors in our community who speak to groups about the Holocaust.

The inclusion of the topic "Rescuers"—stories of courageous individuals who risked their lives to help others—elicited this response: "Before this unit I only knew of the men who did wrong. Now I know there were some people who didn't ignore this madness."

The responses made by our students show that they now possess the necessary tools to understand and appreciate Anne Frank. Since we have seen the positive impact of our changes, we will continue to look for more books and materials in an effort to improve the unit.

BIBLIOGRAPHY FOR ANNE FRANK UNIT
G.W. FEASER MIDDLE SCHOOL, MIDDLETOWN, PENNSYLVANIA

Abells, C. B. (1986). *The children we remember.* New York: Greenwillow Books.
> *The children who lived and died in the Holocaust are remembered in this photographic essay.*

Adler, D. A. (1989). *We remember the Holocaust.* New York: Holt.
> *The text supplemented by first person accounts and original photographs from private collections tells the story of the Holocaust.*

Anti-Defamation League of B'nai B'rith. (1988). *Hate Groups in America: A record of bigotry and violence.* New rev. ed.
> *Information on the major anti-Semitic and racist organizations that have a record of violence. Chapter 7 suggests ways that society can counter the effects of these racists groups.*

Anti-Defamation League of B'nai B'rith and The National Council for the Social Studies. (1985). *The Record: The Holocaust in history 1933–1945.*
> *A sixteen-page newspaper that contains a wealth of information about the Holocaust.*

Appleman-Jurman A. (1988). *Alicia, my story*. New York: Bantam.

> *A heroic girl of fifteen uses her resourcefulness and courage to save herself and help others during the Holocaust. After the war she bravely leads Jews on an underground route to Palestine.*

Arnold, E. (1969). *A kind of secret weapon*. New York: Scribner's.

> *A Danish family risk their lives working for the Danish Resistance during World War II. This story is about loyalty, patriotism, love, and sacrifice.*

Arrick, F. (1981). *Chernowitz*. New York: New American Library.

> *A powerful story of prejudice and hatred. At first Bobby Cherno ignored Emmett Sundback and his remarks but as Emmett's campaign of anti-Semitism gained momentum and the whole school turned against him, Bobby felt the time had come to take action.*

Ashman, C, and Wagman, R. J. (1988). *The Nazi hunters, the shocking true story of the continuing search for Nazi war criminals*. New York: Pharos Books.

> *Text gives information about Nazi war criminals who still remain in hiding around the world.*

Atkinson, L. (1985). *In kindling flame: The story of Hannah Sensesh 1921–1944*. New York: Lothrop.

> *Biography of Hannah Sensesh, a young Jewish woman who gave up her own dreams as a settler in Israel and returned to Europe and to work for the Resistance during World War II. Hannah's bravery was an inspiration for others. The book contains excerpts from Hannah's diary and letters to her mother and brother.*

Atwell, N. (1987). *In the middle: Writing and reading and learning with adolescents*. Portsmouth, NH: Heinemann, Boynton/Cook.

> *A handbook for teaching whole language in the middle school.*

Banyard, P. (1986). *The rise of the dictators, 1919–1939*. New York: Watts.

> *Following World War I the world moved into an economic depression. Powerful dictators arose who offered solutions. Intent on expansion, Mussolini of Italy and Hitler of Germany broke the peace established by the League of Nations and thus the world plunged into another world war.*

Benchley, N. (1974). *Bright candles*. New York: Harper & Row.

> *Sixteen-year-old Jens Hansen and his friends participate in the Danish Resistance when the Germans invade their homeland in 1940.*

Bernbaum, I. (1985). *My brother's keeper: The Holocaust through the eyes of an artist.* New York: G. P. Putnam's.

Text and art tell the story of the Holocaust particularly the Warsaw ghetto. The story is told in simple narrative as the artist describes each piece of art.

Bernheim, M. (1989). *Father of the orphans: The story of Janusz Korczak.* Dutton.

Dr. Korczak dedicated his life to the children of Poland. When the Nazis closed his orphanages, he chose to go with the children first to the Warsaw ghetto and finally to Treblinka death camp.

Bodinger-DeUrinarte, C. and Sancho, A. R. (1992). *Hate crime: Source book for schools.* Los Alamitos, CA: Southwest Center for Educational Equity Southwest Regional Laboratory & Philadelphia: Research for Better Schools.

This book provides background information and resources schools can use to address hate crimes.

Bunting, E. (1989) *Terrible things.* New York: Harper & Row.

This picture book, illustrated by Steven Gammell with powerful black-and-white drawings, is an allegory of the Holocaust. One by one creatures are snatched from the clearing until only one little rabbit remains. He goes off into the world to warn others in hopes that someone will listen.

Carter, V. L. (Executive Producer), Field, F. (Producer), & Grasshoff, F. (Director). (1981). *The Wave.* (videotape). Films, Inc.

A high school history class learns about the power of group conformity when teacher, Ron Jones, recreates a movement resembling the Nazi Movement in Hitler's Germany. Based on a short story by Ron Jones.

Chaikin, M. (1987). *A nightmare in history: The Holocaust 1933–1945.* New York: Clarion.

Traces the roots of anti-Semitism from Biblical times through Hitler's reign of power in Nazi Germany. Special attention is paid to the Warsaw Ghetto and the concentration camp Auschwitz-Birkenau.

The Diary of Anne Frank. (1959). (Video cassette) Twentieth Century-Fox Film Corporation.

Finkelstein, N. H. (1985). *Remember not to forget: A memory of the Holocaust.* New York: Watts.

The story of the Holocaust is told in bold black-and-white woodcuts and brief text. The importance of remembering is emphasized throughout the book. The author explains the meaning of Yom Hashoa, a day on which Jews of the world pause to remember.

Forman, J. (1967). *Ceremony of Innocence*. Hawthorn Books.

> A novel based on the true story of Hans and Sophie Scholl. The story takes place from the time of their arrest by the Gestapo until their executions for treason. Hans and Sophie were members of the "White Rose," a group that published and distributed a pamphlet titled Leaflets of the White Rose *calling for resistance against the Nazis.*

Forman, J. (1967). *Horses of anger*. New York: Farrar, Straus & Giroux.

> A fifteen-year-old German boy lives through the nightmarish last days of Hitler's reign disillusioned and welcoming defeat.

Forman, J. (1968). *The traitors*. New York: Farrar, Straus & Giroux.

> Paul Engle, adopted son of Bavarian minister Noah Engle, hides his Jewish friend and joins a group of traitors in the village of Ravenskirch whereas the Pastor's natural son, Kurt, is a committed Nazi.

Friedman, P. (1978). *Their brothers' keepers*. New York: Holocaust Library.

> The stories of the brave men and women who helped hide and protect Hitler's victims.

Friedman, I. R. (1990). *The other victims: First-person stories of non-Jews persecuted by the Nazis*. Boston: Houghton Mifflin.

> Other groups of people besides Jews suffered at the hands of the Nazis. This book represents the personal stories of some of those people. Included are personal accounts of Christians, Gypsies, deaf persons, homosexuals, and blacks.

Gallaz, C. and Innocenti, R. (1985). *Rose Blanche*. Mankato: Creative Education.

> A picture book about how a child experiences war without understanding it.

Gay, K. (1989). *Bigotry*. Hillside, NJ: Enslow.

> Traces the history of bigotry and racism. Terms like PREJUDICE, BIGOTRY, RACISM, and DISCRIMINATION are defined. Ways groups and individuals can help reduce prejudice are suggested and discussed.

Gehrts, B. (1975). *Don't Say a Word*, trans. by E. D. Crawford. New York: McElderry.

> The story of a German adolescent during World War II. Anna's Jewish friend and her family commit suicide, her first love is killed at the Russian front, her father is imprisoned and executed for treason, and her brother dies while serving with the German army. Originally published under the title: Nie wieder ein Wort davon?

Gies, M. (1987). *Anne Frank remembered: The story of the woman who helped to hide the Frank family*. New York: Simon & Schuster.

The story of the Franks' loyal friend Miep Gies and how she and her husband bravely hid the Frank and Van Daan families until their capture by the Nazis.

Gilbert, M. (1982). *Atlas of the Holocaust*. London: Michael Joseph in Association with the Board of Deputies of British Jews.

Maps, photos, and narratives trace Hitler's war against the Jews. The 316 maps are arranged in chronological order showing the evolution of the Holocaust. Most maps are accompanied by narratives and photos.

Gilfond, H. (1973). *The Reichstag fire, February, 1933: Hitler utilizes arson to extend his dictatorship*. New York: Watts.

An account of the background to and results of the night the German parliament building burned.

Goldston, R. (1967). *The life and death of Nazi Germany*. New York: Bobbs-Merrill.

A history of the Nazi party in Germany.

Goodrich, F. and Hackett, A. *The diary of Anne Frank*. In Anderson, R., Brinnin, J., Malcolm, L. J., & Leeming, D. A. (1989). *Elements of Literature*, second course. New York: Holt, Rinehart & Winston.

Literature book from which the play, The Diary of Anne Frank *by Frances Goodrich and Albert Hackett is read.*

Greene, B. (1973). *Summer of my German soldier*. New York: Dial.

A twelve-year-old Jewish girl, living in Arkansas, befriends a German P.O.W. and hides him in her father's garage after he escapes from a P.O.W. prison near her home. Their friendship leads to disaster for both Anton and Patty when investigators discover what Patty has done.

Hannan, C. (1978). *A boy in that situation: An autobiography*. New York: Harper & Row.

An account of the experiences of a thirteen-year-old Jewish boy in Nazi Germany prior to his escape to England.

Hautzig. E. (1968). *The endless steppe*. New York: Crowell.

The author's account of her childhood in Siberia where her family lived after they were arrested and deported from their home in Poland. In Siberia, the Rudomins were treated as slaves and life was difficult, but they managed to survive and return to Poland after World War II.

International Center for Holocaust Studies, Anti-Defamation League of B'nai B'rith. (1986). *The Holocaust in books and films: A selected, annotated list.* New York: Hippocrene Books.

Judgment at Nuremberg. (1979). (Filmstrip) Media Basics, Inc.
> Dramatization of the Nuremberg Trials of Nazi war criminals following World War II.

Kerr, J. (1971). *When Hitler stole pink rabbit.* New York: Coward, McCann & Geohegan.
> The story of a nine-year-old Jewish girl whose family is forced to leave Nazi Germany and seek refuge in other countries. Based on the author's experience.

Kerr, M. E. (1978). *Gentlehands.* New York: Harper & Row.
> Buddy wants to impress Skye Pennington, a gorgeous, wealthy girl who spends her summers in the seacoast town where his dad is a policeman. He takes her to meet his estranged and eccentric grandfather. His summer is shattered when a Nazi hunter reveals a terrible secret about his grandfather.

Koehn, I. (1977). *Mischling, second degree: My childhood in Nazi Germany.* New York: Morrow.
> Ilse Koehn, like many other German children her age, is a member of the Hitler youth and was even chosen to be a leader. But Ilse is different. Her grandmother is Jewish and that makes Ilse a MISCHLING, a child with one Jewish parent. Her family struggles to keep its deadly secret hidden in order to save Ilse's life.

Kuchler-Silberman, L. (1961). *My hundred children.* New York: Dell.
> The story of the woman who led a group of Jewish children to Israel from Poland.

Landau, E. (1990). *Nazi war criminals.* New York: Watts.
> The story of Nazi war criminals who went into hiding following World War II. Many of these criminals have been found and brought to Justice. The final chapter discusses the Kurt Waldheim controversy.

Lowry, L. (1989). *Number the stars.* New York: Houghton Mifflin.
> Ten-year-old Annemarie Johansen and her family bravely help hide her friend Ellen when Germans invade Denmark in 1943. The Danish Resistance, with the help of the courageous people like Annemarie and her family, manage to smuggle almost all of Denmark's 7,000 Jews to safety in Sweden. Annemarie is called on to show special courage if Ellen and her family are to make it safely to Sweden.

Marrin, A. (1987). *Hitler: Portrait of a tyrant.* New York: Viking, Kestrel.

An account of Hitler's life from his early childhood with a tyrannical father through his early adulthood filled with disappointments and rejections to his swift and powerful political rise as Germany's most deadly leader.

McKissack, P. and McKissack, F. (1990). *Taking a stand against racism and racial discrimination.* New York: Watts.

Examines racism and racial discrimination in the United States. The book discusses organizations that work to combat racism and its effect on society today.

Meltzer, M. (1976). *Never to forget: The Jews of the Holocaust.* New York: Harper & Row.

The book is divided into three sections: "The History of Hatred," "Destruction of the Jews," and "Spirit of Resistance." Factual information is presented along with personal accounts in the form of letters, diaries, poems, and songs. Contains a chronology of events that affected the Jews during the Holocaust.

Meltzer, M. (1982). *The truth about the Ku Klux Klan.* New York: Watts. (out of print)

Discusses the Ku Klux Klan from its beginning after the Civil War to the present day. Final chapters deal with those who join the Klan, why, and what can be done about them.

Meltzer, M. (1983). *The Terrorists.* New York: Harper & Row.

A history of modern terrorism.

Meltzer, M. (1988). *Rescue: The story of how Gentiles saved the Jews in the Holocaust.* New York: Harper & Row.

To help a Jew during the Holocaust could mean the end of a Gentile's life as well. This book tells of the brave Gentiles who risk their own lives and the lives of their families to help save other human beings during a terrible time in history.

Moskin, M. D. (1972). *I am Rosemarie.* New York: Dell.

Rosemarie was a Holocaust survivor. Her story is the story of the victims of the Holocaust. The author states in her notes that Rosemarie is a "composite based on very real people who lived through all the things described in this book. The camps are real and everything that happened there, down to the names of the SS guards."

Natkiel, R. (1985). *Atlas of World War II.* New York: The Military Press.

Contains 85 illustrations and 150 maps with commentary.

Nicholson, M. and Winner, D. (1989). *Raoul Wallenberg: The Swedish diplomat who saved 100,000 Jews from the Nazi Holocaust before mysteriously disappearing.* Milwaukee: Gareth Stevens Publishing.

> *Tells of the life of Swedish diplomat Raoul Wallenberg who saved the lives of 100,000 Hungarian Jews during the Holocaust. Wallenberg disappeared while being taken to meet with the Russians shortly after the liberation of Budapest.*

Organized bigotry: White sheets and swastikas. (1981). (Filmstrip) Current Affairs.

> *Discusses the Ku Klux Klan and neo-Nazis in the United States. Presents their history and philosophies, and discusses the dangers these groups pose to society.*

Orgel, D. (1988). *The Devil in Vienna.* New York: Puffin.

> *Based on the experience of the author, The Devil in Vienna is the story of Inge Dornenwald and Lieselotte Vessely. The two girls have always been best friends. In 1937 everything changes in Vienna. Inge is Jewish and Lieselotte is forced by her father to become a member of the Hitler Youth. Because of the high position Lieselotte's father holds in Hitler's organization, it becomes extremely dangerous for the girls to continue their friendship.*

Reiss, J. (1972). *The upstairs room.* New York: Crowell.

> *After Hitler invaded Holland in 1940, Annie de Leeuw's father wanted to come to the United States, but her mother refused. Her father's only recourse to save his children was to find a Gentile family that would hide them. This is Annie de Leeuw and her sister Sini's story of hiding in the upstairs rooms of a farmhouse in Holland.*

Richter, H. P. (1970). *Friedrich.* New York: Holt, Rinehart and Winston.

> *The tragic story of a German Jewish boy as told by his friend and neighbor. Friedrich's story chronicles Hitler's pogrom against the Jews of Germany. Friedrich's friends stood by and watched as Nazi laws became more and more restrictive; they offered only advice and lacked the courage to really help. Has a chronology of dates for laws and regulations that affected German Jews.*

Richter, H. P. (1972). *I was there.* New York: Holt, Rinehart and Winston.

> *The story of a group of adolescent boys living through the Hitler years in Germany. German teenagers joined the Hitler Youth. At first their duties involved collecting money and scraps of iron, and participating in marches and demonstrations. Finally, when it is clear that Germany is losing the war, a desperate Hitler calls on the Youth to do more than demonstrate. Has a chronology of important dates at the end of the book.*

Rogasky, B. (1988). *Smoke and ashes: The story of the Holocaust*. New York: Holiday House.

Examines the causes and events of the Holocaust. Follows Hitler's plan to exterminate the Jews. Discusses what life was like in the ghettos and concentration camps. A final chapter deals with the Nuremberg Trials, sentencing, and execution of those responsible for the Holocaust.

Roth-Hano, R. (1988). *Touchwood: A girlhood in occupied France*. New York: Four Winds.

After the German invasion of France, Renee Roth and her family are forced from their home in Alsace to seek refuge in Paris. Soon conditions in Paris begin to worsen also and the Roths fear deportation. Arrangements are made to have the girls sent to a Catholic women's residence where it is hoped they can spend the remainder of the war in safety, "touchwood."

Schnabel, E. (1958). *Anne Frank: A Portrait in Courage*; trans. by Richard and Clara Winston. New York: Harcourt, Brace & World.

The author has reconstructed the story of Anne Frank from interviews with forty-two people who remembered her. Originally published in Germany under the title: Anne Frank: Spur eines Kindes.

Shemin, M. (1969). *The empty moat*. New York: Coward, McCann & Geohegan.

Determined to protect her family castle Elizabeth Van Swaenenburg refused to allow the underground to hide refugees in Swaenenburg Castle. As the war continues and Nazi oppression mounts, she realizes that she must find the courage to help.

Siegal, A. (1981). *Upon the head of the goat: A childhood in Hungary 1939–1944*. Farrar, Straus & Giroux.

This Newbery Honor book is the story of a family as it struggles to survive in German occupied Hungary. Nine-year-old Piri's mother's resourcefulness and determination hold the family together until the final moment when they are boarded on trains bound for Auschwitz.

Siegal, A. (1985). *Grace in the wilderness: After the liberation 1945–1948*. New York: Farrar, Straus & Giroux.

Sequel to Upon the head of the Goat. Liberated from Bergen-Belsen concentration camp, fifteen-year-old Piri and her sister Iboya begin new lives as Holocaust survivors in Sweden.

Serraillier, I. (n.d.). *Escape from Warsaw*. (Original title *The Silver Sword*.) New York: Scholastic.

Young children find themselves alone in the rubble of Warsaw. Determined to find their parents, they leave Warsaw on a perilous search for their lost family.

Shirer, W. L. (1961). *The rise and fall of Adolf Hitler.* New York: Random House.
 Describes Hitler's childhood, education, rise to power, political career, and final defeat.

Snyder, L. L. (1961). *Hitler and Nazism.* New York: Watts.
 Describes Hitler's life, the forming of the Nazi party, and his rise to power.

Snyder, T. F. F. and Kaemmer, D. (1986). *Timeliner* (Computer program). Cambridge, MA: Tom Snyder Productions. (Tom Snyder Productions, Inc., 90 Sherman St., Cambridge, MA 02140)

Strasser, T. (1981). *The wave.* New York: Dell and T.A.T. Communications.
 A high school history class learns about the power of group conformity when teacher, Ron Jones, recreates a movement resembling the Nazi Movement in Hitler's Germany. This work is a novelization of a teleplay by Johnny Dawkins based on a short story by Ron Jones.

Streatfield, N. (1976). *When the sirens wailed.* New York: Random House.
 Rather than stay with a new family, three young evacuees try to return to their home in London after their country host dies suddenly.

Taylor, J. and Shaw, W. (1987). *The Third Reich almanac.* New York: World Almanac.
 Presents a chronology of the Third Reich from the birth of Adolf Hitler to the Nuremberg Trials, including the rise of the Nazi party to power.

U.S. Holocaust Memorial Council. (1989). *Fifty years after the eve of destruction:* Days of Remembrance April 30 through May 7, 1989.
 A resource guide for organizing observances for the Days of Remembrance of the Victims of the Holocaust.

U.S. Holocaust Memorial Council. (1992). *Fifty years ago in the depths of darkness:* Days of Remembrance April 26 through May 3, 1992.
 The 1992 resource guide for organizing observances for the Days of Remembrance of the Victims of the Holocaust.

Volavkova, H. (ed.) (1978). *I never saw another butterfly: Children's drawings and poems from Terezin Concentration Camp, 1942–1944.* New York: Schocken Books.
 Children's poems and drawings from Terezin Concentration Camp. In catalogs of drawings and poems at the end of the book, biographical information is given about the children who created them. The work of thirty-nine children is represented in this book.

Wiesel, E. (1982). *Night*. New York: Bantam.

A powerful personal account of a young Jewish boy who along with his family is imprisoned in Nazi death camps.

Wolfe, B. H. (1970). *Hitler and the Nazis*. New York: G. P. Putnam's.

Describes Hitler's rise to power during pre-World War II years, the men who helped him carry out his reign of terror, and his final defeat.

Wuorio, E. L. (1973). *Code: Polonaise*. New York: Holt, Rinehart, and Winston.

The true story of a small band of orphaned children who secretly worked for their country's freedom.

Wuorio, E. L. (1973). *To fight in silence*. New York: Holt, Rinehart, and Winston.

The story of the heroic rescue of Denmark's Jews during World War II, as seen through the eyes of a valiant Norwegian boy and his Danish cousins.

Yolen, J. (1988). *The Devil's arithmetic*. New York: Viking.

Hannah resents her Jewish traditions and wonders why she should have to remember the past and listen to her grandfather's stories. On the evening of the Passover Seder, when she opens the door to welcome the prophet Elijah, Hannah steps back into the 1940s to a Jewish village in Poland. She has become her Hebrew namesake, Chaya. The Hebrew name Chaya had been given to her in honor of her aunt's friend. Chaya and her family are taken away to Nazi concentration camps. Living out the end of Chaya's life makes Hannah understand why the Holocaust should never be forgotten.

Young, Brigadier P. (1981). *The world almanac of World War II*. New York: World Almanac.

A comprehensive reference book on World War II.

Anita Downs has taught elementary school children in both public and private schools. She taught fourth grade at Rochester Elementary School in Rochester, Illinois, and is currently teaching sixth grade at Sacred Heart Catholic School in Pana, Illinois. She has an avid interest in children's literature and its use across the curriculum.

*   *   *

What are the components of thematic history units that center around children's trade books? What strategies might be employed to use thematic history units throughout an entire school year? Anita Downs introduces her strategies for creating thematic units, using a unit that she developed on the Middle Ages as an example. Her formula might easily be used to create other units integrating history, literature, and other subjects.

13

Breathing Life into the Past: The Creation of History Units Using Trade Books

Anita Downs

When I think of history, a rich tapestry of people and events that have moved and shaped our world comes to mind. Yet at the beginning of the school year when I ask my fourth-grade students what comes to mind when they think of history, I invariably receive responses such as it's dull or boring, it's not important, it's "stuff" that has already happened that nobody cares about any more. How sad that the story of our past, the story of ourselves and our development into the people and society we are today, is thought of in such a negative light.

We have only ourselves to blame for these negative attitudes. How has history traditionally been taught in our schools? More often than not, history has been taught to our children using a single textbook to be read aloud by the students or assigned as a series of silent reading assignments. The textbook—which contains little more than the bare facts about events, names, places, and dates—has taken over the role of teacher. The key elements of human experience and involvement are missing. After all, our history is the story of real people whose actions and ideas influenced the events of their time and ours. Yet, history textbooks avoid including the human traits of historical figures, leaving us with faceless, sometimes nameless people whom we have a difficult time caring about. To take out the human quality is to take out any real meaning.

Another reason history textbooks tend to be dry and meaningless to children is that they try to cram too much information into a single year's curriculum. For example, information spanning from the discovery of the New World to the Vietnam War is to be covered during a fifth-grade school year. This means that World War II may be covered in five or six brief pages and the Holocaust in a single paragraph. Therefore, history textbooks do not have the space to present more than one viewpoint or perspective about a historical topic. We all know that any story has more than one side to it.

One solution to the problem of uninspiring history textbooks is the integration of history-related trade books into the regular classroom curriculum. There are many rich and rewarding picture books, biographies, photo essays, and historical novels on the market today that can make time periods, events, and people of the past come alive. Literature is a valuable resource and can be the key to getting children actively and emotionally involved in history. Through literature, children can vicariously relive the past. They can picture more clearly what it was like to travel westward in a covered wagon or experience racial prejudice in the deep South. Through historical trade books our students can experience the lives of others, discover unfamiliar time periods and places, and explore values and beliefs different from their own.

However, the study of history is more than just reading about our past. A teacher who is truly interested and excited about the subject matter being presented can be greatly motivating to students. Teachers should encourage children to play an active role in the learning process through decision making, problem solving, research, and exploration.

The thematic unit is one method of bringing history alive through active research, exploration, and activities based on trade books. For example, I developed and used a thematic unit on the Middle Ages entitled "Castles and Castle Times" with my fourth-grade classes. I found that this method of presenting history can be adapted to meet personal teaching styles, students' individual needs, and whole classroom needs at various grade levels. I decided to employ two strategies to aid in the study and research: First, I let students use trade books to research narrower topics of their choice. The only requirement was that the topic had to deal in some way with the Middle Ages. Second, I devised a series of whole-class activities throughout all areas of the curriculum based on trade books about the Middle Ages. I used both strategies simultaneously. The following pages offer more detailed explanations of the materials and activities used in each of these teaching strategies.

Strategy 1: Individualized Research Using Trade Books

Step 1: Capturing the Students' Interest

Capturing the students' interest in a subject is the first step in whetting their appetites to learn more. I usually grab my students' attention by reading aloud to them. At the beginning of this unit, I often begin by reading Selina Hasting's *Sir Gawain and the Loathly Lady* (1987), one of the many legends associated with King Arthur. I also read several short ghost stories that are found in Beth Smith's factual book, *Castles* (1988). Next I ask my students when these stories might have taken place and where these people might have lived. After this, I divide the children into small groups for brainstorming. They are asked to think about everything they know about castles—when they were built, where they were built, and what sort of people lived in them. Calling the students back into a large group, I record their ideas on the board. This activity naturally moves into an informal classroom discussion in which I present them with introductory information about the Middle Ages. Read-aloud books I have used to help provide background knowledge are *A Journey Through History: The Middle Ages* by Maria Rius (1988) or Robyn Gee's *Castle Times* (1982).

Step 2: Gathering Information

Next, we go to the library to gather all the materials relating to our topic that we can find. I also bring into the classroom any resources that I have collected from other sources. I give my students plenty of time to browse, read, and explore. Then I ask them to record in a spiral notebook any information that they find particularly interesting. Gathering again for a second informal discussion, we share any new information that we have discovered.

Step 3: Individualized, In-Depth Research

In the third step of the individualized strategy, I explain to my students that each of them is to do an in-depth investigation on a narrower topic of their choice dealing with the Middle Ages. As the students brainstorm for possible topics, I write them on the board. At this point I often give them the choice to work individually or in groups of up to five. Below is a list of some possible topic choices for further investigation into the Middle Ages.

- Life in a Castle
- Education
- Villages and Town Life
- Agriculture
- Medicines and Healing
- The Role of Women
- Warfare and Weapons
- The Hunt

- Knights
- Travel and Trade
- Music, Dance, Entertainment
- Stories and Legends
- Feasts
- Pilgrims and Pilgrimages
- Role of Religion

Step 4: Final Project and Presentation

The last step of the individualized method is for students to write a paper and present a final project that deals with their research findings. The final project not only provides the students with a chance to be creative, but also gives them the opportunity to use the higher-level thinking skills. During the time that my students are given to work on their final projects, I schedule meetings with them as needed. Some students need more attention and guidance than others.

The format of the final project should be left up to the students, with the teacher serving only as a consultant or guide. The one requirement that I make concerning format is that each student keep an on-going record in a journal of his or her findings. In this way, I can keep track of the entire process of discovery rather than simply the finished product. Journals are collected and graded periodically. This also serves to keep students motivated and on task, and ensures that all students in a group situation are participating. Below is a list of ideas for final projects that are to accompany a written report:

- Present music or songs from the era.
- Draw a diagram or map.
- Write and illustrate a book.
- Construct a three-dimensional figure.
- Give an oral presentation.
- Create a visual display.
- Design a costume.
- Teach a game from the time period.

Figure 13–1 illustrates the steps involved in this first strategy.

Strategy 2: Activities Based on Trade Books

Students should play an active role in the planning and creation of activities for the entire group. Such was the case with the following activities relating to the Middle Ages. I have attempted to organize them according to subject, although in some cases there is no clear-cut boundary between the various disciplines.

Reading

During the course of our study I usually read aloud Marguerite De Angeli's *The Door in the Wall* (1949) and *Adam of the Road* by Elizabeth Gray (1942). These two novels are wonderful stories and fine sources of information pertaining to the Middle Ages. Also, the students read independently *The Whipping Boy* by Sid Fleischman (1986), a lighter, more humorous novel that children enjoy.

These novels are excellent sources with which to compare and contrast literary elements such as setting, character development, and plot conflict. Trade books also provide many opportunities for participation in

Individualized Research Using Trade Books

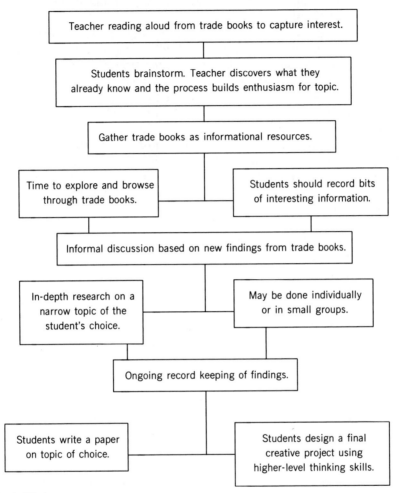

FIGURE 13–1

other related activities, including reader's theater, literature response journals, and informal discussions.

We also used the historical novels to make comparisons among time periods. For example, my students compared the common values and beliefs of two different periods in history, focusing on the differing roles of women.

Social Studies

I believe that a construction of a time line is essential at the beginning of any history unit to give children some perspective. In this particular unit,

I usually use a piece of butcher paper to create a time line together with the class. The children later decorate it, and it is hung somewhere in the room or in the hallway.

During this unit we eventually discuss the various occupations and walks of life that existed during the Middle Ages. By this time, the children have gained some needed background from their earlier independent research and reading. I ask each child to choose a type of person or occupation to investigate further. After the investigation, each student is to write a journal from his or her person's point of view. For example, if a child chooses a knight, he or she is to keep a journal based on what a knight during the Middle Ages might be thinking or experiencing. Parts of the journals will be shared orally in class. They will then be put on display to serve as additional resources about the Middle Ages. The following is a list of occupations or walks of life generated by the students in a brainstorming activity:

People from the Middle Ages
1. Nobles (King, Queen, Lord, Lady)
2. Serf
3. Knight
4. Squire
5. Monk
6. Craftsman
7. Merchant
8. Minstrel
9. Court Jester
10. Nun
11. Crusader
12. Pilgrim

Math

After I read aloud and we discuss Aliki's A *Medieval Feast* (1983), I ask the children to plan a feast for the visiting king. We discuss estimation, and then I ask the students to design a menu and estimate how much bread, meat, fruit, cheese, wine, and so on will be needed to prepare an opulent meal for the king and his party. The party consists of the queen, her ladies in waiting, the king's knights, squires, servants, and members of the court. Of course, the first step in solving the problem is to decide how many people are traveling in the king's party. Children work on this assignment in small groups.

Science and Math

Another activity we participate in during this unit is to study and discuss David Macaulay's book *Castle* (1977). His illustrations and text do an excellent job of explaining exactly how castles were constructed as well as what types of tools were used. A videotaped version of the book is also available.

During this time we also discuss what it was actually like to live in a castle. The children contribute to the discussion by adding information they have discovered in their independent research.

Next, we design and build our own classroom model of a castle. *Castles: A Read and Build Book* by Victoria Prego de Oliver (1975) is a good source for castle construction. This activity requires us to work together in planning, measuring, building, and following directions provided by a trade book.

Music

Listening to music of the era is a fine way to develop music appreciation. Medieval music can be found in music stores and some libraries, particularly at universities. In an ideal situation, you could invite an expert on music from this time period to speak to the class, or a harpist or other musician to perform for the children. Children could also embark on an investigation in trade books to discover if there are any songs we sing today that have been passed down to us from the Middle Ages.

Art

I normally bring in several books about medieval art for the children to look at during their free time. I also call the students' attention to the illustrations found in picture books about this time period. Both *The Middle Ages* edited by Fiona MacDonald (1984) and *Castles of the Middle Ages* by Philippe Brochard (1980), with their reprints of medieval art, are excellent sources for art appreciation.

Next, we design shields and discuss why and how they were used. We discuss the idea of a coat of arms symbolically representing a person or a family. We brainstorm about symbols, and what certain symbols represent. For example, a bear could represent strength, a peacock pride, a fox cunning, and a lion courage. I then ask the children to represent themselves symbolically. Once they have designed their symbols, they place them on their shields.

Another activity involves building a bulletin-board castle out of paper cutouts representing stones. Upon each "stone" the children write one fact that they have discovered about the Middle Ages. No fact may be repeated. In addition to this, I also provide a long piece of butcher paper for the class to use to design a replica of a medieval tapestry. This is usually an optional, free-time activity.

Culminating Activity

A Medieval Day marks the end of our investigation into the Middle Ages. Each child role-plays his or her choice of person based upon our social studies project on occupation or walk of life. Children do their best to dress the parts, creating costumes ahead of time. We also set up a mock feast based upon our research and reading of trade books. The food is to be prepared on a volunteer basis at home and brought to school on the day of the feast. We strive to stay as authentic as possible, using bread trenchers as plates and eating with our fingers. Fingers can be washed in bowls of water between courses as they did in medieval days. Children are seated according to position or rank. Medieval music is played in the background, and our minstrels and jesters perform for entertainment. We play checkers, chess, backgammon, blindman's buff, and bob for apples (all forms of medieval entertainment). This is also the day that students share their independent projects with the class.

The unit on the Middle Ages is a rich and exciting experience for children. Much active learning takes place and students seem to have an unending desire to learn more. Discovering our past is an ongoing process. The process of learning, research, and discovery can be sustained indefinitely with an active, motivating classroom environment and plenty of trade books. There are always more new and interesting facts to uncover, and one area of knowledge and discovery often leads to additional areas to explore.

Implementing trade books in the study of history and other subjects can brighten any curriculum, for it is the power of narrative (in both fiction and nonfiction literature) that stirs the imagination. Barbara Hardy from the University of London says, "We dream in narrative, day dream in narrative, remember, anticipate, hope, despair, believe, doubt, plan, revise, criticize, construct, gossip, learn, hate, love by narrative" (cited in Huck, 1977, p. 363). If narrative is so powerful, shouldn't we as teachers harness this strength when teaching our children? Trade books can provide the power we need to breath life into the past.

RESOURCES

Aliki. (1983). A medieval feast. New York: Harper & Row.

Black, I. (1963). Castle, abbey and town. New York: Holiday House.

Brochard, P. (1980). Castles of the middle ages. New Jersey: Silver Burdett Company.

Buer, W. (1957). Knights and castles and feudal life. New York: G.P. Putnam's.

Cohen, B. (1988). The Canterbury tales. New York: Lothrop, Leed, Shepard Books.

De Angeli, M. (1949). *The door in the wall*. New York: Doubleday.

Fleischman, S. (1986). *The whipping boy*. New York: Greenwillow Press.

Gee, R. (1982). *Castle times*. Tulsa: EDC Publishing Company.

Gerrard, R. (1984). *Sir Cedric*. New York: Farrar, Straus & Giroux.

Gray, E. (1942). *Adam of the road*. New York: Viking Press.

Hartman, G. (1956). *Medieval days and ways*. New York: Macmillan.

Hastings, S. (1987). *Sir Gawain and the loathly lady*. New York: Mulberry Books.

Hindley, J. (1976). *The time traveler book of knights and castles*. London: Unsborn Publishing.

Hodges, M. (1984). *Saint George and the dragon*. New York: Little Brown.

Huck, C. (1977). Literature as the content of reading. *Theory into Practice, 16*, 363–371.

Lanier, S. (1924). *The boy's King Arthur*. New York: Scribner's.

Lasker, J. (1976). *Merry ever after*. New York: Viking.

Lasker, J. (1986). *The tournament of knights*. New York: Harper & Row.

Macaulay, D. (1973). *Cathedral*. New York: Houghton Mifflin.

Macaulay, D. (1977). *Castle*. New York: Houghton Mifflin.

MacDonald, F. (Ed.) (1984). *The Middle Ages*. New Jersey: Silver Burdett Company.

McKinley, R. (1988). *The outlaws of Sherwood*. New York: Greenwillow.

Miquel, P. (1981). *The days of knights and castles*. New Jersey: Silver Burdett Company.

Nye, R. (1968). *Beowulf: A new telling*. New York: Hill & Wang.

Prego de Oliver, V. (1975). *Castles: a read and build book*. New York: Wayland.

Pyle, H. (1903). *The story of King Arthur and his knights*. New York: Scribner's.

Pyle, H. (1946). *The merry adventures of Robin Hood*. New York: Scribner's.

Robinson, M. (1953). *King Arthur and his knights*. New York: Random House.

Rius, M. (1988). *A journey through history: The Middle Ages*. Barron's.

Sancha, S. (1982). *The luttrell village: Country life in the Middle Ages*. New York: Crowell.

Schiller, B. (1965). *The kitchen knight*. New York: Holt, Rinehart and Winston.

Smith, B. (1988). *Castles*. New York: Wayland.

Sutcliff, R. (1981). *King Arthur and the round table*. New York: Dutton.

Twain, M. (1948). *The prince and the pauper*. New York: World Publishing Company.

Uden, G. (1968). *A dictionary of chivalry*. New York: Crowell.

Williams, J. (1968). *The sword of King Arthur*. New York: Crowell.

Winthrop, E. (1985). *The castle in the attic*. New York: Holiday House.

Michael Tunnell has authored a number of articles and books about children's literature, including *The Prydain Companion* (Greenwood, 1989). He has also written three children's picture books (*Chinook!*, *The Joke's on George*, and *Beauty and the Beastly Children*), all forthcoming from Tambourine Books.

Cheryl Hudson has taught both primary grades and special education in New-foundland, Canada. She has just completed her work as a graduate student in the College of Professional Studies at Northern Illinois University.

*   *   *

This bibliography presents a selection of trade books about United States history. Instead of being arranged by genre or historical period (historical fiction, for example, or Colonial America) this list focuses more on the people of history than on the events. It can serve as a beginning point for teachers who desire to incorporate trade books into history courses and other subjects. Many titles suggested in this bibliography have been deemed "notable" by the National Council for the Social Studies and the Children's Book Council. Some titles, however, especially those with older copyright dates, may no longer be in print, but they should be available from school and public libraries. A suggested grade-level range is noted in each entry using the codes P, E, and J (P = Grades K–3; E = 4–6; J = 6–9).

American Historical Literature for Young Readers: An Annotated Bibliography

Michael O. Tunnell and Cheryl Hudson

Americans at War

American Revolution

Avi. (1984). *The fighting ground*. Lippincott. 160 pp. ISBN 0-397-32074-4. Historical Fiction. (E & J)

> Thirteen-year-old Jonathan joins a regiment to fight the British in the revolutionary war. He soon learns that being a soldier is not as glorified as he dreamed. Internal conflict makes this a powerful novel.

Collier, J. L., and Collier, C. (1974). *My brother Sam is dead*. Four Winds. 216 pp. ISBN 0-02-722980-7. Historical Fiction. (E & J)

> Tim Meeker is confused in his loyalties during the American Revolution. His brother Sam runs away to fight the British. His father remains loyal to the king.

Collier, J. L., and Collier, C. (1981). *Jump ship to freedom: A novel*. Delacorte. 198 pp. ISBN 0-385-28484-5. Historical Fiction. (E & J)

> A fourteen-year-old slave boy tries to buy freedom for himself and his mother. Set in Stratford, Connecticut, during and after the American Revolution.

Collier, J. L., and Collier, C. (1983). *War comes to Willy Freeman*. Delacorte. 192 pp. ISBN 0-440-09642-1. Historical Fiction. (E & J)

> Willy, an African-American child, is threatened with being returned to slavery after the death of her patriot father in the Revolutionary War.

Davis, B. (1976). *Black heroes of the American Revolution*. Illus. with prints and maps. Harcourt. 80 pp. ISBN 0-15208560-2 Informational. (E)

Examines the black Americans' involvement in the American War of Independence. Illustrated with original drawings and etchings of this period. Contains bibliography and index.

Edwards, S. (1985). *George Midgett's war.* Scribner's. 144 pp. ISBN 0-684-18315-3. Historical Fiction. (E & J)

Fourteen-year-old George and his father build a barge to carry supplies from Okracoke Island, North Carolina, to George Washington's Continental Army at Valley Forge.

Forbes, E. (1943). *Johnny Tremain.* Houghton Mifflin. 256 pp. IBSN 0-395-06766-9 Historical Fiction. (E & J)

Orphan Johnny Tremain finds himself in the midst of the Boston Revolt of 1775.

Fritz, J. (1973). *And then what happened, Paul Revere?* Illus. by Margot Tomes. Coward. 48 pp. ISBN 0-698-20274-0 Historical Fiction. (P & E)

Humorous story and illustrations of Paul Revere's ride to Lexington and his narrow escapes along the way.

Fritz, J. (1976). *Will you sign here, John Hancock?* Illus. by Trina Schart Hyman. Coward. 74 pp. ISBN 698-20308-9 Biography. (P)

An account of the life of John Hancock, the first signer of the Declaration of Independence and governor of Massachusetts for eleven terms.

Fritz, J. (1977). *Can't you make them behave, King George?* Illus. by Tomie dePaola. Coward. 46 pp. ISBN 0-698-20315-1. Historical Fiction (Picture Book). (P & E)

A view of the American Revolution from the perspective of King George, who never intended to start a war.

Koger, E., Sr. (1976). *Jocko: A legend of the American Revolution.* Prentice. 29 pp. Historical Fiction (Picture Book). (E)

Jocko, the son of a freed slave, remained with George Washington's horse through a snowy, stormy night after being given the job of caring for the horse when he followed his father into war during the American Revolution. Information about the hardships of the Continental soldiers is included.

Longfellow, H. W. (1990). *Paul Revere's ride.* Illus. by Ted Rand. Dutton, 40 pp. ISBN 0-525-44610-9. Poetry (Picture Book). (P, E, & J)

Longfellow's famous poem is further enlivened by Rand's vivid illustrations. Includes a historical note.

Marrin, A. (1988). *The war for independence: The story of the American Revolution.* Illus. with prints and maps. Atheneum. 288 pp. ISBN 0-689-31390-X. Informational. (J)

A carefully researched account of the Revolutionary War. Includes splendid prints, paintings and black-and-white maps, and bibliography and index.

Meltzer, M. (1987). *The American revolutionaries: A history in their own words 1750–1800.* Illus. with prints and photographs. Crowell. 224 pp. ISBN 0-690-04643-X. Informational. (E & J)

Using diaries, journal entries, newspaper articles, and other sources, the author helps readers understand the feelings of the people who lived through the American Revolution.

Meltzer, M. (1991). *Thomas Jefferson: The revolutionary aristocrat.* Illus. with black-and-white photographs. Watts. 256 pp. ISBN 0-531-15227-8. Biography. (J)

The complex, productive life of Thomas Jefferson is examined in this biography. The author addresses questions concerning the contradictions in Jefferson's words and deeds. Includes index.

O'Dell, S. (1980). *Sarah Bishop.* Houghton Mifflin. 184 pp. ISBN 0-395-29185-2. Historical Fiction. (E & J)

A girl from a Tory family is brutalized by the war and eventually flees to a place safe from Patriots and the British alike.

Peterson, H. S. (1973). *Give us liberty: The story of the Declaration of Independence.* Garrard. 96 pp. ISBN 0-8116-6507-0. Informational. (E)

An account of the events leading to the writing of the Declaration of Independence.

Phelan, M. K. (1976). *The story of the Boston Massacre.* Crowell. 146 pp. Informational. (E & J)

Quotations and descriptions from diaries, newspapers, and letters aid in this realistic retelling of the Boston Massacre.

Reeder, R. (1973). *Bold leaders of the American Revolution.* Little, Brown. 226 pp. Biography. (E)

An exceptional account of twelve British and American men and women who were involved with the American Revolution.

Roop, P., and Roop, C. (1986). *Buttons for General Washington.* Illus. by Peter E. Hanson. Carolrhoda. 48 pp. ISBN 0-87614-294-3. Historical Fiction (Picture Book). (P)

Fourteen-year-old John Darragh takes coded messages sewn in the buttons of his coat to his brother at George Washington's camp from his home in British-occupied Philadelphia. Based on a true story of a Quaker family. Easy to read.

Civil War

Beatty, P. (1988). *Be ever hopeful, Hannalee.* Morrow. 224 pp. ISBN 0-688-07502-9. Historical Fiction. (J)

The story of a poor Southern family who moves to devastated Atlanta, Georgia, at the end of the Civil War, as told by fourteen-year-old Hannalee.

Beatty, P. (1991). *Jayhawker.* Morrow. 224 pp. ISBN 0-688-09850-9. Historical Fiction. (E & J)

The story of a young man from Kansas who, during the early years of the Civil War, is involved in freeing slaves from Missouri.

Cosner, S. (1988). *War nurses.* Illus. with photographs and prints. Walker. 120 pp. ISBN 0-8027-6828-8. Informational. (E & J)

Tells of the contribution of nurses to the American Civil War.

Erdman, L. G. (1975). *Save weeping for the night.* Dodd, Mead. 205 pp. Historical Fiction. (E)

Bettie Shelby, wife of Confederate hero General Jo Shelby, took her children and followed her husband into battle during the Civil War. Depicts life on the losing side of the Civil War.

Freedman, R. (1987). *Lincoln: A photobiography.* Illus. with photographs and prints. Clarion. 160 pp. ISBN 0-89919-380-3. Biography. (E & J)

Photographs, prints, and reprints of original documents enhance this account of Lincoln's career and his presidency. Original writings and a list of Lincoln museums, monuments, and memorials are included. The 1988 Newbery Medal winner. Also contains a bibliography and index.

Hiser, B. T. (1986). *The adventure of Charlie and his wheat-straw hat: A memorat.* Illus. by Mary Szilagyi. Dodd, Mead. 40 pp. ISBN 0-396-08772-8. Historical Fiction (Picture Book). (P)

The squire's animals are saved during the Civil War because of Charlie's love for his wheat-straw hat. An Appalachian story.

Hoobler, D., and Hoobler, T. (1977). *Photographing history: The career of Mathew Brady.* Illus. with photographs. G. P. Putnam's. 90 pp. Biography (E & J)

An account of the career of Mathew Brady, the photographer who captured the Civil War with his camera.

Hunt, I. (1986). *Across five Aprils*. 1964. Reprint. Follett/Berkley Pacer. 190 pp. IBSN 0-425-10241-6. Historical Fiction. (E & J)
> *The Civil War years in Southern Illinois are revealed through the eyes of young Jethro Creighton.*

Meltzer, M. (Ed.) (1989). *Voices from the Civil War: A documentary history of the great American conflict*. Illus. with prints. Crowell. 224 pp. ISBN 0-690-04802-5. Informational. (E & J)
> *Brief passages and excerpts from people who experienced this conflict, including information about the people and the events involved. Contains bibliography and index.*

Murphy, J. (1990). *The boys' war*. Illustrated with black-and-white photographs. Clarion. 110 pp. ISBN 0-89919-893-7. Informational. (E & J)
> *An extremely moving book that uses diary entries, personal letters, and archival photographs to describe the experiences of boys, sixteen years old or younger, who fought in the Civil War. Includes bibliography and index.*

Ray, D. (1990). *The story of how the Civil War began*. Illus. with photographs. Dutton, Lodestar. 102 pp. ISBN 0-525-6708-3. Informational. (E & J)
> *An engaging account of the events leading to the outbreak of the Civil War. Causes are examined with varying perspectives represented. Includes index and bibliography.*

Ray, D. (1991). *Behind the blue and gray: The soldier's life in the Civil War*. Illus. with photographs. Dutton, Lodestar. 102 pp. ISBN 0-525-67333-4. Informational. (E & J)
> *This tragic event in American history is humanized through the anecdotes, quotations, and photographs that detail the effects of the Civil War on individual soldiers, both Confederate and Union. Includes bibliography, glossary, and index.*

Reeder, C. (1989). *Shades of gray*. Macmillan, Collier. 152 pp. ISBN 0-02-775810-9. Historical Fiction. (E & J)
> *At the end of the Civil War, twelve-year-old Will, having lost all his immediate family, reluctantly leaves his city home to live in the Virginia countryside with his aunt and the uncle he considers a "traitor" because he refused to take part in the war.*

Weidhorn, M. (1988). *Robert E. Lee*. Illus. with photographs and prints. Atheneum. 160 pp. ISBN 0-689-31340-3. Biography. (J)
> *A view of the Civil War from the perspective of a key Southern figure who was able to inspire an army that was greatly outnumbered.*

The World Wars

Bernbaum, I. (1985). *My brother's keeper: The Holocaust through the eyes of an artist.* Illus. by author and with photographs. G. P. Putnam's. 64 pp. ISBN 0-399-21242-6. Informational. (E & J)

The author tells his personal story of the Holocaust and the Warsaw Ghetto through his paintings. A moving account of a difficult period. Includes bibliography.

Bauer, M. D. (1983). *Rain of fire.* Clarion. 153 pp. ISBN 0-89919-190-8. Historical Fiction. (E & J)

Twelve-year-old Steve has trouble understanding why his older brother Matthew refuses to talk about what he has seen in Hiroshima soon after the dropping of the first atomic bomb.

Chaikin, M. (1987). *A nightmare in history: The Holocaust 1933–1945.* Illus. with photographs and prints. Clarion. 160 pp. ISBN 0-89919-461-3. Informational. (E & J)

The Jewish experience during World War II is focused on through detailed, factual accounts.

Davis, D. S. (1982). *Behind barbed wire: The imprisonment of Japanese Americans during World War II.* Illus. with photographs. Dutton. 166 pp. ISBN 0-525-26320-9. Informational. (J)

Tells of the denial of civil rights to this group of people during World War II.

Devaney, J. (1991). *1941: America goes to war.* Illus. with photographs and maps. Walker. 188 pp. ISBN 0-8027-6980-2. Informational. (J)

This book chronicles the year the United States entered World War II. See other books in the series by Devaney. Includes bibliography and index.

Hahn, M. D. (1991). *Stepping on the cracks.* Clarion. 216 pp. ISBN 0-395-58507-4. Historical Fiction. (E & J)

In 1944, while her brother is overseas fighting in World War II, eleven-year-old Margaret gets a new view of the school bully Gordy when she finds him hiding his own brother, an army deserter, and decides to help him.

Innocenti, R., and Gallaz, C. (1985). *Rose Blanche.* Illus. by author. Creative Education. 32 pp. ISBN 0-87191-944-X. Historical Fiction (Picture Book). (E & J)

The story of a German girl who defies authority by sneaking food to Jews and political prisoners held in a nearby work camp. She becomes another casualty of war.

Landau, E. (1991). *We survived the Holocaust*. Illus. with black-and-white photographs. Watts. 144 pp. ISBN 0-531-11115-6. Informational. (E & J)
Sixteen first-person accounts of surviving the Holocaust.

Lowry, L. (1989). *Number the stars*. Houghton Mifflin. 137 pp. ISBN 0-395-51060-0. Historical Fiction. (E & J)
In 1943, during the German occupation of Denmark, ten-year-old Annemarie and her family risk their lives to shelter their Jewish neighbors and to eventually help them escape to Sweden. Winner of the 1991 Newbery Award.

Marrin, A. (1982). *The airman's war: World War II in the sky*. Illus. with photographs. Atheneum. 216 pp. Informational. (J)
Personal anecdotes are used to explain the experiences of the bomber crews and fighter pilots during World War II. Includes bibliography and index.

Maruki, T. (1980). *Hiroshima no pika*. Illus. by author. Lothrop. 48 pp. ISBN 0-688-01297-3. Informational (Picture Book). (E & J)
A retelling of a mother's account of what happened to her family during the Flash that destroyed Hiroshima in 1945.

Ray, D. K. (1990). *My daddy was a soldier: A World War II story*. Holiday House. 40 pp. ISBN 0-8234-0795-0. Historical Fiction (Picture Book). (P & E)
An account of the experiences and feelings of a young girl whose father is drafted during World War II.

Rogasky, B. (1988). *Smoke and ashes: The story of the Holocaust*. Illustrated with black-and-white photographs. Holiday House. 187 pp. ISBN 0-8234-0697-0. Informational. (E & J)
Through archival photographs and with well written text, this book examines the causes, events, and legacies of the Holocaust. Includes bibliography and index.

Rostkowski, M. L. (1986). *After the dancing days*. Harper. 224 pp. ISBN 0-06-025078-X. Historical fiction. (E & J)
Against her mother's wishes, thirteen-year-old Annie befriends a severely burned young World War I veteran at a veteran's hospital in Kansas.

Schellie, D. (1982). *Shadow and the gunner*. Four Winds. 136 pp. Historical Fiction. (E & J)
World War II is brought to life in this story of the friendship between eleven-year-old Bobby and his eighteen-year-old neighbor. When Billy falls in love with Bobby's sister and goes off to war, it is difficult for Bobby to accept the change in their relationship.

Sender, R. M. (1988). *To life*. Macmillan. 240 pp. ISBN 0-02-781831-4. Historical Fiction. (J)

An account of the trouble and horror faced by the Jewish people after World War II.

Uchida, Y. (1971). *Journey to Topaz*. Creative Arts. 160 pp. ISBN 0-916870-85-5. Historical Fiction. (E & J)

Yuki, a young Japanese American, sees her life fall apart as she and her family are interned in a prison camp in the deserts of Utah.

Yolen, J. (1988). *The devil's arithmetic*. Viking Kestrel. 170 pp. ISBN 0-670-81027-4.

Hannah resents the traditions of her Jewish heritage until an unexplained time shift takes her from her home in contemporary America to a small Jewish village in Nazi-occupied Poland. Hannah soon finds herself in a Nazi death camp.

Vietnam War

Ashabranner, B. (1988). *Always to remember: The story of the Vietnam Veterans Memorial*. Illus. with photographs by Jennifer Ashabranner. Dodd, Mead/G. P. Putnam's. 112 pp. ISBN 0-396-09089-3. Informational (Photo Essay). (E & J)

The story of Jan C. Scruggs, the Vietnam veteran who led the drive for a memorial, and Maya Ying Lin, who designed the memorial. A splendid black-and-white photo essay. Includes bibliography and index.

Bunting, E. (1990). *The wall*. Illus. by Ronald Himler. Clarion. 32 pp. IBSN 0-395-51588-2. Historical Fiction (Picture Book). (P & E)

A boy and his father visit the Vietnam Veterans Memorial and find the name of the boy's grandfather.

Fincher, E. B. (1980). *The Vietnam War*. Illus. with photographs and maps. Watts. 88 pp. ISBN 0-531-04112-3 Informational. (J)

A look at the history of Vietnam, the invasion of Cambodia and Thailand, and the impact of the Vietnam War on America. Includes bibliography and index.

Hauptly, D. J. (1985). *In Vietnam*. Illus. with photographs and maps. Atheneum. 192 pp. ISBN 0-689-31079-X. Informational. (J)

An account of the history and culture of Vietnam, the mistakes made by America, and foreign relations issues. Contains bibliography and index.

Hoobler, D., and Hoobler, T. (1990). *Vietnam: Why we fought*. Illus. with photographs. Knopf. 196 pp. ISBN 0-394-81943-8. Informational. (E & J)

Examines the history of Vietnam's relationships with other nations, involvement of the United States in the conflict, and the effects of the war. Contains index and bibliography.

Lawson, D. (1986). An *album of the Vietnam* War. Illus. with photographs and maps. Watts. 96 pp. ISBN 0-531-10139-8. Informational. (E & J)

A review of the Vietnam War beginning with the French involvement in the 1940s, spanning America's involvement, and ending with the veterans' ticker-tape parade in 1985 in New York City. With index.

Myers, W. D. (1988). *Fallen angels.* Scholastic. 320 pp. ISBN 0-590-40942-5. Historical Fiction. (J)

The story of seventeen-year-old Richie Perry who spends a year in Vietnam in 1967. Includes rough language and the horror of war. Dedicated to Myers's brother who died in Vietnam.

Nelson, T. (1989). *And one for all.* Orchard. 182 pp. ISBN 0-531-05804-2. Historical Fiction. (E & J)

Twelve-year-old Geraldine grapples with the realities of the Vietnam War when her older brother enlists whereas his best friend chooses to protest the war.

Paterson, K. (1988). *Park's quest.* Dutton, Lodestar. 148 pp. ISBN 0-525-67258-3. Historical Fiction. (E & J)

Park never knew his father who died fighting in Vietnam. Though his mother is against it, Park makes a journey to the farm of his paternal grandfather and discovers the reason his mother has refused to tell him about his father.

Warren, J. (1990). *Portrait of a tragedy: America and the Vietnam War.* Lothrop. Illus. with photographs. 206 pp. ISBN 0-688-07454-5 Informational. (J)

A discussion of the causes, events, and aftermath of the most controversial conflict in American history.

Wolitzer, M. (1984). *Caribou.* Greenwillow. 176 pp. ISBN 0-688-03991-X. Historical Fiction. (J)

Becca questions her beliefs when her nineteen-year-old brother goes to Canada in 1970 to avoid being drafted and sent to Vietnam.

Other Conflicts

Carmer, C. (1975). *The pirate hero of New Orleans.* Illus. with drawings. Harvey. 38 pp. Poetry. (P)

A poem about the pirate Jean Lafitte, who helped General Andrew Jackson drive the British from American shores to win the Battle of New Orleans in the War of 1812.

Fritz, J. (1989). *The great little Madison.* Illus. with prints. G. P. Putnam's. 144 pp. ISBN 0-399-21768-1. Biography. (E & J)
Biography of the fourth president of the United States who attended the Continental Congress and the Constitutional Convention. Contains bibliography and index.

Lawson, D. (1989). *The Abraham Lincoln Brigade: Americans fighting fascism in the Spanish Civil War.* Illus. with photographs. Crowell. 176 pp. ISBN 0-690-04699-5. Informational. (J)
Looks at the Abraham Lincoln Brigade and its performance in the Spanish Civil War.

Marrin, A. (1985). *1812: The war nobody won.* Illus. with prints, maps and diagrams. Atheneum. 192 pp. ISBN 0-689-31075-7. Informational. (E & J)
An account of the War of 1812 and other parallel events such as Dolly Madison's escape from the White House, the writing of "The Star Spangled Banner," and Johnny Appleseed's mission. Contains bibliography and index.

Marrin, A. (1991). *The Spanish-American War.* Illus. with photographs. Atheneum. 192 pp. ISBN 0-689-31663-1. Informational. (E & J)
The Spanish-American War and Phillipine insurrection are described in vivid detail. Life in the United States during the time of the War is also described, helping place the events in historical context.

Human Rights

Civil Rights, Slavery

Bacon, M. H. (1975). *Rebellion at Christiana.* Crown. 216 pp. Historical Fiction. (J)
A well-researched account of the part played by the Underground Railway in helping slaves escape the Fugitive Slave Law of 1850. The trial at Christiana, Pennsylvania, where a victory was won for antislavery, is detailed and excerpts from the autobiography of William Parker, a former slave, are included.

Fox, P. (1973). *Slave dancer.* Bradbury Press. 176 pp. ISBN 0-87888-062-3. Historical Fiction. (E & J)
Thirteen-year-old Jessie Bollier, kidnapped on the streets of New Orleans and pressed to service on a slave ship, must play the fife to make the African slaves dance. During this voyage, Jessie witnesses firsthand the misery and sufferings of the African captives.

Hamilton, V. (1988). *Anthony Burns: The defeat and triumph of a fugitive slave.* Knopf. 208 pp. ISBN 0-394-98185-5. Biography. (J)

In 1854, Anthony Burns, a slave, escapes to Boston. He is reclaimed by his master under the Fugitive Slave Act but abolitionists rush to his defense. Includes sections from the Fugitive Slave Act of 1850. Contains bibliography and index.

Harris, J. C. (1989). *Jump on over! The adventures of Brer Rabbit and his family.* Adapted by Van Dyke Parks. Illus. by Barry Moser. HBJ. 48 pp. ISBN 0-15-241354-5. Traditional Tale. (P & E)

Five stories told by African American slaves and first published in 1880 tell of how Brer Rabbit outwits Brer Fox, Brer Bear, and Brer Wolf during a drought. Historical context for the stories is provided by an illustrator's note.

Hooks, W. H. (1990). *The Ballad of Belle Dorcas.* Illus. by Brian Pinkney. Knopf. 40 pp. ISBN 0-394-94645-6. Traditional Tale (Picture Book). (E & J)

This tale of love between freeborn Belle Dorcas and slave Joshua is based on a conjure tale of the Carolinas which blends fantasy with the realities of social injustice.

Lester, J. (1968). *To be a slave.* Dial. 160 pp. ISBN 0-8037-8955-6. Informational. (E & J)

Actual slaves give testimony of their experiences in the southern United States from capture in Africa to the Emancipation. Lester's commentaries and background information add further to the understanding of this period of American history.

Lester, J. (1982). *This strange new feeling.* Dial. 151 pp. ISBN 0-8037-8491-0 Historical Fiction. (E & J)

A fictionalized account of three slave couples' struggle for freedom, based on true stories. Included are notes citing several historical sources.

Rappaport, D. (1991). *Escape from slavery: Five journeys to freedom.* Illus. by Charles Lilly. HarperCollins. 128 pp. ISBN 0-06-021632-8. Informational. (E & J)

True stories of slaves who gained their freedom with help from both blacks and whites. Includes bibliography.

Sanfield, S. (1989). *The adventures of High John the Conqueror.* Illus. by John Ward. Orchard. 128 pp. ISBN 0-531-08407-8. Traditional Tale. (E & J)

Sixteen humorous tales portraying how the slave folk hero High John outsmarted his master. An author's note precedes each tale. With bibliography.

Scott, J. A. (1978). *Woman against slavery, the story of Harriet Beecher Stowe*. Crowell. 169 pp. Biography. (E & J)

The story of Harriet Beecher Stowe, who wrote Uncle Tom's Cabin *and helped change people's perception of slavery.*

Smucker, B. (1978/1979). *Runaway to freedom*. Illus. Charles Lilly. Harper/Trophy 154 pp. ISBN 0-06-440106-5. Historical Fiction, (P & E)

A story of pride and dignity about two slave girls who struggle to reach Canada and freedom.

Winter, J. (1988). *Follow the drinking gourd*. Illus. by the author. Knopf. 48 pp. ISBN 0-394-99694-1. Historical Fiction (Picture Book/Song). (P & E)

A family flees to freedom after Peg Leg Joe, a one-legged sailor, teaches plantation slaves the way to the North with the lyrics of a song containing directions to the Underground Railway. Color illustrations, music, and a historical note are included.

Women's Rights

Adler, D. (1991). *A picture book of Eleanor Roosevelt*. Holiday House. 32 pp. IBSN 0-8234-0856-6. Biography (Picture Book). (P)

A brief account of the life and accomplishments of Eleanor Roosevelt.

DePauw, L. G. (1975). *Founding mothers: Women in America in the Revolutionary Era*. Houghton. 228 pp. ISBN 0-395-21896-9. Informational. (J)

An examination of the struggles and achievements of ordinary women, from slaves to wealthy ladies, during the Revolutionary War.

Felton, H. W. (1976). *Deborah Sampson, soldier of the Revolution*. Dodd. 111 pp. Historical Fiction. (E)

The true story of a woman who joined the army in 1782 during the American Revolution and was found out to be a woman only when she was near death in a hospital. One of America's earliest feminists.

Hoople, C. G. (1978). *As I saw it: Women who lived the American adventure*. Dial. 187 pp. Informational. (E & J)

Documentation of the role and struggles of women in American history. Factual accounts of colonial and pioneer women including a frontier doctor, a Union spy, and an astronomer, collected from journals, diaries, letters, and speeches.

Jacobs, W. J. (1979). *Mother, Aunt Susan and me: The first fight for women's rights*. Illus. with prints and photographs. Coward. 60 pp. Historical Fiction. (E & J)

The sixteen-year-old daughter of Elizabeth Cady Stanton recounts the struggle for women's rights.

Lauber, P. (1988). *Lost star: the story of Amelia Earhart.* Illus. with prints and photographs. Scholastic. 112 pp. ISBN 0-590-41615-4. Biography. (E)
The story of the female aviator who had great dreams but disappeared during a historic flight in 1937. Contains bibliography and index.

Levenson, D. (1973). *Women of the West.* Watts. 88 pp. Informational. (J)
Explores the lives of African American, white, and Native American women in America since 1818.

Lindstrom, A. J. (1980). *Sojourner Truth: Slave, abolitionist, fighter for women's rights.* Illus. by Paul Frame. Messner. 128 pp. Biography. (E)
The life of Sojourner Truth, a former slave, who fought for human rights during the Civil War years.

Oneal, Z. (1990). *A long way to go.* Viking. 54 pp. IBSN 0-670-82532-8. Historical Fiction. (E)
An eight-year-old girl deals with the women's suffrage movement that rages during World War I.

Paterson, K. (1991). *Lyddie.* Dutton, Lodestar. 182 pp. IBSN 0-52567338-5. Historical Fiction. (E & J)
Impoverished Vermont farm girl Lyddie Worthen is determined to gain her independence by becoming a factory worker in Lowell, Massachusetts, in the 1840s.

Peavy, L., and Smith, U. (1985). *Dreams into deeds: Nine women who dared.* Illus. with prints and photographs. Scribner's. 160 pp. ISBN 0-684-18484-2. Biography. (E & J)
A biography of nine women named to the National Women's Hall of Fame: Jane Addams, Marian Anderson, Rachel Carson, Alice Hamilton, Mother Jones, Juliette Gordon Low, Margaret Mead, Elizabeth Cady Stanton, and Babe Didrikson Zacharias. A fictionalized vignette at the beginning of each chapter portrays each as a young girl with dreams. Photographs of each as an adult and a child are included. Contains index.

Rappaport, D. (1990). *American women: Their lives in their words; a documentary history.* Illus. with prints and photographs. HarperCollins. 336 pp. ISBN 0-395-51588-2. Informational. (J)
Diaries, letters, speeches, interviews, and other primary sources reveal the thoughts and ideals of an impressive collection of American women, including

Native Americans, early European settlers, etc. Includes bibliography and index.

Reit, A. (1976). *Alone amid all this noise: A collection of women's poetry.* Four Winds. 118 pp. Poetry. (J)

A collection of poetry stretching over two thousand years of poetry written by women.

Reit, S. (1988). *Behind rebel lines: The incredible story of Emma Edmonds, Civil War spy.* Harcourt Brace Jovanovich, Gulliver. 112 pp. ISBN 0-15-200416-2. Biography. (E & J)

The story of Emma Edmonds who posed as a man during the Civil War while fighting in the Union Army and later served as a spy while working as a nurse in the Confederate field hospitals.

Roosevelt, E. (1984). *Eleanor Roosevelt, with love: A centenary remembrance.* Illus. with photographs. Dutton, Lodestar. 176 pp. ISBN 0-525-67147-1. Biography. (E & J)

A biography of Eleanor Roosevelt written by her son. Recounts her personal and public life and emphasizes the principles by which she lived. Includes a list of autobiographies and an index.

Warren, R. (1975). *A pictoral history of women in America.* Crown, 228 pp. Informational. (J)

The role of women in the history of the United States.

Religious Rights and Freedoms

Blue, R. (1979). *Cold rain on the water.* McGraw. 124 pp. Historical Fiction. (J)

The story of a Jewish family who came to America from Russia to find religious freedom only to find out that they must struggle to find freedom in the new country. Alex, the teenage son, is able to adapt to life in America better than his father who feels that he has lost his roots.

Jacobs, W. J. (1975). *Roger Williams.* Watts. 64 pp. Historical Fiction. (E)

A book about the life of one of the fathers of religious liberty in America and his friendship with the Indians.

Rosenblum, R. (1989). *The old synagogue.* Illus. by author. Jewish Publication Society. 32 pp. Picture book. (E)

Lively black-and-white drawings are used in this story of the establishment, decline, and revival of a synagogue and neighborhood founded by European immigrants.

Prejudice

Adler, D. A. (1989). *A picture book of Martin Luther King, Jr.* Illus. by Robert Casilla. Holiday House. 32 pp. ISBN 0-8234-0770-5. Biography (Picture Book). (P)

Martin Luther King's dream of a world free of hatred and prejudice is accentuated in this story of his life through attractive illustrations and a very readable text.

Coerr, E. (1988). *Chang's paper pony.* Harper & Row. 64 pp. ISBN 0-06-021328-0. Historical Fiction. (Beginning Reader). (P)

Chang and his grandfather, Chinese immigrants who prepare food at a mining camp in the 1850s, must face the prejudice of the miners.

Costabel, E. D. (1988). *The Jews of New Amsterdam.* Atheneum. 32 pp. ISBN 0-689-31351-9. Informational. (P & E)

The story of Jews who came to America from Brazil during colonial times and found out that America did not hold freedom and equality for all.

Durham, M. S. (1991). *Powerful days: The civil rights photography of Charles Moore.* Illus. with photographs by Charles Moore. Stewart, Tabori. 208 pp. ISBN 1-55670-171-3. Informational. (E & J)

This book provides a look into Moore's movement and into the hazards of his work.

Foreman, J. D. (1979). *Freedom's blood.* Illus. with photographs. Watts. 114 pp. Historical Fiction. (J)

A fictionalized account of the murder of civil rights' activists Mickey Schwerner, James Chaney, and Andrew Goodman in Mississippi in 1964.

Haskins, J. S. (1975). *The picture life of Malcolm X.* Illus. with photographs. Watts. 43 pp. Biography. (P & E)

The story of Malcolm X, an important leader in the drive for freedom by the blacks. This account does not deny his early wrongdoings.

Hoffman, E. D. (1979). *Fighting mountaineers: The struggle for justice in the Appalachians.* Houghton Mifflin. 216 pp. Informational. (E & J)

Seven historical events in the fight for social, political, and economic justice by the people of the Southern Appalachians.

Myers, W. D. (1991). *Now is your time: The African American struggle for freedom.* Illus. with photographs and prints. HarperCollins. 292 pp. ISBN 0-06-024371-6. Informational. (E & J)

A history of the African-American struggle for freedom and equality, beginning with the capture of Africans in 1619, continuing through the American Revolution, the Civil War, and into contemporary times. Includes bibliography and index.

Parks, R. (with Jim Haskins). (1992). *Rosa Parks: My story.* Illus. with photographs. Dial. 192 pp. ISBN 0-8037-0673-1. Biography. (E & J)

The autobiography of Rosa Parks, who, on Dec. 1, 1955, refused to give up her seat to a white man on a segregated bus and thus sparked the Montgomery, Alabama, bus boycott. Includes index.

Pascoe, E. (1985). *Racial prejudice.* Illus. with photographs and prints. Watts. 128 pp. ISBN 0-531-10057-X. Informational. (J)

Discusses the prejudice against minorities in the United States and the harm it has done to both those who are discriminated against and those who are prejudiced. Contains bibliography and index.

Schiffman, R. (1981). *Turning the corner.* Dial. 192 pp. Historical Fiction. (J)

A book dealing with religious and political prejudices set during the Great Depression. The words "Jew" and "Red" are painted on the Levine's steps.

Taylor, M. (1976). *Roll of thunder, hear my cry.* Dial. 304 pp. IBSN 1-55736-140-1. Historical Fiction. (E & J)

Set during the depression, this story examines the extreme racial prejudice in the South through the eyes of a proud black child, Cassie Logan.

Taylor, M. (1987). *The gold cadillac.* Illus. by Michael Hays. Dial. 48 pp. ISBN 0-8037-0343-0. Historical Fiction. (E)

A black family encounters prejudice when they drive from Ohio to Mississippi in their new 1950 gold Cadillac.

Taylor, M. (1990). *Mississippi bridge.* Dial. 62 pp. ISBN 0-8037-0426-7. Historical Fiction. (E & J)

Black passengers are ordered off a bus to make room for white passengers in this brief story that is part of the Logan family saga.

Taylor, M. (1990). *The road to Memphis.* Dial. 290 pp. ISBN 0-8037-0340-6. Historical Fiction. (J)

The continuing story of the Logan family. A black youth is provoked into seriously injuring three white boys and enlists Cassie Logan's help in fleeing from Mississippi to Chicago.

Uchida, Y. (1981). *A jar of dreams*. Atheneum, McElderry. 132 pp. Historical Fiction. (E & J)

> *Cultural conflicts are highlighted in this story about eleven-year-old Rinko Tsujimura and her family's struggle with prejudice during the depression in California.*

Walter, M. P. (1982). *The girl on the outside*. Lothrop. 149 pp. Historical Fiction. (E & J)

> *Two students, one black and one white, make a stand for desegregation in this fictionalized story of the integration of Central High School in Little Rock, Arkansas in 1957.*

Governing America
Forming the Government

Faber, D., and Faber, H. (1989). *The birth of a nation: The early years of the United States*. Scribner's. 224 pp. ISBN 0-684-19007-9. Informational. (E & J)

> *An examination of the United States government's first ten years. Contains bibliography and index.*

Fisher, L. E. (1989). *The White House*. Illus. with photographs and diagrams. Holiday House. 96 pp. ISBN 0-8234-0774-8. Informational. (E)

> *Examines changing presidential styles and the architectural history of the White House from its construction in 1792 to today. With index.*

Freedman, R. (1990). *Franklin Delano Roosevelt*. Illus. with black-and-white photographs. Clarion. 208 pp. ISBN 0-89919-379-X. Biography. (E & J)

> *With a masterful use of archival photographs, Freedman brings Franklin Roosevelt to life for young readers. Engaging text presents both the public and private lives of FDR and discusses the praise and the criticism for his policies, programs, and lifestyle. Includes bibliography and index.*

Goode, S. (1983). *The new federalism: States' rights in American history*. Watts. 160 pp. ISBN 0-531-04501-3. Informational. (J)

> *Examines the ongoing debate concerning states' rights by comparing the viewpoints of individuals such as Hamilton, Marshall, Franklin Roosevelt, and Lincoln who favored more federal authority with Jefferson, Burke, and Reagan who preferred a less powerful central government.*

Hoopes, R. (1982). *The changing vice-presidency*. Illus. with photographs. Crowell. 192 pp. Informational. (E & J)

A history of the evolution of the office of vice-president, which includes brief biographies of the vice-presidents of the United States.

Parker, N. W. (1991). *The president's cabinet and how it grew.* Illus. by author. HarperCollins. 40 pp. ISBN 0-06-021618-2. Informational (Picture Book). (E)

Using the author's illustrations to enhance the text, this book explains the purpose, function, and history of each cabinet position.

Provensen, A. (1990). *The buck stops here: The presidents of the United States.* Illus. by author. HarperCollins. ISBN 0-06-024786-X. Biography (Picture Book).

Each president of the United States is highlighted in rhyme and in an illustration that summarizes his major achievements during his administration. A brief historical note on each president is found at the conclusion. Includes bibliography.

Constitution

Anderson, J. (1987). *1787.* Illus. by Alexander Farquharson. Harcourt Brace Jovanovich, Gulliver. 208 pp. ISBN 0-15-200582-X. Historical Fiction. (E & J)

The events ocurring during the time of the writing of the U.S. Constitution are reported by one of James Madison's aides. A blend of fact and fiction. Includes the text of the Constitution. With bibliography.

Faber, D., and Faber, H. (1987). *We the people: The story of the United States Constitution since 1787.* Illus. with prints and photographs. Scribner's. 256 pp. ISBN 0-684-18753-1. Informational. (J)

A historical account of the Constitutional Convention and a discussion of the Constitution as a changing document. Includes the text of the Constitution, a bibliography, and index.

Fritz, J. (1987). *Shh! We're writing the Constitution.* Illus. by Tomie dePaola. Putnam. 64 pp. ISBN 0-399-21403-8. Informational. (E)

This carefully researched beginner's history of the Constitutional Convention includes humorous anecdotes. Contains historic notes and the text of the Constitution.

Hauptly, D. (1987). *A convention of delegates.* Atheneum. 148 pp. ISBN 0-689-31148-6. Informational. (E & J)

Describes the events occurring before and during the Constitutional Convention.

Lawson, D. (1979). *The changing face of the Constitution.* Watts. 188 pp. Informational. (J)

Prohibition, universal suffrage and women's rights, civil rights, and religious freedom are discussed in relation to the U.S. Constitution.

Levy, E. (1987). *. . . If you were there when they signed the Constitution.* Illus. by Richard Rosenblum. Scholastic. 80 pp. IBSN 0-590-40519-9. Informational. (E & J)

Gives basic answers to questions that are often asked about the Constitution.

Meltzer, M. (1990). *The Bill of Rights: How we got it and what it means.* Harper-Collins. 192 pp. ISBN 0-690-04807-6. Informational. (E & J)

Events leading to the writing of the Bill of Rights, the meaning of each amendment, and contemporary interpretations of these constitutional guidelines are covered in this book. Includes bibliography and index.

Spier, P. (1987). *We the people: The Constitution of the United States of America.* Doubleday. 40 pp. ISBN 0-385-23789-5. Informational (Picture Book). (P)

Illustrations of American life, past and present, accompany each phrase of the Preamble to the Constitution. Contains a historical overview and text of the Constitution.

Wise, W. (1975). *American freedom and the Bill of Rights.* Parents. 64 pp. Informational. (E)

A discussion of the Bill of Rights including a history of the events preceding the Constitution, people who participated in writing the Constitution, and the first Ten Amendments.

Economy

Bess, C. (1986). *Tracks.* Houghton Mifflin. 192 pp. ISBN 0-395-40571-8. Historical Fiction. (E & J)

Eleven-year-old Blue and his older brother Monroe ride the rails through Texas and Oklahoma, meeting many people trying to make it through the Great Depression.

Caven, R. (1978). *A matter of money: What do you do with a dollar?* Illus. with photographs. Phillips. 80 pp. Informational. (E & J)

A discussion of money, including its history, credit, banking, taxes, stocks, and bonds.

Field, R. (1988). *General store.* Illus. by Giles Laroche. Little, Brown. 32 pp. ISBN 0-316-28163-8. Poetry (Picture Book). (P)

This early twentieth-century poem gives us a glimpse at the retail business in the past. Enhanced by color illustrations.

Fisher, L. E. (1979). *The factories.* Illus. by the author. Holiday. 62 pp. ISBN 0-8234-0367-X. Informational. (E & J)

Industrialism in New England is looked at from a humanistic view through these accounts of the first textile mill, factory girls, the 1876 Exposition, and sweatshops.

Lens, S. (1985). *Strikemakers and strikebreakers.* Illus. with photographs. Dutton, Lodestar. 176 pp. ISBN 0-525-67165-X. Informational. (J)

Stories of strikes, lockouts, and the growth of unions tell the history of the labor movement in the United States.

Macaulay, D. (1983). *Mill.* Illus. by the author. Houghton Mifflin. 128 pp. ISBN 0-395-34830-7. Historical Fiction. (E & J)

Fantastic illustrations depict mills as they would have looked in the 1800s in New England.

Perez, N. A. (1988). *Breaker.* Houghton Mifflin. 216 pp. ISBN 0-395-45537-5. Historical Fiction. (E)

This story of fourteen-year-old Pat McFarlane, a slate picker in a coal mining town in Pennsylvania at the turn-of-the-century, looks at the development of early labor organizations and at the prejudice toward immigrant workers.

Seldon, B. (1983). *The mill girls: Lucy Larcom, Harriet Hanson Robinson and Sarah G. Bagley.* Illus. with prints and photographs. Atheneum. 200 pp. ISBN 0-689-31005-6. Biography. (J)

The biographies of these three women give the reader insight into issues of work and self-satisfaction at the beginning of the Industrial Revolution in New England.

Thrasher, C. (1982). *End of a dark road.* Atheneum, McElderry. 218 pp. Historical Fiction. (E & J)

Seeley Robinson's second year in high school is complicated by her family's struggle to survive the Great Depression.

Social Structure

Ashabranner, M., and Ashabranner, B. (1989). *Counting America: The story of the United States census.* Illus. with photographs by Melissa Ashabranner, G. P. Putnam's. 112 pp. ISBN 0-399-21747-9. Informational. (J)

Describes how the census, which has changed historically, is conducted, what it ascertains, and why it is undertaken. Includes glossary, bibliography, and index.

Dolan, E. F., Jr. (1984). *The insanity plea.* Watts. 112 pp. ISBN 0-531-04756-3. Informational. (J)

The history and current status of the insanity plea is examined as well as the controversy surrounding it.

Goode, S. (1984). *Violence in America.* Messner. 288 pp. ISBN 0-671-45810-8. Informational. (J)

Deals with the history of violence in America from the time of the first settlers to the present day.

Fleming, T. (1989). *Behind the headlines: The story of American newspapers.* Walker. 160 pp. ISBN 0-8027-6891-1. Informational. (E & J)

An interesting account of the development of the newspaper in the United States and of the people and events that have influenced it. Contains bibliography and index.

Raskin, J., and Raskin, E. (1975). *Guilty or not guilty? Tales of justice in Early America.* Lothrop. 128 pp. Informational. (E)

Ten case histories of early justice in America based upon records of the past. They range from a witchcraft trial in Salem, Massachusetts, to a case of law and order in old Texas.

Weiss, A. E. (1982). *God and government: The separation of church and state.* Houghton Mifflin. 132 pp. ISBN 0-395-32085-2. Informational. (E & J)

Explores how the separation of church and state was established and how it applies to issues today, such as public school prayer and euthanasia.

Weiss, A. (1987). *The Supreme Court.* Enslow. 96 pp. ISBN 0-89490-131-1. Informational. (J)

The emergence of the Supreme Court in the history of the United States is discussed through famous cases and issues. A list of U.S. Supreme Court justices is included along with a bibliography and index.

American Symbols and Monuments

Dowden, A. O. (1978). *State flowers.* Illus. with color paintings. Crowell. 96 pp. ISBN 0-690-03884-4. Informational. (P, E & J)

Discusses the origin and history of each state flower as well as how each was chosen.

Fisher, L. E. (1985). *The Statue of Liberty.* Illus. by author and with photographs. Holiday. 64 pp. ISBN 0-8234-0586-9. Informational. (E)

An account of the construction of the statue in France, its transatlantic voyage, and the assembly of the Statue of Liberty in New York Harbor. Includes an index.

Giblin, J. C. (1983). *Fireworks, picnics, and flags: The story of the Fourth of July symbols*. Illus. by Ursula Arndt. Clarion. 96 pp. ISBN 0-89919-146-0. Informational. (E)

Explores how this country has formed its identity through such symbols as the Liberty Bell and Uncle Sam.

Haban, R. D. (1989). *How proudly they wave: Flags of the fifty states*. Illus. with drawings. Lerner. 112 pp. ISBN 0-8225-1799-X. Informational. (E & J)

Gives information about the background and symbolic meaning of each state flag. Includes a glossary.

Shapiro, M. J. (1985). *How they built the Statue of Liberty*. Illus. by Huck Scarry. Random. 56 pp. ISBN 0-394-96957-X. Informational. (E & J)

Details of the assembly of the Statue of Liberty in the New York harbor, compiled from interviews with the restoration team, make this nineteenth-century engineering feat accessible to young readers. Contains black-and-white sketches based on photographs and diagrams.

St. George, J. (1985). *The Mount Rushmore story*. Illus. with photographs and prints. G. P. Putnam's. 128 pp. ISBN 0-399-21117-9. Informational. (E & J)

Gives a biography of the sculptor Gutzon Borglum and a study of this national monument.

Tower, S. A. (1975). *A stamp collector's history of the United States*. Messner. 64 pp. Informational. (E & J)

Stamps issued on special events tell the history of the United States. Includes an index.

Settling New Lands

Discovery of the Americas

Adler, D. (1991). *A picture book of Christopher Columbus*. Illus. by J. Wallner and A. Wallner. Holiday House. 32 pp. ISBN 0-8234-0857-4. Biography. (Picture Book). (P)

A brief account of the life and accomplishments of Columbus.

Benchley, N. (1975). *Beyond the mists*. Harper. 152 pp. Historical Fiction. (J)

The eleventh-century adventures of the Norsemen, including Leif Eriksson's voyage to the new land.

Ceserani, G.P. (1979). *Christopher Columbus*. Illus. by Piero Ventura. Random. 38 pp. Biography. (P)
   Christopher Columbus's first voyage to the Americas.

Conrad, P. (1991). *Pedro's journal*. Illus. by Peter Koeppen. Caroline House. 84 pp. ISBN 1-878093-7. Historical Fiction. (E & J)
   Written as the diary of a ship's boy, this story presents a personal view of Columbus's first voyage to the Americas.

Fritz, J. (1979). *Brendan the navigator*. Illus. by Enrico Arno. Coward. 32 pp. ISBN 0-698-20473-5. Biography (Picture Book). (P & E)
   History and myth are intermingled in this lighthearted story of this sixth-century Irish saint who may have crossed the Atlantic.

Fritz, J. (1980). *Where do you think you're going Christopher Columbus?* Illus. by Margot Tomes. G. P. Putnam's. 80 pp. IBSN 0-399-20723-6. Biography. (E)
   Revealing positive and negative facets of Columbus's personality, Fritz discusses the explorer's voyages to the New World.

Irwin, C. (1980). *Strange footprints on the land: Vikings in America*. Harper. 184 pp. Informational. (E & J)
   Facts, hypotheses, and controversies about the Norsemen who came to America 500 years before Columbus. Includes maps, bibliography, and index.

Jacobs, F. (1992). *The Tainos: The people who welcomed Columbus*. Illus. by Patrick Collins. Putnam. 107 pp. ISBN 0-399-22116-6. Informational. (E & J)
   Describes the history, culture, and mysterious fate of the first native Americans to welcome Columbus in 1492. Includes bibliography and index.

Kurtz, H. I. (1976). *Captain John Smith*. Watts. 57 pp. Biography. (E)
   An account of the explorer Captain John Smith. Includes maps, prints, drawings, and original documents.

Levinson, N. (1990). *Christopher Columbus: Voyager to the unknown*. Illus. with prints. Dutton, Lodestar. 118 pp. IBSN 0-525-67292-3. Biography. (E & J)
   A generally complimentary biography of Columbus. Includes an index.

Maestro, B., and Maestro, G. (1991). *The discovery of the Americas*. Illus. by Giulio Maestro. Lothrop. 48 pp. ISBN 0-688-06837-5. Informational (Picture Book). (E)

A well balanced account of the early settlement and exploration of the Americas, beginning in 20,000 B.C. and ending in 1522 when Magellan circumnavigated the earth. Includes glossary.

Meltzer, M. (1990). *Christopher Columbus and the world around him.* Illus. with prints. Watts. 192 pp. ISBN 0-531-15148-4. Biography. (J)

Describes the voyages of Columbus, the terrible impact of the Spaniards on the Native Americans, and the ultimate cultural influence of the Native Americans on the white conquerors. Includes an index.

Pelta, K. (1991). *Discovering Christopher Columbus: How history is invented.* Illus. with photographs and prints. Lerner. 112 pp. ISBN 0-8225-4899-2. Informational. (E & J)

Though the voyages of Columbus are the focus of this book, Pelta also examines how historians interpret evidence, often differently. Includes index.

Roop, P., and Roop, C. (Eds.). (1990). *I, Columbus—My journal.* Illus. by Peter Hanson. Walker. 56 pp. ISBN 0-8027-6978-0. Informational. (E)

Columbus's first voyage to the Americas is recounted through carefully selected excerpts from his journal.

Weil, L. (1983). *I, Christopher Columbus.* Atheneum. 48 pp. ISBN 0-689-30965-7. Biography (Picture Book). (P)

A history of the voyages of Christopher Columbus emphasizing that Columbus thought America was actually the Far East and that the friendly Indians were exploited.

Yolen, J. (1992). *Encounter.* Illus. by David Shannon. Harcourt. 32 pp. ISBN 0-15-225962-7. Historical Fiction (Picture Book). (P, E & J)

A Taino Indian boy on the island of San Salvador recounts the story of Columbus's arrival and how he tries to warn his people not to accept these strange, white visitors.

Colonization

Barth, E. (1975). *Turkeys, Pilgrims and Indian corn: The story of the Thanksgiving symbols.* Clarion. 96 pp. ISBN 0-395-28846-0. Informational. (E)

Traces the philosophy of our dependence on the land and contains examples of foods and symbols of harvest festivals. Clears up many misconceptions about the dress and customs of early settlers.

Bulla, C. R. (1981). *A lion to guard us.* Illus. by Michele Chessare. Crowell. 128 pp. ISBN 0-690-04096-2. Historical Fiction. (E & J)

Amanda Freebold and her younger brother and sister flee from London and rejoin their father in the American colony of Jamestown.

Dalgliesh, A. (1954). *Courage of Sarah Noble.* Scribner's. 64 pp. ISBN 0-684-18830-9. Historical Fiction. (P & E)

Eight-year-old Sarah goes with her father into the wilderness while he builds a cabin for the family. She confronts the dangers of the wild and finally must stay with the Indians when her father goes back for the rest of the family.

D'Amato, J., and D'Amato, A. (1975). *Colonial crafts for you to make.* Messner. 64 pp. Informational (Crafts). (E)

Gives clear and concise directions for making such things as miniature rooms and toys.

Dillon, E. (1986). *The seekers.* Scribner's. 144 pp. ISBN 0-684-18595-4. Historical Fiction. (E & J)

When his beloved Rebecca goes to the New World in 1632 with her parents, sixteen-year-old Edward follows her from England to the colonies. Based on actual accounts of this period.

Fleischman, P. (1990). *Saturnalia.* Harper. 113 pp. IBSN 0-06-021912-2. Historical Fiction. (E & J)

In 1681 in Boston, fourteen-year-old William, a Narraganset Indian captured in a raid six years earlier, leads a productive and contented life as a printer's apprentice but is increasingly anxious to make some connection with his Indian past.

Hoople, C. G. (1975). *The heritage sampler: A book of Colonial arts and crafts.* Dial. 132 pp. Informational (Crafts). (J)

Describes the life of the early settlers and contains a collection of Colonial recipes and crafts.

Kessel, J. K. (1983). *Squanto and the first Thanksgiving.* Illus. by Lisa Donze. Carolrhoda. 48 pp. ISBN 0-87614-199-8. Biography (Picture Book). (P)

The lives of the last fifty-five Pilgrims are saved by Squanto, the last living Patuxet Indian and former slave, when he teaches them how to survive the harsh Massachusetts winter. Explains the history of Thanksgiving.

Loeb, R. H., Jr. (1979). *Meet the real Pilgrims: Everyday life on a Plimoth plantation in 1627.* Illus. with photographs and line drawings. Doubleday. 144 pp. Informational. (E)

Photographs of the reconstructed village of Plymouth allow us to view the living conditions of the Pilgrims in early New England.

Patterson, L. (1978). *Benjamin Banneker, genius of Early America.* Illus. by David Scott Brown. Abingdon. 142 pp. Biography. (P & E)

A *fictionalized biography of a free black man who was an intellectual leader in Colonial America.*

Penner, L. R. (1976). *The Colonial cookbook.* Hastings. 128 pp. ISBN 0-8038-1202-7. Informational (Cookbook). (E & J)

Historical and culinary facts of Colonial America along with easy-to-prepare Colonial recipes.

Penner, L. R. (1991). *Eating the plates: A pilgrim book of food and manners.* Illus. with drawings and photographs. Macmillan. 128 pp. ISBN 0-02-770901-9. Informational. (E)

Pilgrim eating habits, manners, and other customs dealing with food are explained in this book. Includes bibliography, glossary, and index.

Perl, L. (1975). *Slumps, grunts and snickerdoodles: What Colonial America ate and why.* Clarion. 125 pp. ISBN 0-395-298923-8. Informational. (E)

A history of cultural changes reflected in the foods of Colonial America. Contains thirteen authentic recipes that can be prepared and enjoyed today.

Sewall, M. (1986). *The pilgrims of Plimoth.* Illus. by the author. Atheneum. 48 pp. ISBN 0-689-31250-4. Historical Fiction (Picture Book). (P)

Depicts the transatlantic voyage and the daily life and responsibilities of the pilgrims who founded Plimoth in 1620. Includes a glossary.

Siegel, B. (1981). *Fur trappers and traders: The Indians, the Pilgrims, and the beaver.* Illus. by William Sauts Bock. Walker. 64 pp. ISBN 0-8027-6397-9. Informational. (E)

Describes the methods by which beavers were hunted, furs prepared for trade, and fur hats were made. Also discusses the importance of the fur trade in early America.

Smith, C. (Ed.). (1991). *The explorers and settlers: A sourcebook on colonial America.* Illus. with prints and photographs. Millbrook. 96 pp. ISBN 1-56294-035-X. Informational. (E & J)

Describes the first explorations and settlements in North America. See the other books in the Sourcebook on Colonial America series.

Speare, E. G. (1983). *Sign of the beaver.* Houghton Mifflin. 135 pp. IBSN 0-395-33890-5. Historical Fiction. (E & J)

Left alone to guard the family's wilderness home in eighteenth-century Maine, Matt is able to survive only when local Indians teach him their skills.

Speare, E. G. (1958). *The witch of Blackbird Pond.* Houghton Mifflin. 256 pp. IBSN 0-395-07114-3. Historical Fiction. (E & J)

In 1687, Kit must move from the Caribbean to a Connecticut Colony, but she finds herself at odds with the colony's stern Puritan lifestyle. This leads to Kit's eventual trial for witchcraft. Winner of the 1959 Newbery Award.

Waters, K. (1989). *Sarah Morton's day: A day in the life of a Pilgrim girl.* Ill. with photographs by Russ Kendall. Scholastic. 32 pp. ISBN 0-590-42634-6. Informational (Photo Essay). (P)

A day in the life of a nine-year-old girl who lived on Plimoth Plantation in 1627 has been recreated in this color photo essay. Verified by journals from this period. Includes a glossary.

Westward Expansion

Alderman, C. L. (1979). *Annie Oakley and the world of her time.* Illus. with photographs. Macmillan. 112 pp. Biography. (E)

A biography of Annie Oakley, a young woman who made history with her sharpshooting abilities. This book pays particular attention to providing accurate information about the time in which she lived.

Anderson, J. (1986). *Pioneer children of Appalachia.* Photographs by George Ancona. Clarion. 48 pp. ISBN 0-89919-440-0. Informational (Photo Essay). (P & E)

Photographs of an extended pioneer family taken at Fort New Salem, a living history museum in West Virginia, bring to life this account of Appalachian settlers in the nineteenth-century.

Brenner, B. (1978). *Wagon wheels.* Illus. by Don Bolognese. Harper. 64 pp. ISBN 0-06-020668-3. Historical Fiction (Beginning Reader). (P)

During a fierce nineteenth-century snowstorm, Osage Indians help a black family traveling west to Kansas.

Brown, D. (1980). *Lonesome whistle: The story of the first transcontinental railroad.* Illus. with photographs and maps. Holt. 144 pp. Informational. (J)

A discussion of the plans to build the transcontinental railroad, which was constructed in the 1860s, and a look at the immigrants who built it. Includes an index.

Blumberg, R. (1987). *The incredible journey of Lewis and Clark.* Illus. with maps, prints, and photographs. Lothrop. 144 pp. ISBN 0-688-06512-0. Informational. (E & J)

An extensive look at the journey of Lewis and Clark, the first explorers to record the geography, wildlife, and people west of the Mississippi River as an attempt to fulfill President Jefferson's dream of a bicoastal United States. Contains historical notes on the text and illustrations, a bibliography, and an index.

Carlson, V. (1974). *John Wesley Powell: Conquest of the canyon.* Harvey House. 158 pp. Informational. (E & J)

A history of the exploration of the Grand Canyon.

Coerr, E. (1986). *The Josefina story quilt.* Illus. by Bruce Degen. Harper. 64 pp. ISBN 0-06-021349-3. Historical Fiction (Beginning Reader). (P)

The story of Faith and her pet hen Josefina traveling with her family to California during the 1850s is recalled by Faith when she sews a patchwork quilt to recount the adventure.

Conrad, P. (1985). *Prairie songs.* Harper. 167 pp. ISBN 0-06-021336-1. Historical Fiction. (E & J)

Lousia's life in a loving pioneer family on the Nebraska prairie is altered by the arrival of a new doctor and his beautiful, tragically frail wife.

Conrad, P. (1991). *Prairie visions: The life and times of Solomon Butcher.* Illus. with photographs by Solomon Butcher. HarperCollins. 96 pp. ISBN 0-06-021375-2. Biography/Informational. (E & J)

Solomon Butcher, who appeared in Conrad's Prairie Songs, actually lived on the Nebraska prairies in the latter part of the 1800s and spent most of his life photographing the homesteaders and writing anecdotes and stories about prairie life. This photobiography is filled with Butcher's stories and with his amazing photographs. Includes bibliography.

DeFelice, C. (1990). *Weasel.* Macmillan. 119 pp. ISBN 0-02-726457-2. Historical Fiction. (E & J)

Alone in the frontier wilderness in the winter of 1839 while his father is recovering from an injury, eleven-year-old Nathan runs afoul of the renegade killer known as Weasel and makes a surprising discovery about the concept of revenge.

Freedman, R. (1983). *Children of the wild West.* Illus. with photographs. Clarion. 112 pp. ISBN 0-89919-143-6. Informational. (E & J)

Life in the American West from 1840 to the early 1900s is captured through photographs. Text and archival photographs focus on the children involved in the move westward.

Freedman, R. (1985). *Cowboys of the wild West.* Illus. with photographs and prints. Clarion. 104 pp. ISBN 0-89919-301-3. Informational. (E & J)

Anecdotal text and fascinating photographs capture the spirit of the nineteenth-century Old West and the cowboy as well as give a historical account of cattle ranching during that time. Includes a bibliography and index.

Harvey, B. (1986). *My prairie year: Based on the diary of Elenore Plaisted*. Illus. by Deborah Kogan Ray. Holiday. 40 pp. ISBN 0-8234-0604-0. Historical Fiction (Picture Book). (P & E)

A true story of homesteading told by nine-year-old Elenore Plaisted, who moved from Lincoln, Maine, to the Dakota Territory in 1889.

Harvey, B. (1990). *My prairie Christmas*. Illus. by Deborah Kogan Ray. Holiday House. 32 pp. ISBN 0-8234-0827-2. Historical Fiction (Picture Book). (P & E)

A pioneer family's celebration of its first Christmas on the American frontier is disrupted when Pa is stranded by a blizzard and may not make it safely home.

Kellogg, S. (1984). *Paul Bunyan*. Illus. by author. Morrow. 40 pp. ISBN 0-688-03850-6. Traditional Tale (Picture Book). (P & E)

Kellogg's zany illustrations bring new life to an old favorite, the American tall tale figure of lumberjack Paul Bunyan. See other picture book versions of tall tales by Steven Kellogg, including Pecos Bill *and* Mike Fink.

Kellogg, S. (1988). *Johnny Appleseed*. Illus. by author. Morrow. 40 pp. ISBN 0-688-06418-3. Biography (Picture Book). (P & E)

Presents the life of John Chapman, or Johnny Appleseed, and describes his love of nature, his kindness to animals, and his planting of apple trees in Pennsylvania and Ohio. Some of the tall tales about Johnny are mentioned, primarily in the author's note.

Lasky, K. (1983). *Beyond the divide*. Macmillan. 264 pp. ISBN 0-02-0751670-9. Historical Fiction. (E & J)

Meribah Simon leaves with her father to join the 1849 Gold Rush when he is shunned by their Amish community. They are abandoned on the trail westward by the others and, though her father eventually dies, Meribah's indomitable spirit helps her to survive. An author's note provides background for the story.

MacLachlan, P. (1985). *Sarah, plain and tall*. Harper. 64 pp. ISBN 0-06-024102-0. Historical Fiction. (E)

A story of life in the Midwest in the mid-nineteenth century. Anna, Caleb, and their father are looking for a mother and wife when Sarah, a young woman from Maine, answers Papa's letter. However, they are afraid that she will not adjust to living on the prairie. The 1986 Newbery Medal winner.

McClung. R. (1990). *Hugh Glass, mountain man.* Illus. with black-and-white prints and a map. Morrow. 176 pp. ISBN 0-688-08092-8. Historical Fiction/Biography. (E & J)

A fictional biography of the legendary fur trapper, focusing on his life after a nearly fatal grizzly bear attack in 1823. Includes bibliography.

Moeri, L. (1981). *Save Queen of Sheba.* Dutton. 116 pp. IBSN 0-525-33202-2. Historical Fiction. (E & J)

After miraculously surviving a Sioux Indian raid on the trail to Oregon, a brother and sister set out to find the rest of the settlers.

O'Dell, S. (1986). *Streams to the river, river to the sea: A novel of Sacagawea.* Houghton. 208 pp. ISBN 0-395-40430-4. Historical Fiction. (E & J)

The story of the expedition of Lewis and Clark to the west coast of America is recounted through a young Shoshone woman who was their interpreter and guide.

Petry, A. (1964). *Tituba of Salem Village.* Includes an introductory note and maps. Crowell. 254 pp. IBSN 0-690-04766-5. Historical Fiction. (J)

In 1692, Tituba, a black slave, becomes the object of suspicion and eventually attack from crazed witch-hunters in Salem.

Sanders, S. R. (1989). *Aurora means dawn.* Illus. by Jill Kastner. Bradbury. 32 pp. ISBN 0-02-778270-0. Historical Fiction (Picture Book). (P & E)

Traveling from Connecticut to Ohio in the 1800s, members of the Sheldon family get caught by a thunderstorm near Aurora, where they settle and build a farm. Includes a note about the historical basis for this story.

Siebert, D. (1990). *Train song.* Illus. by Mike Wimmer. HarperCollins. 32 pp. ISBN 0-02-793581-7. Poetry (Picture Book). (P & E)

The rhyme and rhythm of the text replicate the clickety-clack of trains as readers ride the rails all across America of yesterday and today.

Speare, E. G. (1957). *Calico captive.* Houghton Mifflin. 288 pp. IBSN 0-395-07112-7. Historical Fiction. (E & J)

In 1754, Miriam Willard is captured by the Indians during the French and Indian War. Based on an actual event, this story vividly portrays the experience of the long wilderness trek from New Hampshire to Montreal, where Miriam is sold to the French.

Straight, T. A. (1979). *The price of free land.* Illus. with photographs. Lippincott. 96 pp. Autobiography. (E)

This biography, beginning in 1914 when the author was five years old, and accompanied by photographs from her family album, tells of homesteading in western Nebraska.

Turner, A. (1989). *Grasshopper summer.* Macmillan. 176 pp. ISBN 0-02-789511-4. Historical Fiction. (E & J)

Eleven-year-old Sam tells of his family's move from Kentucky to the southern Dakota Territory in 1874. The hardships of the trip, building a sod house, and planting a crop are vividly portrayed.

Walker, B. M. (1979). *The little house cookbook: Frontier foods from Laura Ingalls Wilder's classic stories.* Illus. by Garth Williams. Harper. 256 pp. ISBN 0-06-446090-8. Informational (Cookbook). (P & E)

Over 100 recipes, accompanied by historical information, present the foods and cooking of Laura Ingalls Wilder's frontier childhood. A carefully researched addition to American History.

Wilder, L. I. (1973). *The little house books.* Harper & Row, Trophy. 9 volumes. ISBN 0-06-440040-9. Historical Fiction. (E)

A boxed set of paperback editions of Laura Ingalls Wilder's beloved fictionalized stories of her life growing up on the American frontier.

Heritage

Immigration

Anderson, J. (1989). *Spanish pioneers of the Southwest.* Illus. with photographs by George Ancona. Lodestar. 64 pp. ISBN 0-525-67264-8. Informational (Photo Essay). (E & J)

This black-and-white photo essay examines the Hispanic cultural roots of the Southwest by recreating a day in the life of Miguel on El Rancho de las Golondrinas, an early settlement near Santa Fe, New Mexico, in the eighteenth century.

Bales, C. A. (1977). *Tales of the elders: A memory book of men and women who came to America as immigrants, 1900–1930.* Illus. with photographs. Follett. 160 pp. Informational. (E & J)

The photographs enhance this account of the people who came to America as immigrants in the early twentieth century.

Cech, J. (1991). *My Grandmother's Journey.* Illustrated by Sharon McGinley-Nally. Bradbury. 40 pp. ISBN 0-02-718135-9. Historical Fiction (Picture Book). (P & E)

Korie's grandmother tells her about the hardships she endured when she immigrated to the United States after World War II.

Clark, A. N. (1978). *To stand against the wind*. Viking. 136 pp. Historical Fiction. (E & J)

Immigration and the Vietnam War cause difficult situations and cultural conflicts in the novel.

Dionetti, M. (1991). *Coal mine peaches*. Illus. by Anita Riggio. Orchard. 32 pp. ISBN 0-531-05948-0. Historical Fiction (Picture Book). (P & E)

Grandfather was a young Italian immigrant who had worked in the coal mines and who was a storyteller. He tells the story of raising his family while helping to build the Brooklyn Bridge.

Fisher, L. (1975). *Across the sea from Galway*. Four Winds. 103 pp. Historical Fiction. (E)

The Donovan family struggles to reach the United States during Ireland's potato famine of the 1840s. When two of the three children are lost at sea off the coast of Massachusetts, the survivor strives to ensure that the family will endure.

Fisher, L. E. (1986). *Ellis Island*. Holiday House. 64 pp. IBSN 0-8234-0612-1. Informational (Photo Essay). (E & J)

A history of immigration through the port of New York, with special focus on the processing at Ellis Island. Contains an index.

Fleming, A. (1988). *The king of Prussia and a peanut butter sandwich*. Illus. by Ronald Himler. Scribner's. 48 pp. ISBN 0-684-18880-5. Historical Fiction (Picture Book). (E)

The immigrational history of the Mennonites who traveled from Prussia to the Russian Steppes and on to the state of Kansas, bringing with them the Turkey Red wheat seed. Includes an author's note and an index.

Freedman, R. (1980). *Immigrant kids*. Illus. with photographs. Dutton. 80 pp. ISBN 0-525-32538-7. Informational. (E & J)

Photographs of children who immigrated to the United States from Europe at the turn of the century show these children at home, at school, at work, and at play.

Harvey, B. (1987). *Immigrant girl: Becky of Eldridge Street*. Illus. by D.K. Ray. Holiday House. 42 pp. ISBN 0-8234-0638-5. Historical Fiction (Picture Book). (E)

Becky, whose family has emigrated from Russia to avoid persecution as Jews, finds growing up in New York City in 1910 a vivid and exciting experience.

Jacobs, W. J. (1990). *Ellis Island: New hope in a new land*. Illus. with black-and white photographs. Scribner. 40 pp. ISBN 0-684-19171-7. Informational. (E)

Archival photographs help recreate the American immigrant experience of being processed at Ellis Island. Restoration of Ellis Island is also covered. Includes index.

Keith, H. (1977). *The obstinate land.* Crowell. 214 pp. Historical Fiction. (E & J)
The story of an immigrant family making a new life in Oklahoma at the turn of the century.

Kidd, D. (1991). *Onion tears.* Illus. by Lucy Montgomery. Orchard. 80 pp. ISBN 0-531-08470-1. Historical Fiction. (P & E)
Nam-Huong has trouble forgetting the horrors she left behind in Vietnam. She also misses her family. With the help of new friends and a supportive teacher, Nam-Huong begins to adjust to her new life.

Lehmann, L. (1978). *Better than a princess.* Nelson. 95 pp. Historical Fiction. (E & J)
Based on the true story of a seven-year-old girl and her brothers who immigrated to America from Europe at the turn of the century and settled in Missouri.

Lehmann, L. (1981). *Tilli's new world.* Dutton, Lodestar. 154 pp. Historical Fiction. (E)
Tilli wants to go to school but her family has other needs. This story of an immigrant family on a Missouri farm in 1880 is based on the life of the author's mother.

Levinson, R. (1985). *Watch the stars come out.* Illus. by Diane Goode. Dutton. 32 pp. ISBN 0-525-44205-7. Historical Fiction (Picture Book). (P)
The transatlantic crossing and arrival in New York of the immigrants of the early 1890s are described through the eyes of a child.

Mayerson, E. W. (1990). *The cat who escaped from steerage.* Scribner. 80 pp. ISBN 0-684-19209-8. Historical Fiction. (E)
A nine-year-old Jewish girl experiences traveling in steerage on a steamship, adopting a stowaway cat, and passing through Ellis Island when her family immigrates to America.

Mays, L. (1979). *The other shore.* Atheneum. 223 pp. Historical Fiction. (J)
The lives of immigrants who worked in the sweatshops on the Lower East Side of New York City are examined in this novel of an immigrant girl who came to America from Italy in 1911.

Moskin, M. (1975). *Waiting for Mama.* Coward, McCann. 96 pp. Historical Fiction. (E)

At the turn of the century, a Russian immigrant family waits in New York City for the mother to arrive from Russia.

Murphy, E., and Driscoll, T. (1974). *An album of the Irish Americans.* Illus. with photographs. Watts. 96 pp. Informational. (J)
An account of Irish immigration to the United States, including the difficulties immigrants encountered and the contributions they made.

Nadler, G. (1981). *Coming to America: Immigrants from southern Europe.* Delacorte. 143 pp. ISBN 0-440-01340-2. Informational. (J)
This book depicts the histories of immigrants from Spain, Portugal, Italy, and Greece, who came to America between 1880 and 1930 during the times of mass immigration.

Sachs, M. (1982). *Call me Ruth.* Doubleday. 134 pp. Historical Fiction. (E)
Rifka (Ruth) and her mother, immigrants to the United States at the turn of the century, have dreams of their new life but are forced to deal with the reality that awaits them in America.

Sandin, J. (1981). *The long way to a new land.* Harper. 64 pp. ISBN 0-940742-24-1. Historical Fiction. (Beginning Reader). (P)
A story about Carl Erik and his family who immigrate to America from Sweden in 1868. The poverty in Sweden, the transatlantic voyage, and their arrival in America are described in five short chapters.

Yep, L. (1975). *Dragonwings.* Harper. 248 pp. IBSN 0-06-026738-0. Historical Fiction. (E & J)
Set in San Francisco at the time of the great earthquake, Dragonwings tells the story of Chinese immigrants, father and son, who must leave the security and protection of the family business and enter the world of the Demon (white) people. 1976 Newbery Honor Book.

Yep, L. (1991). *The star fisher.* Morrow. 160 pp. ISBN 0-688-09365-5. Historical Fiction. (E, & J)
A Chinese-American teenager has trouble fitting in at her West Virginia school. Set in 1927, this story tells of Joan Lee's struggle for identity, as she quarrels with her parents who cling tenaciously to Chinese traditions.

Cultural Diversity in America
NATIVE AMERICANS

Autumn, W. D. (1982). *Ceremony—In the circle of life.* Illus. by Sanyan Tawa Wicasta. Carnival. 32 pp. ISBN 0-9407-24-1. Historical Fiction (Picture Book). (P & E)

Star Spirit explains the circle symbol, which is prominent in Native American life, to Little Turtle.

Benchley, N. (1972). *Only earth and sky last forever.* Harper. 204 pp. IBSN 0-06-440049-2. Historical Fiction. (J)
Dark Elk, a young Indian warrior, joins Crazy Horse's troops and battles Custer at the Little Big Horn.

Bierhorst, J. (1979). *A cry from the earth: Music of the North American Indians.* Illus. with photographs and maps. Four Winds. 114 pp. Informational (Music). (E & J)
An anecdotal account of the role of music and dance in Native American life and a description of the instruments and music.

Bierhorst, J. (1974). *Songs of the Chippewa.* Illus. Farrar. 48 pp. Informational (Music). (P)
Includes songs of the Chippewa translated into English with arrangements for guitar and piano, along with illustrations that depict the Chippewa people, their homes, and their lands.

Bierhorst, J. (1985). *The mythology of North America.* Illus. with prints and maps. Morrow. 256 pp. ISBN 0-688-04145-0. Traditional Tale. (J)
The mythology of eleven North American regions is described. Includes Native American artwork, maps, diagrams, photographs, a bibliography, and an index.

Boesen, V., and Graybill, F. C. (1977). *Edward S. Curtis: Photographer of the North American Indian.* Illus. with photographs. Dodd. 191 pp. Biography. (E & J)
A biography of the man who is best known for photographing the North American Indians.

Connolly, J. E. (1985). *Why the possum's tail is bare and other North American Indian nature tales.* Illus. by Andrea Adams. Stemmer. 64 pp. ISBN 0-88045-069-X. Traditional Tale. (E)
Thirteen tales from North American Indian tribes. Each makes a moral statement supporting an ancient tribal law.

Ekoomiak, N. (1990). *Arctic memories.* Illus. by author. Holt. 32 pp. ISBN 0-8050-1254-0. Informational (Picture Book). (P & E)
Inuit Eskimo lifestyle and culture are revealed through the memories the author has of what was taught him by his grandfather.

Freedman, R. (1987). *Indian chiefs.* Illus. with photographs and prints. Holiday. 160 pp. ISBN 0-8234-0625-3. Biography. (E & J)

Through dialogues and vivid photographs, portrays six Indian chiefs who led their people and struggled to preserve their culture during difficult times.

Freedman, R. (1992). *An Indian winter.* Illus. by Karl Bodmer. Holiday House. 88 pp. ISBN 0-8234-0930-9. Informational. (E & J)
Relates the experiences of the German prince, Maximilian, his servant, and Swiss artist Karl Bodmer as they travel through the Missouri Valley in 1833, living with the Mandan Indians and recording their impressions in words and paintings. Includes bibliography and index.

Glubok, S. (1975). *The art of the Northwest Coast Indians.* Macmillan. 48 pp. Informational (Art). (E)
The artistic expression of the Native Americans from Oregon to southern Alaska is explored through such items as household artifacts, canoes, masks, and totem poles. The significance and uses of these items are discussed. Illustrated with black-and-white photographs.

Glubok, S. (1975). *The art of the Plains Indians.* Macmillan. 48 pp. Informational (Art). (E)
The culture of the Plains Indians is reflected in their art forms. Many pictures are used to show the variety of their art.

Goble, P. (1978). *The girl who loved wild horses.* Illus. by author. Bradbury. 32 pp. ISBN 0-02-736570-0. Traditional tale (Picture Book). (P & E)
Though she is fond of her people, a girl prefers to live among the wild horses where she is truly happy and free.

Goble, P. (1987). *Death of the iron horse.* Illus. by author. Bradbury. 32 pp. ISBN 0-02-737830-6. Historical Fiction (Picture Book). (P & E)
The documented story of how the Cheyenne gained a small victory over the white man by tearing up the railroad tracks with their knives and tomahawks.

Hancock, S. (1975). *The blazing hills.* Putnam. 47 pp. Historical Fiction. (P)
A realistic folktale told every Easter eve in Fredericksburg, Texas, of an event that happened in the spring of 1846 between the Apache and Comanche Indians and the German settlers.

Highwater, J. (1977). *Anpao: An American Indian odyssey.* Lippincott. 256 pp. IBSN 0-397-31750-6. Historical Fiction. (J)
A blending of traditional North American Indian tales and the growing to manhood of an Indian boy. 1978 Newbery Honor Book.

Highwater, J. (1981). *Moonsong lullaby.* Illus. with photographs by Marcia Keegan. Lothrop. 32 pp. ISBN 0-688-00427-X. Traditional Tale. (P & E)

Illustrated with powerful photographs, this lullaby tells of the role the moon plays in Native American culture.

Hoxie, F. E. (1989). *The Crow.* Illus. with photographs and prints. Chelsea House. 128 pp. ISBN 1-55546-704-0. Informational. (E & J)
Tribal origins, effects of European settlers on the Crow, and life of the tribe today are included in this chronological story of the Great Plains Crow Indians. Contains a glossary, bibliography, and index.

Hoyt-Goldsmith, D. (1991). *Pueblo storyteller.* Illus. with photographs by Lawrence Migdale. Holiday House. 32 pp. ISBN 0-8234-0864-7. Informational (Picture Book). (E)
A photoessay that explains the Pueblo practice of preserving traditions by passing them from generation to generation through storytelling.

Mayo, G. W. (1989). *Earthmaker's tales: North American Indian stories about earth happenings.* Walker. 92 pp. ISBN 0-8027-6840-7. Traditional Tale. (E)
Natural phenomena such as floods, fog, snow, storms, volcanoes, and winds are explained in these seventeen North American Indian tales. Includes glossary.

Mayo, G. W. (1987). *Star tales: North American Indian stories about the stars.* Walker. 96 pp. ISBN 0-8027-6673-0. Traditional Tale. (E & J)
Fourteen tales of the Native Americans, including the Blackfoot and Sioux, that explain how they interpret the stars in the night sky. A list of sources and glossary also included.

Morrison, D. N. (1980). *Chief Sarah: Sarah Winnemucca's fight for Indian rights.* Illus. with prints and photographs. Atheneum. 196 pp. Biography. (J)
A self-educated Paiute Indian, Sarah Winnemucca, was the first Native American to have a book published in English. Her battle with the Bureau of Indian Affairs for Indian rights is also discussed.

O'Dell, S. (1960). *Island of the blue dolphins.* Houghton Mifflin. 184 pp. IBSN 0-395-06962-9. Historical Fiction. (E & J)
Based on the true account of an Indian girl who spent eighteen years alone on an island off the coast of California. The 1961 Newbery winner.

O'Dell, S. (1970). *Sing down the moon.* Houghton Mifflin. 137 pp. ISBN 0-395-10919-1. Historical Fiction. (E & J)
In 1864, Bright Morning, a Navajo girl, is first captured by Spanish slavers and later must march on the Trail of Tears with her people to a new reservation.

Sewall, M. (1990). *People of the breaking day.* Illus. by author. Atheneum. 48 pp. ISBN 0-689-31407-8. Informational (Picture Book). (P & E)

The lifestyle of the Wampanoag Indians as they lived at the time of the Pilgrims is highlighted. This is a companion volume to Sewall's The Pilgrims of Plimoth.

Shetterly, S. H. (1991). *Raven's light: A myth from the people of the Northwest coast.* Illus. by Robert Shetterly. Atheneum. 32 pp. ISBN 0-689-31629-1. Traditional Tale (Picture Book). (P & E)
A Native American creation myth based on the traditional stories of the Northwest tribes.

Sneve, V. D. H. (Comp.) (1989). *Dancing teepees: Poems of American Indian youth.* Illus. by Stephen Gammell. Holiday House. 32 pp. ISBN 0-8234-0724-1. Poetry. (E & J)
Themes of youth and the importance of the spoken word are echoed in these nineteen poems from the oral tradition and from today's North American Indian tribal poets.

Stanley, F. (1991). *The last princess: The story of Princess Ka'iulani of Hawai'i.* Illus. by Diane Stanley. Four Winds. 40 pp. ISBN 0-02-786785-4. Biography. (E)
Princess Ka'iulani becomes Queen of Hawai'i and battles in vain to help her people maintain control and ownership of their island home.

Strete, C. K. (1979). *When Grandfather journeys into winter.* Illus. by Hal Frenck. Greenwillow. 86 pp. Historical Fiction (Picture Book). (P)
An explanation of life and death told through the relationship between an Indian grandfather and his grandson.

Wallin, L. (1984). *In the shadow of the wind.* Macmillan, Bradbury. 216 pp. ISBN 0-02-792320-7. Historical Fiction. (J)
The story of a white boy and an Indian girl, both teenagers, who fall in love during 1835, despite the struggle of the Creek Indians to save their land from the greedy white settlers.

Yolen, J. (1990). *Sky dogs.* Illus. by Barry Moser. Harcourt. 32 pp. ISBN 0-15-275480-6. Traditional Tale (Picture Book). (P, E & J)
A young motherless boy in a tribe of Blackfoot Indians is present when his people see horses for the first time.

Yue, D., and Yue, C. (1984). *The tipi: A center of Native American life.* Illus. by David Yue. Knopf. 96 pp. ISBN 0-394-96177-3. Informational. (E & J)
Explains the tipi of the Plains Indians in detail and also shows how the Native Americans adjusted perfectly to their environment. Contains index.

AFRICAN AMERICANS

Adler, D. (1989). *Jackie Robinson: He was first.* Illus. by R. Casilla. Holiday House. 48 pp. ISBN 0-8234-0734-9. Biography. (P & E)
Traces the life of the talented and determined athlete who broke the color barrier in major league baseball in 1947 by joining the Brooklyn Dodgers.

Bang, M. G. (1976). *Wiley and the hairy man.* Illus. by the author. Macmillan. 64 pp. ISBN 0-02-708370-5. Traditional Tale. (P & E)
A southern folktale with vivid illustrations of brave Wiley and his wise mother.

Bryan, A. (Comp.) (1982). *I'm going to sing: Black American spirituals.* Illus. by compiler. Vol. 2. Atheneum. 54 pp. (P, E, & J)
Contains words and music to these folk songs, and woodcut illustrations to enhance them.

Collier, J. L. (1985). *Louis Armstrong: An American success story.* Macmillan. 176 pp. ISBN 0-02-722830-4. Biography. (E & J)
A biography of this musical genius, who came from a poor black family in New Orleans and never had a music lesson but became one of the greatest jazz musicians of all time. Includes information about his recordings, a bibliography, and an index.

Davis, O. (1982). *Langston: A play.* Delacorte. 146 pp. ISBN 0-385-28543-4. Historical Fiction (Play). (J)
This portrait of Langston Hughes weaves many of his poetic works into a play about his life.

Golenbock, P. (1990). *Teammates.* Illus. by Paul Bacon. Harcourt. 32 pp. ISBN 0-15-200603-6. Biography (Picture Book). (P & E)
The story of Jackie Robinson and Pee Wee Reese and the breaking of the color barrier in major league baseball.

Hamilton, V. (1985). *The people could fly: American Black folktales.* Illus. by Leo and Diane Dillon. Knopf. 192 pp. ISBN 0-394-96925-1. Traditional Tale. (E & J).
A collection of twenty-four tales told in Black English and portraying the struggles of the black slaves in America. Includes bibliography.

Haskins, J. (1982). *Black theater in America.* Illus. with photographs. Crowell. 184 pp. ISBN 0-690-04128-4. Informational. (J)
The history of black theater from the time of the minstrel shows to today, featuring a host of black actors and writers. Explains how black theater has grown despite protest and discrimination.

Haskins, J. (1987). *Black music in America: A history through its people.* Illus. with photographs. Crowell. 208 pp. ISBN 0-690-04462-3. Informational (Music). (J)

A history of black musical styles from the time of the slaves in America to today. Includes a discussion of the acceptance of and prejudice against black music today. Includes bibliography and index.

Haskins, J. (1990). *Black dance in America.* Crowell. 232 pp. ISBN 0-690-04657-X. Informational. (J)

Surveys the history of black dance in America, from its beginnings with ritual dances of African slaves, through tap and modern dance to break dancing. Includes an index.

Haskins J. (1991). *Outward dreams: Black inventors and their inventions.* Illus. with photographs. Walker. 128 pp. ISBN 0-8027-6993-4. Biography. (E & J)

A collective biography which tells the stories of several black inventors who overcame prejudice to share their achievements with the world. Includes bibliography and index.

Jackson, F. (1975). *The black man in America, 1932–1954.* Watts. 96 pp. Informational. (E)

Part of a series on the lives of African Americans, this volume focuses on black leaders in the labor unions, the arts, religion, and sports.

Meltzer, M. (1984). *The Black Americans: A history in their own words 1619–1983.* Illus. with photographs. Crowell. 320 pp. ISBN 0-069-04418-6. Informational. (J)

Covers 350 years of black history in America and explores the struggles of African Americans to gain equality.

San Souci, R. D. (1989). *The talking eggs: A folktale from the American South.* Illus. by Jerry Pinkney. Dial. 32 pp. ISBN 0-8037-0620-0. Traditional Tale (Picture Book). (P & E)

Southern culture in reflected in this Creole tale of a good sister, a bad sister, and a greedy mama who get just rewards from an old woman. Detailed illustrations enhance this tale. A 1990 Caldecott Honor Book.

Tobias, T. (1975). *Arthur Mitchell.* Crowell. 32 pp. ISBN 0-690-00662-4. Biography. (P)

A portrait of Arthur Mitchell that deals with the troubles he encountered while becoming a leader in professional ballet.

Turner, G. T. (1989). *Take a walk in their shoes.* Illus. by Elton C. Fax. Cobble-hill. 160 pp. ISBN 0-525-65006-7. Biography. (E)

Biographies of fourteen successful African Americans including Martin Luther King, Jr., Rosa Parks, Frederick Douglass, and Mary McLeod Bethune. A short skit accompanies each.

Walter, M. P. (1985). *Brother to the wind.* Illus. by Leo and Diane Dillon. Lothrop. 32 pp. ISBN 0-688-03812-3. Traditional Tale. (E)

An unusual African American tale in which Emeke's desire to fly becomes a reality with the help of Good Snake.

Yarbrough, C. (1979). *Cornrows.* Illus. by Carole Byard. Coward. 44 pp. ISBN 0-698-20462-X. Historical Fiction. (P & E)

A look at the history of the African American through the symbol of the hairstyle of cornrows.

HISPANIC AMERICANS

Aardema, V. (1991). *Borreguita and the coyote: A tale from Ayutla, Mexico.* Illus. by Petra Mathers. Knopf. 40 pp. ISBN 0-679-80921-X. Traditional Tale (Picture Book). (P & E)

A Mexican folktale about a lamb who is able, more than once, to keep a coyote from eating her.

Blue, R. (1973). *We are Chicano.* Watts. 64 pp. Informational. (E)

The ethnic heritage of the Hispanics is revealed through a twelve-year-old boy's feelings for his family and his culture.

Comins, J. (1974). *Latin American crafts and their cultural backgrounds.* Lothrop. 128 pp. Informational. (E)

Gives instructions for making Latin America crafts from both the past and present.

Griego, M., et. al. (Comp.) (1981). *Tortillitas para mama and other nursery rhymes, Spanish and English.* Illus. by Barbara Cooney. Holt. 32 pp. ISBN 0-8050-0285-5. Traditional Tale (Poetry) (P & E)

Lullabies and nursery rhymes from Latin America presented in both Spanish and English.

Hewett, J. (1990). *Hector lives in the United States now: The story of a Mexican-American child.* Illustrated with black-and-white photographs by Richard Hewett. HarperCollins. 48 pp. ISBN 0-397-32278-X. Informational. (E)

This photo essay examines the daily life and aspirations of a Mexican-American boy whose parents have applied for the right to remain in the United States.

Meltzer, M. (1982). *The Hispanic Americans.* Illus. with photographs by Morrie Camhi and Catherine Noren. Crowell. 149 pp. ISBN 0-690-04110-1. Informational. (E & J)

An account of the history of Hispanic Americans in the United States from 1492, including the struggles to gain bilingual education and the fight against discrimination.

Van Laan, N. (1991). *The legend of El Dorado: A Latin American tale.* Illus. by Beatriz Vidal. Knopf. 40 pp. ISBN 0-679-80136-1. Traditional Tale (Picture Book). (P & E)

A mighty king offers his gold-covered body to the serpent of the lake. Ever since then, the treasures of El Dorado have been hidden in the depths of Lake Guatavita.

ASIAN AMERICANS

Bunting, E. (1982). *The happy funeral.* Illus. by Vo-Dinh Mai. Harper. 40 pp. Historical Fiction (Picture Book). (P & E)

Chinese American customs and traditions are revealed in this story of the death and funeral of young Laura's grandfather.

Demi. (1980). *Liang and the magic paintbrush.* Illus. by the author. Holt. 40 pp. ISBN 0-8050-0220-0. Traditional Tale (Picture Book). (P & E)

Liang spoils the greedy emperor's plans with his wit in this ancient Chinese folktale.

Lee, J. M. (1985). *Toad is the uncle of heaven: A Vietnamese folk tale.* Illus. by the author. Holt. 32 pp. ISBN 0-03-004652-1. Traditional Tale (Picture Book). (P)

A clever toad convinces the King of Heaven to save Earth from a long drought in this retelling of an old folktale from Vietnam.

Lord, B. B. (1984). *In the year of the boar and Jackie Robinson.* Illus. by Marc Simont. Harper. 176 pp. ISBN 0-06-024004-0. Historical Fiction. (E)

A ten-year-old Chinese immigrant pledges her allegiance to the flag in this story of Chinese immigrants in Brooklyn in the late 1940s.

Mahy, M. (1990). *The seven Chinese brothers.* Illus. by Jean Tseng and Mou-sien Tseng. Scholastic. 40 pp. ISBN 0-590-42055-0. Traditional Tale (Picture Book). (P & E)

Seven amazing Chinese brothers, each with a wondrous power, join forces to overthrow a cruel Chinese emperor.

Quayle, E. (1989). *The shining princess and other Japanese legends.* Illus. by Michael Foreman. Arcade. 104 pp. ISBN 0-55970-039-4. Traditional Tale. (E)

Ten witty Japanese tales of heroes and villains, demons and dragons, greed, and a childless couple whose dreams come true.

Reit, S. (1973). *Rice cakes and paper dragons.* Dodd, Mead. 80 pp. Historical Fiction. (P)
The story of a Chinese American girl living in San Francisco and how she celebrates the Chinese New Year.

Say, A. (1990). *El Chino.* Houghton Mifflin. 32 pp. ISBN 0-395-52023-1. Historical Fiction (Picture Book). (P & E)
This is the inspirational story of a Chinese American who eventually becomes the first Chinese bullfighter.

Sung, B. L. (1977). *An album of Chinese Americans.* Illus. with photographs. Watts. 65 pp. Informational. (E & J)
A portrait of the Chinese in America and the hardships and loneliness they have endured in their struggle to maintain their identity.

Uchida, Y. (1983). *The best bad thing.* Atheneum, McElderry. 132 pp. ISBN 0-689-50290-7. Historical Fiction. (E)
The story of Rinko, a twelve-year-old Japanese American girl, and her family who are living in California. She learns that something bad can turn into something good and that people are not always as they appear to be.

Waters, K., and Slovenz-Low, M. (1990). *Lion dancer: Ernie Wan's Chinese New Year.* Illustrated with photographs by Martha Cooper. Scholastic. 30 pp. ISBN 0-590-43046-7. Informational (Picture Book). (P & E)
Ernie participates in his first Lion Dance, part of the Chinese New Year celebration. The setting is Chinatown in New York City. Includes horoscopes of each of the twelve animals in the Chinese lunar calender.

Yee, P. (1990). *Tales from gold mountain: Stories of the Chinese in the New World.* Illus. by Simon Ng. Macmillan. 64 pp. ISBN 0-02-793621-X. Short Stories. (E & J)
A collection of eight stories reflecting the gritty optimism of the Chinese, who overcame prejudice and adversity to build a unique place for themselves in North America.

Yep, L. (1989). *The rainbow people.* Illus. by Patrick Benson. Holt. 80 pp. ISBN 0-8050-1206-0. Traditional Tale. (E)
Twenty magical Chinese American tales of adjusting to life in America. Cultural context is provided for each group of stories.

Yep. L. (1991). *Tongues of jade*. Illus. by David Wiesner. HarperCollins. 192 pp. ISBN 0-06-022471-1. Traditional Tales. (E & J)

A collection of folktales kept alive and part of the Chinese-American culture by nineteenth century Chinese immigrants. Yep retells these tales within a historical context.

EUROPEAN AMERICANS

Clark, A. N. (1975). *Year walk*. Viking. 197 pp. Historical Fiction. (J)

Flashbacks to Spain aid in exploring the culture of the Basques in Idaho.

Geras, A. (1990). *My grandmother's stories: A collection of Jewish folk tales*. Illus. by Jael Jordan. Knopf. 96 pp. ISBN 0-679-90910-9. Traditional Tales. (E & J)

Ten humorous Jewish tales told by a wise grandmother to her granddaughter.

Kurelek, W. (1985). *They sought a new land*. Tundra. 48 pp. IBSN 0-88776-172-0. Informational (Picture Book). (E & J)

The many facets of European immigration and the contribution of European immigrants in the settling of North America are examined in both illustration and text.

Meltzer, M. (Ed.) (1982). *The Jewish Americans: A history in their own words 1650–1950*. Illus. with photographs and prints. Crowell. 167 pp. ISBN 0-690-04228-0 Informational. (E & J)

Contains excerpts from diaries, journals, and letters of Jewish Americans that express what life in America means to them. The editor prefaces each selection with a historical note. Contains index.

Meyer, C. (1976). *Amish people*. Atheneum, McElderry. 138 pp. Informational. (E)

An explanation of the life of the Amish focusing on food, language, school, and customs with emphasis on the role that religion plays in their way of life. A brief history of the Amish from sixteenth-century Europe to twentieth-century America.

O'Shea, P. (1987). *Finn Mac Cool and the Small Men of Deeds*. Illus. by Stephen Lavis. Holiday. 96 pp. ISBN 0-8234-0651-1. Traditional Tale. (P & E)

Finn Mac Cool and the Small Men of Deeds solve the mystery of the king's kidnapped children in this Irish folktale.

Pellowski, A. (1980). *The nine crying dolls: A story from Poland*. Illus. by Charles Mikolaycak. Philomel. 32 pp. ISBN 0-399-20752-X. Traditional Tale. (P & E)

A Polish tale of the results of a woman trying to quiet her crying baby.

Pellowski, A. (1982). *Winding Valley farm: Annie's story*. Illus. by Wendy Watson. Philomel. 192 pp. ISBN 0-399-20863-1. Historical Fiction. (E)

The story of a Polish American family and their six-year-old daughter, Annie, who live on a farm in Wisconsin in the early 1900s. This third novel in a series is based on the author's ancestors.

Traditions and Celebrations in America

Alcott, L. M. (1989). *An old-fashioned Thanksgiving*. Illus. by Michael McCurdy. Holiday House. 32 pp. ISBN 0-8234-0772-1. Historical Fiction (Picture Book). (E & J)

Set in the New Hampshire hills in the 1820s, this book shows a family preparing for a Thanksgiving meal. Illustrated with colored woodblock prints. Originally written for St. Nicholas Magazine *in 1881.*

Anderson, J. (1985). *Christmas on the prairie*. Photographs by George Ancona. Clarion. 48 pp. ISBN 0-89919-307-2. Informational (Photo Essay). (P & E)

Allows the reader to think about why Christmas is celebrated as it is today in America by taking a look at how it was celebrated on the prairie in the 1800s. Many of our present traditions come from these early celebrations.

Howard, E. F. (1989). *Chita's Christmas tree*. Illus. by Floyd Cooper. Bradbury. 32 pp. ISBN 0-02-744621-2. Historical Fiction (Picture Book). (P)

Chita, the daughter of one of the city's first black doctors, experiences Christmas in Baltimore in the early 1900s.

Kimmel, E. (1989). *Hershel and the Hanukkah goblins*. Illus. by Trina Schart Hyman. Holiday House. 32 pp. ISBN 0-8234-0769-1. Traditional Tale (Picture Book). (P)

Hershel of Ostropol single-handedly saves Hanukkah by defeating a series of increasingly dreadful goblins. Lively and humorous illustrations. A note about the celebration is provided by the author. A 1990 Caldecott Honor Book.

Perl, L. (1989). *The great ancestor hunt*. Houghton Mifflin. 104 pp. IBSN 0-89919-745-0. Informational. (E & J)

A guide for tracing one's ancestors via various means. An appendix describes how to use a number of available government resources. Includes an index and a bibliography.

Schwartz, A. (1974). *Cross your fingers, spit in your hat*. J.B. Lippincott. 160 pp. ISBN 0-397-31531-7. Informational. (E & J)

Superstitions about such topics as love and marriage, money, ailments, travel, the weather, and death. With bibliography.

Swanson, J. (1983). *The spice of America.* Illus. by Priscilla Kiedrowski. Carolrhoda. 96 pp. ISBN 0-87614-252-8. Informational. (E)

Fifteen interesting and unusual stories from America's past, including how the doughnut got its hole, and how we got an official Thanksgiving Day.

Walter, M. P. (1989). *Have a happy . . .* Illus. by Carole Byard. Lothrop. 112 pp. ISBN 0-688-06923-1. Historical Fiction (Picture Book). (E)

Kwanzaa, the African American celebration of cultural heritage, is explored on eleven-year-old Chris's Christmas birthday.

Weitzman, D. (1975). *My backyard history book.* Little, Brown. 127 pp. IBSN 0-316-92901-8. Informational. (E & J)

Activities and projects, such as making time capsules and rubbings and tracing genealogy, demonstrate that learning about the past begins at home.

Religions

Ammon, R. (1989). *Growing up Amish.* Illus. with photographs. Atheneum. 102 pp. ISBN 0-689-31387-X. Informational. (E)

Focuses on the homes, work, and schooling of a Pennsylvania Dutch community to depict the Amish way of life. Also, the history of the Amish movement is covered. Includes bibliography and index.

Rice, E. (1982). *American saints and seers: American-born religions and the genius behind them.* Four Winds. 229 pp. Informational. (J)

An account of the various religions that have emerged in America, including the Mormons, Christian Scientists, Shakers, and American Indian religions.

Yolen, J. (1976). *Simple gifts: The story of the Shakers.* Viking. 115 pp. Informational. (E & J)

A history of the emergence of the Shakers in America, an almost extinct group today.

American Life in the 1800s and Early 1900s

Baylor, B. (1983). *The best town in the world.* Illus. by Ronald Himler. Scribner's. 32 pp. ISBN 0-684-18035-9. Historical Fiction (Picture Book). (E & J)

A poetic description of a small town in the Texas hills in the early 1900s.

Blos, J. W. (1979). *A gathering of days: A New England girl's journal, 1830–32.* Scribner's. 144 pp. ISBN 0-684-16340-3. Historical Fiction. (E & J)

The story of Catherine, a fourteen-year-old New Hampshire farm girl who keeps a journal, gives the reader a feeling for the way life was in the past.

Blumberg, R. (1989). *The great American gold rush.* Macmillan, Bradbury. 135 pp. ISBN 0-02-711681-6. Informational. (E & J)

Describes the emigration of people from the east coast of the United States and from foreign countries to pursue the dream of discovering gold. Includes a bibliography and index.

Callaway, K. (1982). *The bloodroot flower.* Knopf. 198 pp. Historical Fiction. (E & J)

A story of twelve-year-old Carrie Usher and her family in the northern Minnesota woods in the early 1900s. Recounts some of the strange and frightening events in their lives.

Costabel, E. D. (1983). *A New England village.* Atheneum. 48 pp. ISBN 0-689-30972-4. Historical Fiction (Picture Book). (P & E)

The reader is given a sense of life in rural nineteenth-century New England through simple text and black-and-white drawings of houses, schools, and people.

Durell, A. (Comp.) (1989). *The Diane Goode book of American folktales and songs.* Illus. by Diane Goode. Dutton. 64 pp. ISBN 0-525-44458-0. Traditional Tale. (P & E)

This collection of Americana comprises seven familiar songs and nine short folktales. Includes captivating illustrations.

Finsand, M. J. (1983). *The town that moved.* Illus. by Reg Sandland. Carolrhoda. 48 pp. ISBN 0-87614-200-5. Historical Fiction. (P & E)

When the people of Hibbing, Minnesota, learned that they had built their town on top of a Mesabi iron ore deposit, they moved their town. Based on a true story.

Fleischman, P. (1991). *The borning room.* HarperCollins. 101 pp. ISBN 0-06-023785-6. Historical Fiction. (E & J)

The life of her family is chronicled as Georgina lies on her death bed in the borning room and remembers growing up on the Ohio frontier. She recalls the generations of children and adults who were born or who died in the borning room, a special place in her family home. The story spans from the days of slavery until World War I.

Fisher, L. E. (1992). *Tracks across America: The story of the American railroad, 1825–1900.* Illus. with photographs, maps, and drawings. Holiday House. 192 pp. ISBN 0-8234-0945-7. Informational. (E & J)

Examines the development of the railroad in the United States from its nineteenth-century beginnings to the end of that century. Includes bibliography and index.

Freedman, R. (1991). *The Wright brothers: How they invented the airplane.* Illustrated with photographs. Holiday House. 128 pp. ISBN 0-8234-0875-2. Biography. (E & J)

Freedman uses archival photographs taken by the Wright brothers and their contemporaries to strengthen an already strong biography and history of the beginning of aviation. Includes index. 1992 Newbery Honor Book.

Glazer, T. (Comp.) (1988). *Tom Glazer's treasury of songs for children.* Illus. by John O'Brien. Doubleday. 256 pp. ISBN 0-385-23693-X. Informational (Song). (P, E & J)

Words and sheet music for 130 American folk songs. Historical annotations are included with each song. Also contains a bibliography and an index of first lines.

Haley, G. E. (1986). *Jack and the bean tree.* Illus. by the author. Crown. 48 pp. ISBN 0-517-55717-7. Traditional Tale (Picture Book). (P & E)

This English folktale retold in Appalachian style allows us to look at the Appalachian way of life through the story of Jack's adventure with the giant in the sky. Illustrated with paintings.

Hall, D. (1979). *Ox-cart man.* Illus. by Barbara Cooney. Viking. 40 pp. ISBN 0-670-53328-9. Historical Fiction (Picture Book). (P)

A nineteenth-century New Englander loads the results of his family's work into an ox-cart and travels to Portsmouth Market to sell the goods and buy supplies for the coming year.

Hartford, J. (1986). *Steamboat in a cornfield.* Illus. with photographs and prints. Crown. 40 pp. ISBN 0-517-56141-7. Historical Fiction. (P & E)

The true story of the steamboat Virginia *that was trapped in a cornfield in 1910 is told using rhythm, rhyme, and photographs.*

Hendershot, J. (1987). *In coal country.* Illus. by Thomas B. Allen. Knopf. 40 pp. ISBN 0-394-98190-1. Historical Fiction (Picture Book). (P)

Life in an Ohio coal-mining town in the 1930s is told from a child's viewpoint, using poetic text and pastel and charcoal illustrations.

Hodges, M. (1989). *Making a difference: The story of an American family.* Scribner's. 196 pp. ISBN 0-684-18979-8. Biography. (J)

Traces the lives and accomplishments of the extraordinary Mary Sherwood and her five children, who played an important part in bringing great changes in higher education and voting rights for women, opportunities for government service, and awareness of the need to preserve the country's natural wonders. Includes an index.

Holland, I. (1990). *The journey home.* Scholastic. 212 pp. ISBN 0-590-43110-2. Historical Fiction. (E & J)

Two orphan sisters in the late 1800s leave New York on the orphan train to seek a new home in the West.

Johnson, H. L. (1975). *Picture the past: 1900–1915.* Lothrop. 96 pp. Informational. (E)

Original prints and photographs depict life from 1900 to 1915 in America.

Lewis, C. (1987). *Long ago in Oregon.* Illus. by Joel Fontaine. Harper. 64 pp. ISBN 0-06-023840-2. Poetry. (P, E & J)

Seventeen poems of life in Oregon in 1917, as well as vignettes of the life of a little girl, her family, and friends during this period.

Loeper, J. J. (1979). *Mr. Marley's Main Street confectionary.* Illus. with prints and drawings. Atheneum. 72 pp. Informational. (E & J)

An enchanting account of the history of ice cream, candy, crackerjacks, soda pop, and other treats and how they came to America. Takes a look at the old-time candy shop as well.

Loeper, J. J. (1984). *Going to school in 1876.* Illus. with prints. Atheneum. 96 pp. ISBN 0-689-31015-3. Informational. (E & J)

Personal anecdotes recreate the lives and the schooling of nineteenth-century American children.

O'Kelley, M. L. (1983). *From the hills of Georgia: An autobiography in paintings.* Illus. with paintings by the author. Atlantic-Little, Brown. 32 pp. ISBN 0-316-63800-5. Autobiography. (P & E)

An autobiography of this folk painter told through her paintings of Georgia in the early 1900s, where she grew up.

Osborne, M. P. (1991). *American tall tales.* Illus. by Michael McCurdy. Knopf. 128 pp. ISBN 0-679-80089-1. Traditional Tales. (E)

Nine tall tales from the United States, including the stories of Davy Crockett, John Henry, Pecos Bill, Sally Ann Thunder, and Stormalong, are found in this volume, along with background notes and a bibliography.

Rylant, C. (1982). *When I was young in the mountains.* Illus. by Diane Goode. Dutton. 32 pp. ISBN 0-525-42525-X. Historical Fiction (Picture Book). (P)

The author pleasantly recalls her loving family and her childhood in the mountains of Appalachia.

Rylant, C. (1984). *Waiting to waltz: A childhood.* Illus. by Stephen Gammell. Macmillan, Bradbury Press. 48 pp. ISBN 0-02-778000-7. Poetry. (E & J)

Illustrated with black-and-white pencil drawings, this collection of thirty poems tells about the life and relationships of the author growing up in a small town in Appalachia.

Sandler, M. W. (1977). *The way we lived: A photographic record of work in vanished America.* Illus. with photographs. Little, Brown. 120 pp. Informational. (E & J)

An account of rural life and industrialism in America around the turn of the twentieth century.

Saunders, S. (1982). *Fish fry.* Illus. by S. D. Schindler. Viking. 32 pp. Historical Fiction (Picture Book). (P)

The story of the annual catfish picnic celebration in Piney Woods in rural Texas depicts life there at the turn of the century.

Smith, E. B. (1982). *The farm book.* Illus. by the author. Houghton Mifflin. 64 pp. ISBN 0-395-32951-5. Historical Fiction (Picture Book). (E & J)

Watercolor illustrations adorn this portrayal of life on a New England farm in early 1900.

Van Rynbach, R. (1991). *Everything from a nail to coffin.* Illus. by author. Orchard. 48 pp. ISBN 0-531-08541-4. Informational (Picture Book). (P & E)

Highlights a disappearing part of Americana, the general store. This book traces the history of an actual general store in Glastonbury, Connecticut, from 1874 to the present.